☞ **W9-BRM-590**

WITHDRAWN

SCENE
OF THE
C

JULIAN EARWAKER & KATHLEEN BECKER

SCENE OF THE CRIME

A Guide to the Landscapes of
British Detective Fiction

Foreword by P D James

AURUM PRESS

Title (pages 2–3) picture: Wensleydale, Yorkshire
Half title (page1) picture: Bath Abbey (detail of West Front)

First published in Great Britain
2002 by Aurum Press Limited,
25 Bedford Avenue, London WC1B 3AT

Map on page 6: www.lib.utexas.edu/maps

A catalogue record for this book is
available from the British Library.

ISBN 1 85410 821 2

10 9 8 7 6 5 4 3 2 1
2006   2005   2004   2003   2002

Printed in Singapore by Imago

Contents

Sandwood Bay

Skye

Raasay

INVERNESS

The Cairngorms

ABERDEEN

SCOTLAND

PERTH

Ardpatrick Point

GLASGOW   EDINBURGH

Kirkcudbright

Holy Island
(Lindisfarne)

Morpeth   Blyth

NEWCASTLE
UPON TYNE

Durham

NORTHUMBRIA

Lake District

Richmond

Yorkshire Dales   North York Moors

Oswaldkirk

YORKSHIRE

Blackpool   Slaidburn   YORK

Haworth   Hull

LIVERPOOL   LEEDS

The Wirral   Halifax

Anglesey   MANCHESTER   Doncaster

Llandudno   SHEFFIELD

Bangor   Chester   Buxton   Peak District

Porthmadog   Leek   Lincoln

Snowdonia   Stoke-on-Trent   Skegness

Shrewsbury   Nottingham   Cley-next-the-Se

THE MIDLANDS   Cromer

Aberystwyth   Leicester   NORWICH   Happisb

Corby   EAST ANGLIA   The Broads

Stourbridge   BIRMINGHAM   Ely   Dunwi

WALES & THE MARCHES   Newmarket   Diss

Offa's Dyke   CAMBRIDGE   THE FENS

Hereford   Colchester

Gloucester   Luton   Felixstowe

Monmouth   Burford   SOUTH-EAST   Mersea

Rhondda Valley   Forest of Dean   OXFORD   Chelmsford   Maldon

SWANSEA   CARDIFF   THE COTSWOLDS   LONDON   Margate

Windsor   HOME COUNTIES

BATH   Guildford   Maidstone   Canterbury

Stogursey   Glastonbury   THE SOUTH   Midhurst   The Downs

Arundel   Brighton   Hastings

Crediton   Corfe Mullen   Poole   Portsmouth

Lydford   EXETER   Isle of
Purbeck

Holywell   Princetown   THE SOUTH-WEST   Torquay

Zennor   Penzance   Dartmoor   Dartmouth   St Peter Port

Land's End   Newlyn   Falmouth   Guernsey

LONDON (detail)

Harringay

Camden   Islington

Paddington   City   East End

Westminster   Greenwich

Kensington   Brixton

Wimbledon

Foreword
by P D James

I suspect I am not the only writer of detective fiction whose creative imagination is sparked off, not by a character or an interesting and original method of murder, but by the setting of the crime. This is not to say that setting is more important than the other elements of fiction – character, plot and structure. All four must be held in creative and symbiotic tension, and the whole narrative written in compelling language if the book is to survive beyond its first months of publication. Many people, if challenged to say which is the most important, character, plot or structure, would opt for character. But the setting is the place where the characters live, move and have their being, and unless it is as convincing to the reader as it is to the writer, the novel, however exciting and credible and however well structured, will lose much of its power.

Setting is, of course, important in all fiction and the place is sometimes so dominant that it virtually becomes a character and even gives a name to the work; *Wuthering Heights, Mansfield Park, Howard's End* and *Middlemarch* are four titles which immediately come to mind. But setting is particularly important to the crime novelist. Firstly, it sets the mood of the work, whether of suspense, horror, mystery, psychological darkness, or the excitement of vicarious danger. We see the effectiveness of setting in Conan Doyle's *The Hound of the Baskervilles*; the gloomy mansion and the eerie horror of the fog-shrouded moor. *The Hound of Wimbledon Common* would hardly provide such a frisson of terror. Setting both influences and reveals character, particularly in its description of people's houses and rooms since we can tell so much from the artefacts with which people choose to surround themselves and the ambience in which they live. Setting can profoundly influence plot and can have a symbolic importance, as does the black tower in my novel of that name, or the church of Fenchurch St Paul's in Dorothy L Sayers' *The Nine Tailors*. Setting can help establish credibility by rooting the sometimes bizarre events of the plot in the firm soil of recognized place. If all these aims are to be achieved, the setting must come alive for the reader. Sight, sound, smells, architecture, flora and fauna, patterns of speech and local customs all contribute to that sense of reality which draws the reader into a recognizable world. And places, like people, cannot shake off their past.

Even the most powerful locations do not come unencumbered by memories of old battles, old rivalries and ancient tragedies. The murkier streets of Edinburgh still speak of Burke and Hare, as the East End does of Jack the Ripper.

Although crime novelists can and do use settings with which they are not personally familiar and which require careful research to come alive, most are more at home in places they know and which exert a lasting fascination for them. H R F Keating provides a most prominent exception; he set his Ghote novels in India with remarkable credibility even before he visited that country. But most crime writers choose to set their novels in parts of their own country in which they feel particularly at home or which evoke in them a powerful emotional response. One reason for eschewing foreign locations, however attractive, exciting or evocative, is that detective fiction, as opposed to other forms of crime writing, invariably involves police procedure even if the detective is an amateur. We move most confident on familiar ground.

So potent is the influence of place on the creative imagination that we associate many writers of detective fiction with their particular habitats. Agatha Christie seems most at home in St Mary Mead, that fictional English village where murder may be committed, but where the discovery of a body on the study floor seldom lastingly disturbs the sleepy respectability of that inter-war village. In strong contrast, Dashiell Hammett, Raymond Chandler and Ross MacDonald are the novelists of California, a world which they largely portray as an urban jungle, violent, decadent and morally corrupt, in which the detective is frequently as much at odds with organized law and order as he is with the criminals, and in which the police detective in Chandler's *The Long Goodbye* 'solves crime with the bright light, the soft sap, the kick to the kidneys, the knee to the groin, the fist to the solar plexus, the night stick to the base of the spine'. Few English detective stories portray such a violent world, although the best of the writers are well aware of the violence and social anarchy which underlies even apparently prosperous cities. Ian Rankin sees Edinburgh as a schizophrenic city where the dimly-lit alleys of a Jekyll and Hyde city are only a short walk from the distinguished architecture and imposing streets of the Edinburgh of international culture and splendid architecture.

But the detective story does not have to be set in the murky underworld of squalor and crime to promote its frisson of danger and unease. Sometimes a contrast is as effective. The poet W H Auden, who dearly loved detective fiction, wrote that he could only fully enjoy it if the setting was the great good place where order, peace, normality and hierarchy enhance the horror of the most contaminating crime. The effective use of contrast is particularly seen in Wilkie Collins' *The Moonstone*, which T S Eliot described as 'the first, the longest and the best' of modern detective stories. Here, the comfortable, ordered domesticity and upper-class respectability of the Verinder's house is menaced by external forces of darkness symbolized by the dark horror of the shivering sands. To the crime writer nothing is as it seems, no place can be guaranteed to be safe and horror lurks even in the familiar and peaceful place where we feel most at home.

We can recognize the topography of the author's mind in the places they choose. Cyril Hare, himself a judge, is most at home in the law courts and legal chambers. Margery Allingham uses the run-down squares of post-war London and the wide skies of the East Coast as her settings. Colin Dexter has made Oxford as famous for murder as it is for its dreaming spires, while Ellis Peters treads the stones of Shrewsbury's haunted cloisters. It is not unusual for crime writers to combine real places with imaginary settings, so that the topography – whether house, village, town or landscape – is recognizable but the location where the murder takes place is imaginary. This is a convenient way of increasing credibility but avoiding the danger of using too specific a place.

Detective fiction, because its effectiveness depends so much on an eye for detail and a sympathetic involvement with the minutiae of daily living, can tell us much about the social mores of the age in which it was written. Here, too, setting is important. If we want to know what it was like to work in a city office in those insecure and dangerous years between the wars, we read Dorothy L Sayers' *Murder Must Advertise*. In *The Nine Tailors* the same author takes us into her own familiar landscape of East Anglia where she was brought up and shows us that remote hierarchical and now dying world of the fenland village. James McClure, in his novels featuring Lieutenant Tromp Kramer and his Zulu assistant, Bantu Detective Sergeant Mickey Zondi, shows us with subtlety and truth more about South Africa in the days of apartheid than many a sociological or political report. Christianna Brand's *Green for Danger* takes us into a wartime hospital, making use of her own experience as a Red Cross nurse.

It is because setting is so fundamental to detective fiction that aficionados of the genre come in organized groups to visit the places associated with their best-loved books and authors. Now, with this volume, they have both a substitute for the physical journey and a guide, not only to real places, but to the physical origins of fictitious settings and the relationship of the writer to the place which has given rise to the novel. This is in itself an exercise in detection, and one of the most fascinating which crime writing affords.

© P D James

Introduction

Detective fiction has come a long way from the Victorian 'detective fever' of Wilkie Collins' *The Moonstone*, through the Golden Age between the two world wars, into today's hugely popular, varied – and increasingly regionalized – form. Private eyes, amateur sleuths and police detectives are now more firmly rooted in place than ever, often linked by distinctive themes – gardening, archaeology, religion, history, nature, the theatre – within areas. Over 250 authors feature in this guide, but emphasis is given to writers whose sense of place is strongest, and whose series detectives provide a continuity and deeper attachment to particular locations.

Scene of the Crime is ordered geographically from north to south (Outer London moves clockwise from the north). Primary locations are highlighted in **BOLD CAPS**, other key locations in **bold**. Within chapters, the text follows a broadly chronological order, beginning with historical novels and continuing by age of author. Where available, authors' dates are listed with their main entry (as are the authors' real names where writing under a pseudonym). An asterisk* indicates that further entries exist for this writer. Awards all refer to the Crime Writers' Association (CWA) annual awards. Ranks of police detectives often change as a series progresses, and will not necessarily be the same for each of the books referenced. Tinted boxes indicate book quotes ⟨...⟩ or author quotes ▭. Whilst space does not permit a full bibliography of the more than 600 books referenced, the tools of today's electronic age, as well as libraries and bookshops, will complement the details provided. Wherever possible, differing US book titles have been given.

Fictional places are always in 'quotation marks'; only real places are boldened ('XYZ Hall' was inspired by **ABC Manor**). All murder and mayhem described in this book is fictional – by illustrating influences, inspirations or models it is not suggested that criminal activities are in any way related to the real-life locations. Whilst some places are open to the public, many remain private homes, and should be respected as such.

This guide provides a new perspective on a favourite literary form, capturing the essence of individual authors' landscapes and settings, blending specific locations with broader backdrops. Whether read on the road, or in the comfort of the armchair, all the evidence points in one direction – to the *Scene of the Crime*.

CHAPTER ONE

Scotland

'I've found the crime novel to be the perfect form
to be writing about the state of modern Scotland.'

Ian Rankin

Land of the ancient Celts, Scotland occupies over one third of the land mass of Britain but accounts for only one tenth of its population. The country's most sparsely populated, stunningly beautiful and timeless landscapes are found in the **HIGHLANDS AND ISLANDS** to the north and west. Centuries of struggle against a harsh climate and harsher invaders, coupled with a history of bloody feuding, enduring legend and irrepressible romanticism, encompass figures as varied as Macbeth, Bonnie Prince Charlie and the Loch Ness monster. Traditional Highland representations of peat smoke, whisky and fishing nets captured in the poetry of **George Mackay Brown** (1921–) now mesh with new

At the edge of the world – **Sandwood Bay** and Am Buachaille stack, scene of the crime in **Gwen Moffat**'s *Miss Pink at the Edge of the World* (1975).

A skilled climber and professional guide, **Gwen Moffat** combines her passion for climbing and interests in wildlife and the environment with traditional detective fiction.

technologies and modern living. With few people, and very few violent deaths, the most likely Highland invasion today is by tourists or clouds of dreaded midges. Alongside issues of conservation and commerce, the arrival of outsiders offers detective writers every opportunity to exploit the tensions and conflicts within small, traditionally close-knit communities.

The fishing village of **Kinlochbervie** lies just twelve miles short of **Cape Wrath** at the very north-western tip of mainland Britain. Not far from here, a walk through craggy peat bog pitted with lochs leads to the remote and stunning **Sandwood Bay**. The wide sweep of clean, pink-tinted sand, translucent waters, rock pools and boulders studded with semi-precious stones is so idyllic it resembles a film set. Buttressed at either end against the stormy Atlantic Ocean by ancient red sandstone sea-cliffs crowded with seabirds, the bay feels about as far removed from humanity as possible.

'Landscape is absolutely essential to my writing,' says **Gwen Moffat*** (1924–), who renames Sandwood Bay 'Calava Bay' in one of her favourite mysteries, *Miss Pink at the Edge of the World* (1975). The arrival of Miss Melinda Pink – wealthy Justice of the Peace, outdoor enthusiast and incurable snoop – coincides with the visit of a couple of unpleasant young men intent upon climbing the 'Old Man of Scamadale' (modelled on the embattled **Am Buachaille** sandstone stack at the south end of the bay). With them comes the threat of 'progress' for the local community and the finely balanced environment. The appearance of killer whales in Calava Bay bodes ill for the unwelcome visitors, but it is human brutality that leads Miss Pink into a double murder investigation:

> Now, westwards, she saw the bay that was called Calava demarcated by splendid headlands jutting into the pale and shining sea… She stared in an enchantment that had nothing to do with climbing; she could admire a cliff for its lines unassociated with the quality of the rock. There were skerries and rocky islands, and in that brilliant but silent world the seascape had an air of unreality. It was like the coastline of Valhalla.

Some 90 miles north of mainland Scotland, between **Orkney** and the **Shetland Islands**, tiny **Fair Isle** inspired **Ann Cleeves**'* *Murder in Paradise* (1988). Cleeves met her husband, an RSPB officer, whilst working on the island. A world-famous bird reserve, Fair Isle is the perfect location for expert amateur ornithologist and detective George Palmer-Jones to investigate the death of a young girl in a cliff-top fall. In a traditional, vulnerable community, Palmer-Jones is aware of the risks involved: 'This is a special place, precarious,' he says. 'If I meddle I might endanger its survival.'

Moffat moves to the west coast to make the crossing over to **Skye**, the largest island of the Inner Hebrides, in *Over the Sea to Death* (1976). Dominating the skyline here are the spectacular **Cuillin**, a jagged-edged range forming one of Britain's most exciting and challenging mountain ridges. Based on Moffat's own climbing on the abrasive gabbro of the Cuillin, Miss Pink witnesses passions running high amongst a small group of professional guides and committed climbers staying in a hotel in 'Glen Shira' (**Glen Brittle**). Moffat's continuing interest in ecology and the environment is reflected in *Quicksand* (2001), a non-series mystery set on a small island in the Outer Hebrides. When a TV crew arrives to survey the island, the first thing they do is trample on the

The 'dinosaur's spine' of **The Cuillin** mountains on the Isle of Skye is the scene of conflict in **Gwen Moffat**'s *Over the Sea to Death* (1976).

eggs of a nesting tern colony. As tensions in the local community reach a murderous intensity, it is clear that eggs are not the only things about to get broken.

'The morrow dawned wet and stormy, being one of those Hebridean days of which Dr Johnson complained that they presented all the inconveniences of tempest without its sublimities.' The well-documented Highland travels of essayist and polymath **Dr Samuel Johnson** (1709–84) and his Scottish biographer **James Boswell** (1740–95) provide ample source material for the eighteenth-century mysteries of 'histo-detector' **Lilian de la Torre*** (pseud. Lilian McCue, 1902–93). In *Dr Sam: Johnson, Detector* (1946), the first of her four Dr Sam short story collections written across forty years, de la Torre charts the duo's 'long-cherished scheam [*sic*] of visiting the Western Islands of Scotland'. In wholehearted pursuit of Scottish mystery and history, Dr Sam and Boswell meet up with 'Prince Charlie's Ruby' – Flora Macdonald – on Skye, and explore the far-flung Hebridean island of **St Kilda**. 'The Second Sight of Dr Sam Johnson' interweaves historical fact with legend: while the island of **Raasay** struggles with the lawlessness following the 1745 Jacobite Uprising, there are echoes of Loch Ness in the sinister 'Kelpie Pool' (a kelpie is a mythical water monster).

A keen climber, **Manda Scott*** (1962–) opens *Stronger Than Death* (1999), the third novel in her Kellen Stewart series, with a gripping

'Looking up, all I could see was rock' – **Manda Scott** researching for *Stronger Than Death*.

description of a rock climb surrounded by sea off **Ardpatrick Point**, near Klapdale Forest. The passage is based on a real climb in Cornwall completed by Scott on her thirtieth birthday, which resulted in a form of epiphany and the beginning of her writing career:

'I was sitting right at the top of this incredible rock. It was a beautiful day, the sun was shining – we were three rope pitches up, so about 150 foot up – and the sea spray was coming right up in front of me, little tiny droplets and it was like magic… with rainbow crystals in the air, it was absolutely beautiful. And I just sat there, bringing the others up and thinking if I don't start now, it's not going to happen. And I went back and I started *Hen's Teeth*.'

In the compelling, compassionate *No Good Deed* (2001), undercover agent Orla McLeod brings a young boy to a fictional village between **Milton** and **Camusteel** on the **Applecross Peninsula**, overlooked by the bulk of **Sgur A'Chaorachain**. Hiding at her mother's cottage in the shadow of the mountains, Orla should feel safe. Instead she finds herself being dragged back into a painful past, and torn between two worlds:

> …she watched the mist make waves against the background of the sky and listened to the wash of the sea and the distant avarice of the gulls and tried to remember that this was the world in which she belonged and that the other half was the delusion… Of the two parts of her, the half that was of the cottage looked out on a landscape that had not changed since her teens and never wanted to leave, while the half that was of Glasgow screamed frustration at the lack of action and wanted desperately to return. Had she woken in the city, it would have been the other way round.

Strategically placed at the head of **Loch Ness** and the mouth of the **Moray Firth**, the Highland capital of **INVERNESS** was the birthplace of **Josephine Tey*** (pseud. Elizabeth MacKintosh, 1896–1952), who returned home in the mid-1920s and rarely left thereafter. Tey was an immensely private person, who for most of her mysteries steers clear of familiar Highland landscapes, preferring to filter them through the character of Detective-Inspector Alan Grant. A native of **Strathspey**, one of the most beautiful valleys in the **Cairngorms**, Grant is a classic gentleman detective of Scotland Yard, a wealthy bachelor who enjoys the challenge of detection almost as much as fishing (Tey's father was a keen fisherman). Only at the last does Tey draw her detached and

Fishing for clues… one of **Josephine Tey**'s favourite pastimes.

In *Blood Proof* (1997), **Bill Knox*** places his police detective Colin Thane on one of **Speyside**'s famous 'whisky trails' to tackle a case of arson and violent death in a remote glen. On the flight to Inverness, Thane looks out over the 'naked granite rock' of the **Cairngorms**, the 'tall, bald mountain peaks scarred by deep gullies, and no visible sign that human life had ever come their way'. Knox knowledgeably interweaves traditional Highland industries (whisky distilling, sheep, cattle, salmon and deer farming) with the motives for murder.

claustrophobic detective close to the invitingly open spaces of home in the atmospheric *The Singing Sands* (1952):

> It was a grey morning, and still. The landscape was tidy and bare. Tidy grey walls round bare fields, bare fences along the tidy ditches. Nothing had begun to grow yet in this waiting countryside. Only a willow here and there by a culvert side showed live and green in the half-shades. It was going to be all right. This was what he had needed; this wide silence, this space, this serenity. He had forgotten how benevolent the place was; how satisfying. The near hills were round and green and kind; beyond them were farther ones, stained blue by the distance. And behind all stood the long rampart of the Highland line, white and remote against the calm sky.

Travelling up on the Euston/Inverness sleeper, Grant picks up a slip of paper from the carriage floor bearing a curious message: 'The beasts that talk, The streams that stand, The stones that walk, The singing sands… That guard the way To Paradise.' So begins an intriguing trail and murder mystery which, inevitably, steers Grant away from his planned fishing at the tiny settlement of **Clune**, south of Inverness on the **Aviemore** road. The familiar Tey themes of isolation, deception and criminal vanity lead Grant to the fictional Hebridean island of 'Cladda', site of the singing sands.

Investigating crime in the fictional village of 'Lochdubh' in north-west Scotland, young police constable Hamish Macbeth is the creation of Glasgow-born **M C Beaton*** (pseud. Marion Chesney, 1936–). Endowed with hair of 'that true Highland red that sometimes looks as if it has purple lights', Macbeth is a crofter as well as the village bobby, and cunningly uses his affected rustic casualness to his advantage when dealing with suspects – particularly the snobbish English. Lochdubh consists of 'a huddle of houses built in the eighteenth century to promote the fishing industry in the Highlands' and 'a curve of eighteenth-century cottages' nestling at the foot of two great peaks. In *Death of a Gossip* (1985), Macbeth is troubled by the arrival of a fishing party, and rightly so, as one of them is soon found strangled. In *Death of a Cad* (1987), a love-smitten Macbeth watches miserably as the object of his affection brings her fiancé home to the family castle. But when one of the engagement party is killed on a grouse shoot, Macbeth quietly asserts himself on the investigation and back into his sweetheart's affections.

A severed arm flying through the air, shoot-outs and a deep-frozen monkfish in the hands of a policeman looking forward to retirement – all ingredients from **Christopher Brookmyre**'s* (1968–) hilarious crime novel *One Fine Day in the Middle of the Night* (1999). Focused on a school reunion on an offshore oil rig-cum-paradise resort in the **Cromarty Firth**, Inspector Hector McGregor remains largely at the periphery of events, as a gang of unbalanced criminals unleashes chaos. Acerbic tongue very firmly in cheek, Brookmyre tackles Scotland's favourite clichés and harshest realities.

Durable, coarse-grained and solid, granite is the favoured building material of **ABERDEEN**, North Sea oil capital, fishing port and focal point of the north-east Scottish coast. Oppressively grey and gloomy in cloud, the hard-hewn façades of the 'Granite City' glitter like treasure in the sunlight, earning Aberdeen its alternative tag of the 'Silver City'. But it was 'black gold' that won the city its fortune as east coast oil money

Aberdeen docks and oil terminals – the North Sea oil capital stands solidly behind the 'Cairnburgh' of **Bill Kirton**'s DCI Jack Carston series.

came gushing into Aberdeen in the 1970s, with this unforeseen spending power also lending Scotland's third-largest city a broad cultural mix.

'Granite – hard, grey and heavy – carries dour, unyielding associations. Consequently, outsiders think of Aberdonians as close, impenetrable folk,' says **Bill Kirton** (1939–). He believes this view of Aberdonians to be a myth, but the Granite City is seldom seen as soft in Kirton's hard-hitting 'Cairnburgh' series featuring Detective Chief Inspector Jack Carston. Closely modelled on Aberdeen, Cairnburgh is, however, located some thirty miles west of the real Granite City. Jack Carston first appears in *Material Evidence* (1995), leading an investigation into the brutal murder of a financial consultant killed in her quayside home. Tough but caring, Carston is an unusually stable, happily married detective, who enjoys good food and wine, and walks in the park to savour the views over the city to the distant Cairngorms. Housing and architecture are central themes in Kirton's writing and, despite the transformation of Cairnburgh wrought by the 'Midas Eighties', often reflect the more traditional character of the city: 'Even this late in the year, there were still plenty of blooms, brazen and exciting against the granite. They were the only outward show of joy. The houses behind them were solid, closed against the elements and the curiosity of strangers.'

Having grown up far south in the city port of Plymouth, Kirton acknowledges that in the boats, nets and hard-edged life of the fishing community there lay 'the seeds of what I respond to in Aberdeen'. Kirton continues his exploration of Aberdeen's 'sense of separation from the other Scottish centres' in *Rough Justice* (1996). With his wife away in Inverness, Carston is left to investigate interlinked cases of violence, intimidation, squatting, corruption and a murder outside Cairnburgh's only nightclub.

'More than just places to keep out the cold and rain… The stone was hard, massive, elegant' – **Bill Kirton**'s *Rough Justice* steers a course through **Aberdeen**'s granite streets.

Born and raised in Aberdeen but living in one of the 'quiet semi-detached red sandstone houses' in the city of **PERTH**, GP and amateur sleuth Jean Montrose is the creation of surgeon **C F Roe** (pseud. Francis Roe, 1932–). Occupying the west bank of the **River Tay**, and ringed with castles and fertile fields, Perth was Scotland's medieval capital. It provides a suitable backdrop for a series of mysteries in which 'wee doc' Jean escapes her quarrelsome family to assist Inspector Douglas Niven with valuable medical and psychological insights, as well as straightforward common sense. In *Death by Fire* (1990), Jean tackles an apparent case of spontaneous human combustion and a spell of black magic in the deserted tower on **Kinnoull Hill**. When a salmon poacher fishes the body of the local squire's daughter out of the Tay in *A Death in the Family* (1993), investigations are blocked by Niven's anxious

'To Jean, the river looked cold, evil and unforgiving, quite unlike its usual sparkling appearance, as if its normal joyfulness had been unmasked to reveal its underlying sinister self' – running beside the city of **Perth**, the **River Tay** provides the scene of the crime in *A Death in the Family*.

superiors. Fortunately, the dead woman was also a patient at Jean Montrose's busy surgery. The watery imagery continues in *A Classy Touch of Murder* (1997), an exploration of ancestry that transports the whole Montrose clan out to nearby 'Strathalmond' Castle, run by an Earl who takes his family history very seriously: 'their family was like a long river; each of them successively responsible for the next stretch, and what they did during their stewardship determined the course and size of the river, maybe forever'.

For traditional Scottish hunting, shooting and fishing, look no further than the mysteries of **Gerald Hammond** (1926–), whose main series characters are dog-breeder John Cunningham, gun expert Keith Calder and angler Walter James. Hammond places his characters in the lowlands of **Fife** and around the town of 'Newton Lauder' in the **Eastern Borders**. His fast-paced outdoor investigations are brimful of technical detail, and often interwoven with elements of Scottish law. Conservationists and opponents are dismissed out of hand in Hammond's wholehearted and expert appreciation of field sports and dogs. *A Shocking Affair* (1999) cleverly brings his main series characters together. When a friend of the Cunninghams agrees to deliver a field dog to an old friend in Newton Lauder, it seems like the perfect opportunity for some leisurely shooting and fishing. But there is scarcely time to land a few trout and bag a few pigeons before murder strikes.

The junction of **Loch Tay** and **Loch Earn**, looking towards the picturesque village of **Killin**, where **Joyce Holms*** ran a B&B for some ten years. Holms' intrepid trainee lawyer 'Fizz' Fitzgerald frequently returns here, to the fictional hamlet of 'Am Bealach' where she grew up, to visit her grandfather and to recuperate from the traffic and crowds of Edinburgh. The area provides the setting for *Foreign Body* (1997), a mystery that originated from a newspaper report about the discovery of an abandoned tent.

There can be few cities so perfectly suited to crime fiction as **EDINBURGH**. Beyond its imposing façades and wealthy tourist walkways lurk the spirits of a legendary criminal past, while a short walk off the **Royal Mile**, dimly-lit alleyways and hidden closes hint at a darker side to the city's grandeur. The juxtaposition of **New Town** and **Old Town** is perhaps the most immediate reminder of a duality that is much stronger here than in most cities. As far back as Tudor times the great Scots poet **William Dunbar** (?1456–?1513) noted that Edinburgh was

Jekyll and Hyde city – the light and dark of **Edinburgh** viewed from **Calton Hill**.

a city with two faces, but today's crime writing owes more to the literary heritage endowed by Edinburgh novelist **Robert Louis Stevenson** (1850–94) and his classic Gothic tale *The Strange Case of Dr Jekyll and Mr Hyde* (1886). From his home at **17 Heriot Row**, young Robert undoubtedly heard tales of the eighteenth-century cabinet-maker William Deacon Brodie – respectable merchant by day, burglar of his clients' houses by night. For all the contemporary buzz of the capital city of newly devolved Scotland, it is the lamplit, foggy evenings of 'Auld Reekie' ('Old Smoky') that exert the strongest influence on contemporary Edinburgh crime writers.

Stevenson's contemporary, novelist and Sherlock Holmes creator **Arthur Conan Doyle***, was born on 22 May 1859 in a flat (no longer standing) at **11 Picardy Place**. He is commemorated here, next to a busy roundabout, by a statue of Holmes. Although, like Stevenson, Conan Doyle locates his greatest creation in fashionable London, the influence of his home city remains visible in his work. Conan Doyle also studied medicine at Edinburgh University, where he worked under Doctor Joseph Bell, a deductive genius specializing in outpatient diagnosis, who provided the model for the most famous and enduring detective in crime fiction.

Alanna Knight: 'The Victorian Edinburgh I'm writing about is still there... the streets that Faro walked and the places that he knew... I can walk the paths and touch the stones.'

'Edinburgh is a great place for a murder, because it has a bloody, a very bloody history,' says historical crime novelist **Alanna Knight**, whose research into the life and works of Robert Louis Stevenson led directly to the creation of her popular Victorian detective, Inspector Jeremy Faro. 'I knew Edinburgh in Victorian times better than I knew any other place,' says Knight, whose former home at **Dryden Place** provides the model for Faro's house at 9 'Sheridan Place', looking out to fine views: 'Edinburgh's extinct volcano, Arthur's Seat, filled the horizon from the drawing-room window, while the dining room offered an undulating, sun-shimmering vista of the Pentland Hills.' There is a genuine sense of place and time in Knight's books, with a strong vein of social justice running through them. Her favourite Faro mystery is *Blood Line* (1989), in which Queen Victoria is expected to make an informal visit to Edinburgh. When a man's body is discovered on the rocks below the castle, Faro finds himself thrown into a dangerous investigation with links to his past.

The Faro series extends to a new generation in *The Inspector's Daughter* (2000), in which Faro's daughter, Rose McQuinn, returns home to Edinburgh to step into her father's shoes and investigate a brutal murder. The year is 1895, it is a decade since she left, and Rose finds Edinburgh much-changed, with Sheridan Place empty and up for sale, and her favourite views obscured by 'streets of tenements five storeys high'. Her thoughts echo down the centuries and, in today's bustle of new-build, remain as pertinent as ever:

'Wrapped in ancient sinister majesty', **Edinburgh Castle** provides the scene of the crime in **Alanna Knight**'s *Blood Line*.

> The changes in the city of Edinburgh since the sixteenth century were no less remarkable to my eyes than what had happened to the skyline in the past ten years and was doubtless fated to continue into the next century. Progress was with us in full fever as the clang of hammers and the mast rigging of scaffolding told of yet another building arching its outline against the sky.

In *Death Knock* (2000), **Frederic Lindsay** illustrates the contrast in character between Edinburgh and Glasgow by a simple invitation (or not) to tea: 'You'll have had your tea?' says one of the characters. 'You've heard that one?… in Glasgow, it's, have you had your tea? I love Edinburgh people, been here twenty years, but that's the difference. *You'll have had your tea*, they ask you here, eh?'

Born in Glasgow, **Frederic Lindsay** (1933–) moved eastwards to Edinburgh in 1981, and when the city had become 'a net of personal connections and layered experience', published *Kissing Judas* (1997). This brooding, complex thriller introduces Edinburgh Detective Inspector Jim Meldrum, a man of indecent integrity determined to right a wrong whatever the personal cost. Inspired by the real-life story of Glasgow detective John Trench, whose pursuit of the truth led to him being hounded and framed by his colleagues, *Kissing Judas* tackles miscarriage of justice under the fall-out of the brutal undercover war in Northern Ireland.

Although Meldrum lives in a flat on **Leith Walk**, he spends plenty of time on the opposite side of the city at **Bruntsfield**. With Edinburgh Castle a frieze on the horizon, this is familiar territory for Lindsay, who once lived in **Warrender Park Crescent**, scene of the opening murder in *Kissing Judas*. Meldrum is aware that his revisiting of the Edinburgh landscape is very much defined by who he is and what he does: 'everyone who lived in a city held a different map of it in mind. It just happened his was a stranger one than most, marked as it was with stains of blood.' From the tall Victorian terraces and open greenery of Bruntsfield, it is a short walk down to the **Greenbank** area of **Morningside Road**, where Meldrum investigates the death of a beautiful red-headed woman in *Death Knock* (2000). The attractive red-head turns out to be a successful local businessman, and Meldrum finds himself teamed with a criminal profiler who has a suspiciously strong understanding of the murder.

Frederic Lindsay on **Bruntsfield Links**, site of his first home in Edinburgh, and scene of the crime in *Kissing Judas*.

'When I worked as a detective in the city, I found it intriguing to discover how many 'ordinary' middle-class people were pushed – by jealousy, greed, or sheer frustration – into taking the law into their own hands.' **Joyce Holms** in 'Fizz' territory: **Bailey Fyffe's Close** on the Royal Mile.

Nothing is what it seems in this cunning, convoluted mystery, and Frederic Lindsay delights in blurring the distinctions between law-maker and law-breaker, male and female identity, and between Edinburgh and Glasgow.

Joyce Holms* (1935–) was also born and educated in Glasgow. Holms entered the world of private investigation quite by chance when she went in search of some sticky tape one morning and walked straight into an Edinburgh detective agency. She came out with a job that opened her eyes to the city and provided ample material for a writing career. If ever the duality of Edinburgh needed personifying, then Holms' unlikely sleuthing team of 'thick-skinned, pragmatic and frequently selfish' law student Fizz Fitzgerald and solid, conservative Tam Buchanan could apply for the job. When she is not busy goading the more conventional and more restrained Buchanan, or leafing through law books, single-minded Fizz likes nothing more than sticking her nose into other people's business. Characterized by mordant humour and snappy dialogue, with a scent of romance hanging tantalizingly in the air, their interaction sparkles like an Edinburgh street in the rain. From her top-floor tenement eyrie in **Bailey Fyffe's Close**, at **107 High Street** on the Royal Mile, Fizz can enjoy fine views of the 'rumbustious mish-mash' of the Old Town.

By contrast, Tam Buchanan works from **17 Charlotte Square** in the civilized New Town, with a mews property close by in **Dean** village. *Bad Vibes* (1998) sees Fizz temping at the reception of an Edinburgh hotel ('existing on a student's grant in Edinburgh was like trying to read a newspaper in a howling gale') where an elderly German gentleman

Quintin Jardine – teamwork is central to his best-selling Bob Skinner mysteries.

The headquarters of Lothian and Borders Police HQ at **Fettes**, well known to many of Edinburgh's fictional detectives.

Paul Johnston predicts a bleak future for the city in his Quintilian Dalrymple series.

is found dead in his bath. Suspicions aroused, Fizz's madcap investigation into an arts scam takes her and Buchanan to an artists' community outside the city and on to the **Isle of Arran**. In the keenly observed, wise-cracking *Mr Big* (2000), Fizz drags her grandpa into an investigation, as Buchanan is called to defend a man accused of murdering Edinburgh's 'Mr Big'.

Having worked in Edinburgh for over thirty years, as spin doctor to 'the powerful, rich and notorious', **Quintin Jardine** (1948–) introduces his own 'big' Edinburgh player, CID Chief Superintendent Robert 'Bob' Skinner, in *Skinner's Rules* (1993). While Jardine's terse prose plays on the contrasts 'between the dark, narrow streets and closes of the Old Town, and the classical airiness of the Georgian city', the action focuses more on the resolute character of tough-talking Skinner and his overworked colleagues. Edinburgh is internationally famous for its Festival, but Skinner can be forgiven for having mixed feelings about it: he almost loses his life in *Skinner's Festival* (1994) when a deadly and determined group of nationalists set out to persuade the Secretary of State for Scotland to declare independence. With 'playing football, watching football, talking about football' a high priority for Jardine, and teamwork an essential part of police investigation, *Thursday Legends* (2000) centres on the tight-knit bunch of officers ably led by hard-tackling Skinner. Increasingly deskbound at **Fettes Police Headquarters**, family man Skinner eagerly anticipates the wholehearted contests of Thursday-night football at the local sports centre. But when an ex-team member is found brutally murdered, Skinner needs all his skill and control to find the killer.

Another member of the new wave of Scottish crime writers dubbed the 'Tartan Mafia' is Edinburgh-born **Paul Johnston** (1957–). His futuristic series featuring Quintilian Dalrymple is set in the 2020s in a bleak, dystopian Edinburgh city-state. Britain has fractured into warring regions and the guardians of the city have modelled their social order on Plato's Republic, with strict enforcement of rules and regulations by their harsh civil servants, the 'auxiliaries'. Tourism is the life-blood of the new Enlightenment, and the Festival is now a year-round event, with ordinary citizens banned from entering the tourist zone. Meanwhile, the royal yacht Britannia lies bullet-riddled and abandoned beneath the ruins of the **Forth Rail Bridge**, **Holyrood Palace** is empty and ransacked, and prestigious **Fettes College** – where Johnston was educated – has been 'blown to pieces' in a war against drugs gangs.

In a narrative laced with wry humour, and a philosophical base befitting the 'Athens of the North', Johnston tackles serious issues along the way. In *Body Politic* (1997), Edinburgh is supposedly devoid of crime, but Dalrymple (who lives at **13 Gilmore Place**, an unspectacular Edinburgh side-street) encounters numerous corpses on the trail of a serial killer and finds corruption and cover-ups along the way. When Dalrymple shadows a suspect, hiding opposite the lavish splendour of **Heriot Row**, Johnston pays tribute to the past:

I took cover in the bushes lining the lower edge of Queen Street Gardens... I was shivering in the gloom, trying to convince myself I wasn't wasting my time... I forced myself to concentrate on the elegant Georgian façade across the road. Nearby was number 17, where Robert Louis Stevenson lived as a boy. Perhaps he had the first intimations of Dr Jekyll here when the mist was swirling around, swallowing the drumming of horses' hooves from passing carriages. The doctor and his sinister doppelganger seemed very close.

The 'elegant Georgian façade' of **17 Heriot Row**, former home of **Robert Louis Stevenson**.

'*Body Politic* revolves around a metaphorical conceit,' says Paul Johnston. 'The regime is seen in terms of the human body, so violence against an individual is also an assault on the state.' As the series progresses, however, this 'body' begins to look increasingly sick: afflicted by severe rationing in *The Bone Yard* (1998) and drought through global warming in *Water of Death* (1999). In *The Blood Tree* (2000), Johnston compares an increasingly dysfunctional Edinburgh with the unexpected democracy of nearby Glasgow, highlighting centuries of mutual mistrust.

Reaching deep into the city's darker and more dangerous recesses, freely accessing the city's criminal past and present, Inspector Rebus creator **Ian Rankin** (1960–) has few illusions about his homeland: 'I wrote the first one to try and tell people in the wider world that there was more to Edinburgh than the castle, tartan, shortbread and whisky. That there was actually a real, living, breathing city, and, when I was living here in the eighties, with real, living, breathing problems. It had the worst Aids and heroin rates in Western Europe per capita, and yet Edinburgh was ignoring that and going along as if it was still this great historic capital.' Born in **Cardenden**, Fife, some 15 miles north of Edinburgh, Rankin binds his narratives so tightly to the urban fabric that the city becomes a character in its own right.

A vividly drawn, essentially solitary character, Inspector John Rebus first appears in *Knots and Crosses* (1987), where he is forced to confront demons from his past and a serial killer dubbed the 'Edinburgh Strangler'. Rebus is a fallible man running on Jack Daniels and ready to do a deal with the devil if necessary. Operating out of **St Leonard's** police station, he spends too much time in pubs, such as the compact, unpretentious **Oxford Bar** on **Young Street**. His love life is often fraught, though he enjoys a form of security with the aptly named GP Dr Patience Aitken (who lives in **Oxford Terrace**). But it is Big Ger' Cafferty,

'*Dr Jekyll and Mr Hyde* really sums up Edinburgh,' says **Ian Rankin**, best-selling figurehead of Britain's regional detective fiction: 'Edinburgh is a very Presbyterian, reserved place, where you might never get to speak to your next-door neighbours, or people in a bus queue wouldn't talk to you. Edinburgh crime tends to be hidden, furtive, it's conspiracies and things that are happening in the dark, behind thick stone Georgian walls. It's the city of Deacon Brodie, of people who seem to be one thing but are actually something else.'

In *Set in Darkness* (2000), work is well under way at the new Scottish Parliament site in **Holyrood**. Building sites can be dangerous places, but when a young man's corpse is discovered behind a fireplace at **Queensbury House**, and a prospective MSP is found dead on site, it is clear that Rebus, 'standing in the midst of one of the biggest building sites in Edinburgh's history', isn't investigating industrial accidents.

arch-villain, alter ego, and Rebus's likely nemesis, who seems to understand him best.

Rankin's work, which has won him numerous accolades and awards, has a strong political bite, and is not afraid to tackle social realities. Typical of his style is *Mortal Causes* (1994), linking a brutal murder and the Edinburgh Festival with sectarianism and gunrunning to violent Protestant Loyalists in Northern Ireland. Continuing the theme of duality, Rankin explores the religious and social divides across from the tourist traps of **Princes Street** and the festival haunts, to the poverty and despair of an estate in 'Pilmuir' (from the real-life **Pilton** and **Muirhouse**). But the novel opens in the claustrophobic **Mary King's Close**, a part of hidden Edinburgh:

> They were in the close proper now, a narrow and fairly steep roadway between stone buildings. A rough drainage channel ran down one side of the road. Passages led off to dark alcoves… Rebus looked around. The place wasn't damp or chilled or cobwebbed. The air seemed fresh. Yet they were three or four storeys beneath road level. Rebus took the torch and shone it through a doorway…
>
> 'That's the wine shop,' the constable said. 'The butcher's is next door.'
>
> So it was. It consisted of a vaulted room, again whitewashed and with a floor of packed earth. But in its ceiling were a great many iron hooks, short and blackened but obviously used at one time for hanging up meat.
>
> Meat still hung from one of them.
>
> It was the lifeless body of a young man.

Arden Street, Marchmont – where **Ian Rankin** lived as a student and first started writing. When Rebus is not driving around in his battered Volvo, he likes listening to rock music in his first-floor flat here.

The capital of Scotland in all but name, **GLASGOW** sprawls across the head of the **Firth of Clyde** on the west coast. Like Edinburgh, it is a city of contrasts, but Glasgow does not hide its problems down narrow closes and behind heritage façades. In its wide, American-style grid of central avenues, shining new office blocks and refurbished hotels sit cheek-by-jowl with decaying red sandstone shopfronts and the gap-toothed defiance of open wasteland. Architectural gems do battle with huge high-rise housing schemes, while the proudly shabby **East End** is swiftly bypassed by tourists hurrying towards the vibrant **West End**. Alongside the **River Clyde**, massive crane towers stand as stark reminders of an industrial heritage almost entirely lost, and trains on the 'Clockwork Orange' underground system scurry along like rats in a run around a city whose heart is cruelly cleaved in two by the M8 motorway.

Its real-life crime statistics may make uncomfortable reading, but Glasgow retains an integrity that permeates much of its detective fiction, drawing more on a landscape of working-class criminality than middle-class misdemeanour. Steeped in symbolism and socialism, the city's contemporary literary scene has been led by the distinctive voices and

In *Boiling a Frog* (2000), **Christopher Brookmyre*** unleashes his investigative journalist Jack Parlabane onto an unsuspecting Edinburgh in the throes of 'post-Festival depression'. Sniffing out political conspiracy, blackmail and worse, Parlabane breaks into the headquarters of the Scottish Catholic Church only to end up mopping out prison cells with the stench of disinfectant strong in his nostrils. A satirist who frames his work within the crime genre, Brookmyre is wickedly funny as he lets loose an unrestrained tirade against Scotland's embryonic political Establishment.

Glasgow viewed from Garnethill – 'Two cities less than fifty miles apart, but to him Glasgow felt utterly different from Edinburgh, the new buildings brasher, the old more run down, the streets full of a darker energy with pavements crowded or suddenly, in mid-morning, eerily empty.'

Frederic Lindsay, *Death Knock* (2000)

'The Court confronts Glasgow Green like a warning' – the old **High Court** of Glasgow on Jocelyn Square, focal point for **William McIlvanney**'s Detective Inspector Laidlaw and **Bill Knox**'s Chief Detective Inspector Colin Thane.

bruised political prose of **Alasdair Gray** (1934–) and **James Kelman** (1946–). Merging elements of Greek and Elizabethan drama with his own unique style, the poet and novelist **William McIlvanney** (1936–) exposes the 'dual nature' of 'most things Scottish… both rough and genteel' in his debut detective novel, *Laidlaw* (1977). A genuine *tour de force*, this novel is indisputably Glaswegian: a tale of hard men and hard crime set in a hard city. Detective Inspector Laidlaw is a man wracked by inner demons – a believer in justice but sceptical of the all-too fallible systems of law enforcement. Like the city he polices, Laidlaw is a mass of contradictions: 'potentially a violent man who hated violence, a believer in fidelity who was unfaithful, an active man who longed for understanding'. A loner, prone to migraine and cold waves of despair, Laidlaw is a big man, a hard man himself, but also an intelligent and sensitive soul, a man more likely to stand accused of 'moral aggression' than physical assault.

'Big darknesses housing old griefs, terrible angers,' Glasgow's derelict tenement blocks are the novel's symbolic landscape and 'prisons for the past'. Still trapped in this past is Bud Lawson, a figure hewn from stone: '…his nature ran on tramlines. It had only one route. If you weren't on it, you were no part of his life.' Lawson is a man for whom violence is the only form of expression, for whom approaching the police is normally unthinkable – until one night his daughter fails to return home. When the girl's body turns up in a dense clump of bushes in **Kelvingrove Park**, Laidlaw knows he must move fast to find the killer before the 'natural justice' of the hard men and their gangs takes its course.

Laidlaw occupies a city and a society in the throes of transition, and lays bare the paradoxes of both new and old. McIlvanney's powerful and poetic prose offers a style almost uniquely Scottish in

'The park's charade of warmth' – **Kelvingrove Park** provides the scene of the crime in **William Mc Ilvanney**'s *Laidlaw*.

its depiction of landscapes sculpted by both compassion and cruelty. In the long-awaited sequel, *The Papers of Tony Veitch* (1983), Laidlaw hears the cryptic dying words of an alcoholic vagrant, and his subsequent investigations reveal a city that simply does not appear to care. With a powerful sense of place, *Strange Loyalties* (1991) takes both creator and character back to their pasts: McIlvanney's native **Kilmarnock**, twenty miles to the south-west of Glasgow, providing the model for 'Graithnock'. As Laidlaw returns to find out why his brother had to die, he discovers that 'the landscape was more than a landscape. It was also a private ordnance map of questions and messages to me. The countryside and the villages I passed through seemed to make an innocent statement about the coexistence of people and nature, but the subtext for me was the strangeness of what I had become.'

In a long-running series featuring Chief Detective Inspector Colin Thane and the fictional 'Millside' (modelled on the old **Maryhill**) Division, **Bill Knox** (1928–99) focuses on the routines of policing observed through his years as a crime reporter in the city. Many of the landscapes of Knox's absorbing police procedurals have now changed as Glasgow's facelift continues unabated. Standing close to the banks of the River Clyde, the landmarks of the old **High Court** building and adjacent **City Mortuary**, and their daily trade in the after-effects of criminality, served as a major source of inspiration.

Thane and DI Philip Moss track a thief who has killed a policeman during an audacious daylight robbery in *Deadline for a Dream* (1957). Knox's first novel provides a study of social pressure and simple human greed, and the portrayal of ambitious young reporter turned killer David Renfield is often sympathetic. The landscape of Glasgow reflects the void between the reality and aspirations of Renfield's life:

Bill Knox – respected Glaswegian journalist and creator of the 'Millside' police procedurals, pictured at Aviemore.

he simply does not have the means to sustain visits to smart bars and the 'wallie close' (traditional tiled finish) of his girlfriend's family: 'tiled, clean, neat, voicing a respectability which shuddered at the soot-stained stone and plaster poverty of its more down-at-heel tenement equivalents in other parts of the city.' The crime itself is enacted beside wasteland and factories, where the incongruity of a Rolls-Royce (collecting the factory wages each week) against a backdrop of Clyde-side cranes 'vague through smoke and haze' makes the robbery almost inevitable. That it is a middle-class reporter stealing working men's wages is significant, and the trade-off of a bag of cash for a young police officer's life is equally unacceptable. Its honour threatened, the city duly demands retribution. With the word out on the street, slowly, inevitably, the full force of Glaswegian justice tightens around the killer's young neck.

The spiral staircase – many of the city's detective stories revolve around life in Glasgow tenements.

Knox was raised in the middle-class suburbs, but through his compact and careful prose describes the poverty, slums and deprivation witnessed in Glasgow through the 1950s and 60s. The Millside series ran parallel to the transformation of Glasgow from a city of heavy industry and shipbuilding to today's technology and service industries. The intuitive, headstrong Thane and more reserved, diligent Moss move on to hi-tech crime in *The Interface Man* (1989) and *Death Bytes* (1998). The unfinished manuscript of Knox's final novel, *The Lazarus Widow* (1999), was completed by **Martin Edwards***. Through this tale of big-money international fraud runs the **River Clyde**, patrolled by the enigmatic figure of the 'Riverman' (based upon a real character), whose life is dedicated to pulling bodies (some living, some long dead) out of its chilly waters.

'My first winter in Glasgow was the coldest for fifty years or more. I thought, if this is what a Scottish winter is like, I won't be able to survive here.' Icy rain and freezing winter winds were blowing around Glasgow's tower blocks and tenements when **Peter Turnbull*** (1950–) entered the city in 1977 as a young social worker. Shocked and angered to learn that the community of **Easterhouse** had 'more people living in it than the city of Perth – with just one shopping centre and four pubs', Turnbull wrote his atmospheric debut *Deep and Crisp and Even* (1981). In the grip of the coldest winter for many years, Glasgow is grinding to a halt as PC Hamilton walks his beat along **Argyle Street** (close to **Buchanan Street**). When he sees a man stagger out of an alleyway before him, Hamilton thinks it must be a drunk:

Born in **Kirkcaldy**, Fife, **Val McDermid*** cut her teeth as a journalist in Glasgow before branching out into crime writing. Her series character, Glaswegian reporter Lindsay Gordon, was probably the first openly lesbian character in British crime fiction. In the face of tabloid prejudice, Lindsay has to prove the innocence of a previous lover in *Final Edition* (1991), set in the newspaper world, with Glasgow proudly donning its mantle of European City of Culture.

The 'Big Freeze', January 1978, **Buchanan Street** – scene of the dramatic finale to **Peter Turnbull**'s chilling *Deep and Crisp and Even*.

The snow lay in an even mantle, disturbed only by his footprints, and the reflected lights enabled him to see a long way. He could see the name over a shop at the end of the street and even fancied that he could pick out individual bolts in the Central Station railway bridge and, turning the other way, he could make out the blue of the clock face at Glasgow Cross. It was very still and very quiet and the only people there were himself and the dead man.

The officers of Glasgow's 'P Division' live unspectacular, averagely paid lives investigating crime and confronting violence and death on a daily basis. But the prospect of a psychopath stalking the streets fills them with a 'stomach-wrenching, heart-stopping fear'. Operating from **Charing Cross** Police Station, DI Donoghue and DS Ray Sussock grow increasingly frustrated as they chase shadows in the hunt for a serial killer dubbed 'Slow Tom'. In his series tackling drugs, poverty, homelessness and abuse in a distinctive, stylized voice, Turnbull charts a changing city; building his landscapes out of the 'schemes' (housing estates), tenements, closes and bars ('The Auld Hoose' is a windowless

Sighthill cemetery and tower blocks – the social landscape of Glasgow's notorious 'schemes' is explored widely by the city's detective fiction writers.

The **Cuillin** on the **Isle of Skye** provide an atmospheric setting for Miss Pink's investigations in **Gwen Moffat**'s climbing mystery *Over the Sea to Death* (1976).

The 'strong shadows and huge sky' of the **Northumberland** coast near **Whitley Bay** – a landscape that features prominently in the novels of **Ann Cleeves**.

Slumbering Mersey giant – the waterfront of **Liverpool** with its trademark Liver Birds high above a city that is home to the series sleuths of **Martin Edwards** and **Ron Ellis**.

York by night – the city's detective fiction looks into the shadows of its historic and tourist façades.

'purpose-built drinking factory'). In *The Man with no Face* (1998), a killing that appears to be an underworld settling of accounts leads Sussock and his colleagues into a labyrinth of insurance fraud, kidnapping and murder. From the discovery of a faceless body in **Winton Drive** near the bohemian profusion of the West End, into the grim tenements of Easterhouse, and on to the outlying town of **Kilsyth**, Turnbull's beautifully cadenced prose zeroes in on Glasgow's 'emotional chemistry, the spirit of the city'.

The traditional landscapes of Glasgow's detective fiction explore a distinctly patriarchal society; where the city still echoes to the hammering of the shipyards, where raised voices are harsh and whisky-furred, and where conflict is resolved by clenched fist or cold steel blade. But new landscapes are emerging, casting a welcome feminist perspective on the city.

To the north of the city centre, **Garnethill** is the highpoint of Glasgow, with extensive views across to the towers of **Sighthill** in the east and to Kelvingrove and the university in the west. Despite some grandiose architecture, this is not a wealthy quarter. Riddled with old tunnels and shafts from the mining of garnets, the most precious commodity here today is the Mackintosh heritage of its Art School. **Denise Mina** (1966–) places her reluctant sleuth and champion of lost causes, Maureen O'Donnell, in a flat at the top of Garnethill in **Buccleuch Street**.

'Glasgow has the perfect landscape for urban thrillers' – **Denise Mina** at the **Garnethill** viewpoint, close to the home of her protagonist, Maureen O'Donnell.

> '···' 'I came back to Glasgow when I was 20, and really fell in love with the city. It was a very dirty city for a long, long time and all the buildings were black and it was very depressing. Then during the 1970s and 80s a lot of the buildings were cleaned up and underneath the black soot the buildings were yellow and red sandstone and absolutely beautiful. I couldn't believe it, because we always thought Glasgow was the ugliest place in the world.'

Hard-drinking, heavy-smoking, self-doubting O'Donnell is introduced in *Garnethill* (1998), the first part of Mina's powerful trilogy of abuse, mental illness, poverty and institutional failure. When Maureen's lover is found in her flat with his throat slit from ear to ear, the finger of suspicion not only points in her direction, it prods her firmly towards the edge of insanity. Crackling with livewire Glaswegian dialogue, this is a shocking, funny, deeply moving tale using Mina's experience of geriatric and terminal-care nursing. Her Glasgow is epitomized by the gritty determination, self-deprecating humour and fundamental decency of Maureen O'Donnell, and *Garnethill* is ultimately a tale of courage, survival and redemption. In an area of great poverty and deprivation, the tall, dark red-brick needle of the **Ruchill** Hospital tower (formerly a fever hospital for contagious diseases, then a general hospital) encapsulates the major themes of the trilogy continued in *Exile* (2000) and *Resolution* (2001).

The all-pervading odour of formalin is a familiar smell in the fiction of veterinary surgeon and anaesthetist **Manda Scott***, whose scalpel-sharp Kellen Stewart trilogy opens with *Hen's Teeth* (1996). Scott's all-action debut explores the dark depths of grieving and death in a plot of multi-million pound drug racketeering. Therapist Kellen Stewart and pathologist Lee Adams make a formidable team as the action moves from a claustrophobic, high-pressure medical world, via West End bars and eating houses, to the relative tranquillity of a horse farm in the **Campsie Hills,** just south-west of **Earl's Seat** ('The Ben'). Scott's precise,

'She looked across to the north side and saw the jagged tower of the Ruchill fever hospital stabbing at the sky. It was watching her, looking into her house' – the symbolic Victorian hospital tower at **Ruchill** haunts Maureen O'Donnell in **Denise Mina**'s *Exile.*

hard-edged prose has a frightening intensity at times, and the burn-out commitment of her characters is personified by Dr Nina Crawford in the veterinary chiller *Night Mares* (1998).

'If one lives in Galloway, one either fishes or paints. 'Either' is perhaps misleading, for most of the painters are fishers also in their spare time. To be neither of these things is considered odd and almost eccentric...' **Dorothy L Sayers*** sets the scene for *Five Red Herrings* (1931) (US: *Suspicious Characters*) far away from the urban realities of Glasgow, in attractive **Kirkcudbright** in the south-west of Scotland. Lord Peter Wimsey arrives in the elegant Georgian town with its picturesque waterfront for a holiday just as Campbell, a highly unpopular painter, is found murdered. Suspicion falls on six other painters, and five of these are the proverbial red herrings. Far from being a fish out of water, Lord Peter appears to be in his element:

> ...Wimsey's soul purred within him as he pushed the car along. The road from Kirkcudbright to Newton-Stewart is of a varied loveliness hard to surpass, and with a sky full of bright sun and rolling cloudbanks, hedges filled with flowers, a well-made road, a lively engine and the prospect of a good corpse at the end of it, Lord Peter's cup of happiness was full.

The picturesque harbour of Kirkcudbright – D L Sayers holidayed here each year from 1929 to 1932, staying at 14a High Street which she describes in *Five Red Herrings* with its 'brilliant blue gate'.

CHAPTER TWO

Northumbria

For many, this would be the first time they had
experienced the splendours of Northumberland: the long sweep of
the beaches, the castles and tower houses, the majestic rise of
the Cheviots in the hinterland.

Roy Lewis, *The Ghost Dancers* (1999)

Bamburgh Castle provides a
romantic Arthurian backdrop
to **Roy Lewis'** *An Uncertain
Sound* (1978).

Comprising modern-day **Northumberland, Tyne & Wear** and **Durham**,
the region of **NORTHUMBRIA** is bounded to the west by the **Pennines**,
England's mountainous backbone, and to the east by the relentless
pounding of the North Sea. Once a great Anglo-Saxon kingdom,
Northumbria is littered with evidence of centuries-old conflict along a
disputed borderland: to the south, **Hadrian's Wall** is a famous reminder
of 400 years of Roman occupation, while a chain of impressive castles
and fortifications all the way up to the **Cheviot Hills** and the Scottish
border point to long years of Anglo-Scottish conflict. More recently, the

vagaries of economic policy dictated from afar have torn the heart out of communities founded on traditional industries such as coal-mining, engineering and ship-building. This is the land of the **Venerable Bede** (673–735), whose *Historia Ecclesiastica Gentis Anglorum* earned him the title of 'Father of English History', but also of popular novelist **Catherine Cookson** (1906–98), a native of the south Tyneside dockyards. The region's detective fiction reflects such contrasts.

NORTHUMBERLAND juxtaposes the raw beauty of England's wildest national park – vast tracts of wide-open moorland, scattered farms and heavily forested hills – with some of the country's worst pockets of post-industrial blight. Happily tramping the untamed moors and windswept coastline to explore the historic sites of England's northernmost county is Arnold Landon, an unassuming planning officer-cum-archaeologist and amateur sleuth created by **Roy Lewis*** (1933–). Based in the county town of **Morpeth**, Arnold's job takes him round many of the county's more mystical and romantic sites and involves him in archaeology, medieval building research – and murder.

'I shall continue to root my books in the north-east' – **Roy Lewis**, creator of the Arnold Landon and Eric Ward mystery series.

   A Secret Dying (1992) takes Arnold Landon deep into the bowels of a Northumberland castle, where he stumbles across the *sudarium*, a fragment of cloth reputedly used to bind the face of Christ in death. The cloth resurfaces in *The Cross Bearer* (1994) as the centrepiece of an exhibition in Morpeth, where Arnold swiftly finds himself drawn into the mystique of the Knights Templar and on a sordid trail of modern-day corruption and political shenanigans. The landscapes of the series reflect Arnold's enjoyment of the outdoors: surveying, photographing and walking. Arnold's practised eye roams across the folds and shadows of the land, alighting on lost villages and long-buried history, his thoughts often in 'tumult with the noise of centuries' as he recreates life, passions and deaths from past days:

> They… drove along the valley, down from the fell, along the wooded gorge that led eastwards towards the coast; across small medieval pack-bridges and through tiny hamlets tucked away under the craggy outcrops… The sun, lower in the sky, now sent long shadows across the field. Sheep scattered as they walked near the boundary hedge, and Arnold pointed out… where the old village would have lain. The long shadows emphasized the folds in the ground; the indentation that would have been the old main street of the village, and the irregular mounds which would once have been the dwelling houses, dragged down to their foundations in disuse, and covered by the accumulation of centuries. Heather and gorse grew there now in profusion, ash trees spread magnificent branches above the quiet earth, and a bank of sycamores leaned across the waters of the small, winding stream that would have served the village long ago.

Iris Collier uses the deeply spiritual landscape of **Holy Island** (Lindisfarne) for the setting of her crime debut *Spring Tide* (1995), featuring DI Douglas McBride and Sergeant Venerables in a tale of religious fanaticism and murder. Young archaeologist Anna Fitzgerald provides the crucial link to the distant past and, captivated by the elements on this desolate coast, to the Northumbrian landscape. The north-eastern duo of McBride and Venerables return in *Requiem* (1997).

Northumberland National Park – 'It's the emptiness. Miles and miles of empty space,' says **Ann Cleeves**.

Raised beneath the skies of North Devon, where with 'strong, far-away horizons you could never feel shut in', **Ann Cleeves** 'fell in love with Northumberland the minute I saw it'.

The dozen years that **Ann Cleeves*** (1954–) spent in the north-east left her with a lasting impression of the openness of its people and surroundings. Curiously, although Cleeves is fond of Northumbria's yawning spaces and dramatic landscapes, it is the small, tightly knit communities here that provide the focus for many of her novels. In *Another Man's Poison* (1992), the detecting duo of renowned amateur ornithologist George Palmer-Jones and his wife Molly arrive in the fictional Pennine area of 'Crowford', where Molly plans to visit her aunt. Alive, Molly's aunt has been proving a nuisance to the local landowner and ambitious politician. Dead, she turns out to be even more troublesome, as the investigation into her murder pokes into every nook and cranny of the landowner's tragic family past. Tackling issues of estate management, gamekeeping and conservation, the rural economy comes under close scrutiny too.

An ex-pit village lad who operates from the police station in 'Otterbridge' (based on **Morpeth**) and lives in the quiet village of 'Heppleburn' (a composite of **Earsdon** and **Holywell**), Detective Inspector Stephen Ramsay is Cleeves' second series detective. One of the strongest Ramsay novels, *The Baby Snatcher* (1997), is a taut and disturbing mystery based on the tiny, bleak, former power station village of **North Blyth**, on the coast between **Newbiggin-by-the-Sea** and **Whitley Bay**. Here, on the isolated 'Headland', where a woman has been

murdered and children keep mysteriously disappearing and reappearing, Ramsay must gain the trust of a wary community in a striking, if ravaged, landscape.

Though still rooted firmly in the Northumberland landscape with its 'strong shadows and huge sky', *The Crow Trap* (1999) is a brooding one-off detective thriller signalling a departure from series detection. Its title derives from the gamekeeper's device used to lure crows to their death by using a live crow trapped in a cage, and is an appropriate metaphor for this edgy mystery. When three women are thrown awkwardly together to form an environmental survey team, each brings her own emotional baggage, and each has her own story of betrayal.

Kielder Water, deep in the Northumberland National Park and the largest man-made reservoir in Europe, becomes 'Cranford Water' in **Ann Cleeves'** *The Sleeping and the Dead* (2001). In the 'driest summer since the reservoir was built', the story probes beneath the surface as DCI Peter Porteous investigates the discovery of a body that has lain undisturbed for over twenty years, against the disconcerting silence of 'Cranwell' village.

No-nonsense, big-hearted **NEWCASTLE-ON-TYNE** has undergone a facelift in recent years, with major redevelopment of its post-industrial areas – especially along the river where its economic might was founded.

'The beach was almost empty... and the power station at the north of the bay seemed close enough to touch.' The isolated industrial community of **North Blyth** provided the inspiration for the 'Headland' of **Ann Cleeves'** *The Baby Snatcher* (1997).

'The Quayside was the right location for him: it kept him in touch with Newcastle and the north, reminded him of his roots, kept his feet on the ground, made him face realities…' – Newcastle's **Quayside** is a focal point for Eric Ward, who first appears in **Roy Lewis'** *A Certain Blindness* (1980), and for the writing of **Martyn Waites**.

The demise of Newcastle's core industries and docklands plunged the Tyneside giant into severe economic recession. Today's resurgent city has much to offer, though areas of dereliction remain, with the contrasts between the high-rises of **Scotswood** and the affluent Victorian terraces of **Jesmond** offering ample scope for detective fiction.

Below the chunky steel girders of the **Tyne Bridge**, built in 1928 as a striking symbol of Newcastle's vital relationship with the river, lies the regenerated, highly photogenic **Quayside**. Eric Ward, the former police officer, solicitor and company director created by **Roy Lewis***, has an office here, overlooking the ships and busy dockside. Eric's practice is well placed for shipping and marine work, and Lewis uses his own legal expertise to immerse Eric in hostile takeovers, fraud and murder in the fields of finance and shipping. Eric is a seasoned traveller, and in *A Kind of Transaction* (1991) moves between Spain, Singapore and Northumbria on the trail of a missing executive and high-level marine fraud.

The concept of importing the 'literary reportage' of American *noir* and hard-boiled writing to the streets of Newcastle is evident in **Martyn Waites'** (1963–) poignant and pacy debut novel, *Mary's Prayer*

(1997). Travelling up from London to cover the funeral of a local drug dealer and former schoolfriend, investigative reporter turned tabloid hack Stephen Larkin is soon reacquainted with an old flame. But when she sets him on the trail of a murderer, Larkin discovers just how dangerous his home city can be. Waites grew up in the West End of Newcastle before moving to nearby **Birtley** – a thinly disguised version of which appears as Larkin's former home town of 'Grimley'. Newcastle's Quayside and Swing Bridge are integral to the story, as are the famous 'Toon' nightlife and drinking culture: 'I try to do the geography of the city by the pubs and their clientele,' says Waites, 'using this as a microcosm of different sections within the city':

'I think Newcastle is a very *noir* kind of city in a way, architecturally it's very suggestive' – **Martyn Waites**.

> He stood in the freezing cold and the pouring rain. The Tyne was slapping angrily at the soaked wooden jetty on which he stood, all weather-eaten and mossed, its banks perilously close to breaking. He was in the shadows, looking out. He could hear the occasional car passing overhead, see right along the waterfront. Directly in front of him was the Tyne Bridge, with the floating night-club moored beneath it; tonight its half-hearted disco lights seemed to cast a depressing pall on the mud-grey water. On the other side of the river the bars and buildings were in darkness; the last straggling Sunday drinkers had gone home hours ago.

Larkin's genuine anger at the rotten remnants of 'broken post-war promises and dodgy land deals', which created the 'crumbling high-rise hell' of housing schemes, resurfaces in *Little Triggers* (1998). In this hard-hitting sequel Waites interweaves the issues of piecemeal urban regeneration, high-level corruption and child abuse. Trying to influence local politics for the better, Larkin's blackmail scheme drags him into a nightmarish world of violence and abuse, and leads to a truly shocking climax.

Due south of Newcastle, rising majestically above the **River Wear**, **Durham Cathedral** is an uplifting sight. Aside from writing a history of the cathedral and many other religious works, former Dean of Durham **Cyril Alington** (1872–1955) found inspiration in England's finest Norman-Romanesque cathedral for a number of clerical mysteries. Featuring two archdeacons as detectives in the cathedral city of 'Garminster', *Archdeacons Afloat* (1946) and *Archdeacons Ashore* (1947) were followed by *Gold and Gaiters* (1950), which centres on the cathedral library and the theft of Roman gold coins.

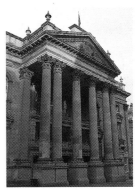

'Newcastle was always reality to me,' wrote **Nancy Spain** (1917–64), who was born in **Jesmond**. A successful journalist, Spain created sleuth Miriam Birdseye and wrote ten detective novels, nine of which were comic capers loaded with sexual politics. *Cinderella Goes To The Morgue* (1950) is set in and around the impressive neo-classic **Theatre Royal** of her native 'Newchester-on-the-Tame'.

CHAPTER THREE

Yorkshire

'I've been able to send Dalziel and Pascoe out to a 'Mid-Yorkshire' that's got everything; it extends into every bit of Yorkshire: right to the coast, down to the coalmining areas, up to the Moors, across to the Dales and the great metropolitan hubs as well.'

Reginald Hill

England's largest historic county has always considered itself a place apart. Yorkshire is the territory of literary detectives as distinctive as its geography: the remote beauty of the **Yorkshire Dales** and **Yorkshire Moors** national parks, miles of spectacular coastline, and major cities such as **Leeds**, **York** and **Sheffield**. Yorkshire's detective fiction offers an insight into conflicting ways of life, from ancient rural landscapes, traditional crafts and the monastic vestiges of religious power, to mighty industrial landscapes and the high-rises of thriving multicultural conurbations. Yorkshire folk may be renowned for their obduracy and dour humour, but there is a strong community spirit and social conscience reflected in the region's detective fiction. Above all this, hanging like a moorland mist, is the spirit of the **Brontës** and the brooding romance of *Wuthering Heights*.

John Wainwright – an early pioneer of the Yorkshire police procedural.

John Wainwright's (1921–) *Death in a Sleeping City* (1965) introduced a powerful new voice to the British police novel. The debut of this working police officer probes the brutality of organized crime in an unspecified Northern city sandwiched between North Riding and County Durham. Subsequent novels depict widely varied Yorkshire landscapes, but Wainwright was born in **Hunslet**, a south **Leeds** suburb where a tree was a tram-ride away and the air was choked by industrial smog. Twenty years with the West Riding Constabulary lends authority and authenticity to his novels. Wainwright's series features several main detectives, most of them Yorkshiremen and proud of it. *Blayde RIP* (1982) details the life of Chief Superintendent Robert Blayde, a Wainwright regular, and is set in the tiny village of **Huby**, midway between **Otley** and **Harrogate**. In *The Man Who Wasn't There* (1989), Chief Inspector Lyle is on the trail of gangland killers and an informant in the 'Lessford' police force. There is a powerful sense of place in the dehumanizing urban sprawl where some three million people are crammed into 'Lessford' and 'Bordfield'. The Lessford landscape is

Yorkshire moors and dales between **Swaledale** and **Wensleydale**.

particularly unforgiving, and its inhabitants 'all seemed to carry the look – the curse – of absolute defeat'. Lyle's escape route is provided by the 'endless zig-zag of drystone walls', the hypnotic rise and fall of the grassy **Pennines** and the 'distant, isolated farmsteads, with no apparent means of access or egress. The skyscape of layers of clouds, each layer moving at a different pace from its fellows. The flocks of sheep, each flock bunched together like a huge, po-faced family; the isolated trees permanently bent away from the prevailing wind; the distant hills and beyond them, more hills, and beyond *them* and in the hazy, purple distance, even more hills.'

One of the undisputed modern masters of the police procedural and recipient of the Diamond Dagger, **Reginald Hill*** (1936–) came to Yorkshire in the late 1960s. The 'eclectic, not specific' Yorkshire of Hill's stylish novels, underpinned by an understanding of human nature as strong as his ear for dialogue and dialect, aims to distil an essence of Yorkshire rather than present a literal landscape. **Doncaster**, in South

An Advancement of Learning (1971) draws on the college where **Reginald Hill** taught for many years (**High Melton**, near Doncaster) – education and learning are major themes in Hill's work.

Reginald Hill, the doyen of Yorkshire crime fiction.

Yorkshire, inspired *A Clubbable Woman* (1970), introducing confrontational, crude and contradictory 'Fat Man' Superintendent Andy Dalziel (pronounced 'Dee-elle') and stressed but rather more civilized, fastidious Detective Chief Inspector Peter Pascoe.

The long and proud tradition of coalmining, and its rapid and painful demise, are explored in *Under World* (1988), the moving, unsentimental story of a young man coming home to 'ride the pit' and to discover how his father really died. Set in the mining community of 'Burrthorpe' in the aftermath of the national miners' strike, the novel portrays a universe of real hardship peopled with proud, insular Yorkshiremen, where ugly terraces reflect uncertain times. Old vengeances die hard here, and the recovery of bones from a disused pit shaft point to bloodshed ahead. Setting off 'along the crest of the ridge so that he remained in the world of trees and leaves and earth and sky for as long as possible', the young miner is soon confronted with the 'graffiti on the blue sky, the dark tower of the winding gear, the conveyor like a ramp into the bowels of a convict ship, the scatter of low sullen buildings all squatting amid mounds of their own waste. The pit-head, whose ugliness only hinted at the vileness of the organism beneath.'

The 'Under World' of a coalface.

... Enscombe is not remote by modern standards. But as the road began to narrow and the valley sides to steepen, Peter Pascoe felt a disproportionate sense of remoteness. Everywhere there were signs of man's presence – the walls built out of stones painfully cleared from the green pastures alongside the shining river, the sheep grazing between them, the whitewashed farmhouses, the road itself – but nowhere was there anything to persuade of man's permanence. Good old heartless, witless nature seemed lurking everywhere, ready to rush back in the minute man dropped his guard.

Pictures of Perfection (1994)

'I was always more likely to be wearing my hiking boots walking round the Dales or Moors than I was walking the mean streets of downtown Bradford,' says Hill, whose landscapes have gradually become more rural as the series progresses. The author's skill at entwining physical and psychological landscape reaches its apogee in *On Beulah Height* (1999), a masterpiece tapping into the anxieties of children and parents, against a background of Yorkshire lore and legend. When three children disappeared from the valley community of 'Dendale' fifteen years ago, Dalziel was unable to solve the case. Then Dendale was flooded – carrying overtones of diluvian punishment – to create a new reservoir. When a child goes missing from the next valley along, Dendale returns to haunt Dalziel. The key themes of loyalty and rootedness are reflected by a prime suspect whom Sergeant Edgar Wield sees as a creature possessed by place, someone 'that I reckon you couldn't uproot, only break off at ground level'.

'Monday morning, start of a new week, air bright as ice in a crystal glass, brandy-gold sun pouring from delft-blue sky, the old bracken glowing on rolling moors, the trees still pied with their unblasted leaves, the pastures still green with their unmuddied grass, as October runs into November and thinks it's September still.'

Reginald Hill, prologue to *The Wood Beyond* (1996).

The ancient centre of **YORK** is a beautiful heritage cluster of narrow medieval streets inside a solid ring of old city walls – more than two miles of walkway broken by gateways, or 'bars' – in the shadow of the largest Gothic building in Britain. England's second city through much of the Middle Ages, York is the ideal location for **Candace Robb**'s historical mysteries. Robb conjures up fourteenth-century York in a series featuring Welshman Owen Archer, a passionate, intelligent and honourable man, once captain of the King's archers but now returned from the Hundred Years War with only one eye. In *The Apothecary Rose* (1993), Owen investigates the death of two knights of the realm in **St Mary's Abbey**, founded in 1086 as a Benedictine abbey in riverside grounds, and by Archer's day the largest wool trader in York. Owen's investigations lead him to Wilton's Apothecary on the corner of **Stonegate** and **Davygate**, where he finds a sleuthing partner in Wilton's gorgeous herbalist wife Lucie.

The wool trade features prominently in *The Lady Chapel* (1994), a tale of court intrigue, devout aspiration and mercantile quarrelling, in which Owen is called in to investigate the death of a Guildsman in the Minster yard whilst in the company of a mysterious hooded woman. The only

York-born **Domini Highsmith** sets her late twelfth-century mysteries in nearby **Beverley**. With help from nurse Elvira, Father Simeon has to contend with corrupt clergy and medieval thievery. Highsmith lives in the shadow of Beverley's magnificent Minster, and took her inspiration for Simeon from the tomb of the Unknown Priest in its North Transept.

witness is a young boy, Jasper: 'The minster loomed high above him to his right, a towering darkness that echoed with breezes and the skittering of night creatures… Jasper hurried past the towers, stumbling in his fear of being alone in this place best left to God and the saints at nightfall.'

York may no longer be the most important city in Yorkshire, but it still retains 'the very special flavour of history still alive in modern times,' says **Barbara Whitehead** (1930–). 'Traditionally, it has been regarded almost as a holy city.' Whitehead's York Mysteries, investigated by Detective Chief Inspector Robert Southwell, chart a changing cityscape and shatter a few illusions about this 'serene city…, this hidebound, conventional place'. Born in **Sheffield**, Whitehead spent over thirty years in York and her mysteries move freely around the city's rich historical locations. The focal point of the Minster becomes the scene of a fictional crime in *The Dean it was that Died* (1991), while in *Playing God* (1988), an infamous rock star cast – or rather miscast, in the opinion of many good burghers of York – to play Jesus in one of the thirteenth-century York Mystery Plays, comes to grief during the dress rehearsal. The real-life York Mystery Plays used to be performed in the open air of the beautifully laid out **Museum Gardens**, against the backdrop of the ruined arches of **St Mary's Abbey**.

The Killings at Barley Hall (1995) take place during the restoration of **Barley Hall** (open to the public) just off **Stonegate** but point back to the Hall's turbulent history and connections with Richard III. In Whitehead's most popular mystery, *The Girl with Red Suspenders* (1990), the real Ship Inn at **Acaster Malbis**, a tiny village on the **River Ouse** south-west of York, provides the location for some crucial scenes.

'We don't just occupy a place, the place also occupies us… We don't just live in a place, it is where our imaginations are set in motion. It is our point of discovery, it is where we discover other people and therefore ourselves' – **John Baker** (1942–) was born in the small east coast resort of **Filey**, just north of **Hull**, but has lived in York for many years. An idealist wrapped in a pessimist's cloak, Sam Turner is the caring, world-weary private investigator of Baker's series exploring city life beyond the medieval walls, where the remnants of ancient history distract from problems unchanged through the centuries: inequality, discrimination, violence, poverty and loneliness.

Sam first appears in *Poet in the Gutter* (1995) as an alcoholic celebrating every day without a drink and attending a men's group. Sam is a big **Raymond Chandler** (1888–1959) fan, and as everyone else in the group seems to be inventing their lives, he pretends to be a private investigator. When one of the members asks for Sam's help in checking up on his wife, the detection starts for real, and Sam is soon discussing details in the old-fashioned comfort of York's traditional meeting place, **Betty's**, on the corner of **St Helen's Square**. Surveillance work seems fun – until his client is found murdered at home and the job turns into bodyguarding the alluring, less than distraught widow, the original Chandleresque femme fatale.

'For many years, I worked constantly on the records of the city of York, transcribing, editing, indexing… recording the inscriptions on its gravestones, and reading its old newspapers.' **Barbara Whitehead** uses her research in the 'York Cycle of Mysteries'.

'There must be a ghost in every other building in this town.' *Walking with Ghosts* (1999), Baker's favourite novel, finds Sam employed by an insurance company to investigate the death of a political lobbyist's wife, whose life was insured for £2.5 million. As Sam faces up to his own wife's impending death, a ghost from their past moves ever closer to home. The city's contrasting social landscapes are symbolized by the team that Sam assembles, notably the 'hameless [*sic*] and hungry' waif Geordie and his dog Barney, who Sam first meets camped in a shop doorway near the **Coppergate Centre**. Romantic, lyrical and compassionate, *Shooting in the Dark* (2001) continues Baker's themes of social exclusion, loss and obsession, as Sam turns bodyguard-cum-

'York is not just about Romans or Vikings or medieval walls, it's about money and power and poverty and sleaze,' says **John Baker**, pictured here near York's **Millennium Bridge**.

The first crime writer to recognize York's criminal potential behind its heritage façade was **Maurice Procter***, who placed abrasive Detective Superintendent Philip Hunter in 'Yoreborough' for novels such as *I Will Speak Daggers* (1956).

The old city walls and **York Minster**, Britain's largest Gothic church, have been walked by fictional detectives since medieval times.

detective for a beautiful blind woman. Using blindness as the meta-phorical key, Baker turns pre-Christmas York into a mirror for Sam's troubled conscience.

'People here always walk the walls because it's quicker than walking the pavements,' says **Peter Turnbull***, whose CID Detective Inspector George Hennessey would like to see a one-way system introduced on York's crowded walls. Hennessey operates from a fictitious police station at the south-western **Micklegate Bar** overlooking the sluggish waters of the Ouse. The gently undulating **Vale of York** provides the setting for the harrowing police procedural *Embracing Skeletons* (1996), which opens with the discovery of the burnt body of a young boy on bleak **Marston Moor**, six miles west of York, and still resounding with the battles of the English Civil War.

Born in **Rotherham**, schooled in **Sheffield** and now living in **Leeds**, Turnbull is pleased to connect with his Yorkshire roots in a compact city without high-rises, and a surface quiet only disrupted '...when the agricultural workers or the miners come into town on a Saturday

Peter Turnbull at the entrance to one of York's ancient 'snickleways' (narrow cobbled alleyways), **Lund's Court** (formerly Mad Alice Lane).

'The world wasn't constructed with consciousness, it was fashioned out of fear and greed, and all of its inhabitants were in hiding. They were on the street, in open view, but each of them was purblind to the predicament of the others' – a homeless man in the busy shopping street of **Stonegate** reflecting **John Baker**'s concerns in *Shooting in the Dark*.

'It struck me how easy it would be to arrange an undetectable murder in that place' – **Trfyan** in **Snowdonia** provides the inspiration for **Glyn Carr**'s climbing mysteries.

'It's a very changeable landscape, and it does have a Gothic sort of element' – moorland heather in the **Yorkshire Dales National Park**, close to **Peter Robinson**'s 'Eastvale'.

The **Ellis Peters** window in the **Abbey of St Peter and St Paul, Shrewsbury** – commemorating one of the best-loved storytellers of historical detective fiction.

evening, wanting their beer'. 'Mind you,' jokes the pathologist in *Fear of Drowning* (1999), 'when we do get murders in the Vale… they have a certain class about them, don't you think? I mean, grubby pit village stabbings on Saturday night belong to South Yorkshire, West Yorkshire has its share of senseless violence, but we in North Yorkshire, particularly in the Vale, have murders of class.' Sure enough, the middle-aged couple who mysteriously vanish from their bungalow in a village on the Ouse appear to have been classy, until their dead bodies emerge from a very ordinary shallow grave.

'The mist that had pervaded the town all day began to thicken into soup. The Humber bubbled away, cooking algae and a mixture of aquatic cryptogams up into a roke that rolled off the river and enveloped the city and the surrounding countryside' – *The Chinese Girl* (2000) is the first instalment of **John Baker**'s Hull-based series featuring ex-con Stone Lewis. Rediscovering the town after more than a decade in prison, Stone sets out to help a young 'Chinese' woman he finds on his doorstep.

Micklegate Bar, the most important of the medieval gates of York, where 'the severed heads of traitors, rebels and enemies of the Crown were once displayed', and where **Peter Turnbull**'s series detective DI George Hennessey contemplates modern-day crime and punishment.

'It stands alone on the hill top, a sentinel for all to note and there is nothing around it save green grass, deciduous trees and oceans of fresh moorland air laced with the multifarious scents of rural England' – **Nicholas Rhea**'s former police house at 'Aidensfield' (**Oswaldkirk**) remains much as described in *Constable on the Hill* and is still occupied by the local police sergeant.

Tucked-away **Glaisdale**.

In the midst of the vast, heather-covered, forested expanse of the **NORTH YORKSHIRE MOORS**, the village of **Goathland** is an incongruous site: a brightly painted film-set village luring coachloads of visitors into the commercial centre of the 'Heartbeat' industry. The television series 'Heartbeat' featuring Constable Nick Rowan was inspired by the gently nostalgic 'Constable' novels of **Nicholas Rhea** (pseud. Peter N Walker, 1936–). 'The idea of the Constable books initially was to show a village bobby's life within a community, not crime fiction as such,' says Rhea. Based on his own experiences in the North Yorkshire Police, *Constable on the Hill* (1979) is an unashamedly light-hearted look back at the life and crimes of 1960s rural North Yorkshire. Rhea was born a few miles to the north-west of Goathland in the isolated former mining village of **Glaisdale** on the River Esk, but the literary heart of 'Constable Country' beats further south in the unpretentious surroundings of **Oswaldkirk**, where Rhea lived and worked as a young police officer.

The beautiful village of 'Aidensfield' takes its name from Oswaldkirk's modern Roman Catholic church of **St Aidan's**. Young Nicholas Rhea has to overcome the initial reserve of the locals, but his competent use of local dialect, discretion and easy-going authority soon thaws the initial frostiness. He has his hands full with local rogue Claude Jeremiah Greengrass (reminiscent of a colourful **Frank Parrish*** character) ensconced in the 'Aidensfield Arms', scheming more misdemeanours. In *Constable at the Gate* (1997), Greengrass' poaching dog Alfred manages to fall into a disused pit shaft, while time continues to stand still in *Constable Over the Bridge* (2001), a story of stolen sandwiches, shoplifting ladies, rummaging for old socks in dustbins – and visiting Royalty.

Omens of Death (1997) begins a light-hearted series featuring highly superstitious Inspector Montague Pluke, whose passion for horse-troughs and knowledge of moorland folklore prove invaluable in solving North Yorkshire crime. With the 'panache and romance' of a **Charlotte Brontë** (1816–1855) character, Detective Superintendent Mark Pemberton is a man who, says Rhea, can 'walk through a ploughed field without getting his feet dirty'. In *Death of a Princess* (1999), Pemberton's visit to a thinly veiled Glaisdale to investigate the shooting of the local landowner is also a journey back into Rhea's past: 'If you walk down Mill Wood, there's an old Mill House (private), with a field beyond it and the river flowing down by the side,' says Rhea. 'This was my childhood haunt. The bridge mentioned in that book, the house on the hill where the family lived, it's all there.'

High up on the north-eastern edge of the North Yorkshire Moors National Park, **Mulgrave Castle** (private) near **Whitby** provides the likely inspiration for the Verinder family home in **Wilkie Collins'** (1889–1924) classic *The Moonstone* (1868), which remained **Ngaio Marsh**'s* favourite detective novel all her life. When Collins visited in 1861, he probably had little idea that this landscape would inspire what is one of the very first English detective stories. As Sergeant Cuff investigates the theft of a priceless Indian diamond, he is drawn towards 'the most horrible quicksand on the shores of Yorkshire' along the nearby coast: 'The heave of the main ocean on the great sand-bank out in the bay, was a heave that made no sound. The inner sea lay lost and dim, without a breath of wind to stir it. Patches of nasty ooze floated, yellow-white, on the dead surface of the water. Scum and slime shone faintly in certain places, where the last of the light still caught them on the two great spits of rock jutting out, north and south, into the sea. It was now the time of the turn of the tide – and even as I stood there waiting, the broad brown face of the quicksand began to dimple and quiver – the only moving thing in all the horrid place.'

A land of rolling green pastures and windswept moors, wooded valleys, limestone scars, rivers, crags and caves, the **YORKSHIRE DALES** can be both inviting and forbidding, something that **Peter Robinson** (1950–) exploits to the full in his powerful fiction. Resident for the last quarter of a century in Canada, Robinson hones an insider's knowledge and an outsider's perspective of his native Yorkshire to perfection in the locales of his series featuring moody Detective Chief Inspector Alan Banks. Born in **Castleford**, Robinson grew up on the **Armley** and **Bramley** council estates of western Leeds, but even in an urban landscape where the potential for violence was very real, the Dales were already his 'big back garden'. Though becoming increasingly industrial, Robinson's fictional town of 'Eastvale' was inspired by the historic market town of **Richmond** high above the river Swale, while 'Swainsdale' absorbs elements of both **Wensleydale** and **Swaledale**.

A precursor to the Constable novels was **Gil North**'s (pseud. Geoffrey Horne, 1916–) Sergeant Caleb Cluff, a kind of Yorkshire Maigret. *Sergeant Cluff Stands Firm* (1960) opens the long-running series in the peaceful Yorkshire Dales market town of 'Gunnershaw', where obstinate but likeable Cluff becomes suspicious of a woman's 'suicide'. Inspector Mole might sometimes disapprove, but Cluff's methods work.

Peter Robinson, creator of
DCI Alan Banks.

'The change in light, the play of light and shadow over the
dale sides, the clouds massing behind the tops there, just ready
to come over; you might get a streak of sunshine on one area and
the rest will be in shadow, and the clouds flitting across. It's a very
lively landscape, it's always changing, it's always moving. And it
does have that real Gothic element, up on the moors especially,
very Brontë-ish. I've set a number of scenes on the tops, in bad
weather: just the heather and the sheep. So it has a moodiness, a
gloom about it as well, but can also be suddenly, surprisingly
beautiful.'

Richmond, gateway to the
Dales and the inspiration
behind Peter Robinson's
'Eastvale'. From the windows
of the police station, Alan
Banks overlooks the town's
cobbled market square with
the church and flagstone-
roofed cottages.

Banks first arrives in the Dales in *Gallows View* (1987), hoping for a quiet life. By the time he investigates the particularly brutal shooting of a financial consultant in *Dry Bones that Dream* (1995), it is clear that the quiet life is in short supply. Against the tranquillity of a rural setting, Banks enters the dead man's world, where nothing is quite as it should be, and discovers a complex network of hi-tech international money laundering, murder and pornography. The development of Banks into a more lonely, isolated character is reflected in his living environment when he acquires a former labourer's cottage, 'a typical Dales mix of limestone, grit and flag', which Robinson envisages as being just outside **Gayle**, near **Hawes**, in Wensleydale. Inspired by **Thrushcross Reservoir**, just north of **Otley**, *In a Dry Season* (2000) joins what Robinson jokingly calls the 'Reservoir Noir' school of crime writing inspired by the blisteringly hot summer of 1995 that dried out lakes, rivers – and reservoirs. In this complex, deeply satisfying mystery, the receding waters of 'Thornfield' Reservoir reveal the long submerged village of 'Hobbs End' (**West End**, flooded in the late 1960s). When a young boy finds the skeleton of a woman, a long-buried story from World War II gradually emerges and Banks moves closer to understanding how the past and present impact on the case.

The commercial capital of Yorkshire (Marks & Spencer started from a local market stall) and Britain's fourth-largest city, **LEEDS** is rapidly exchanging its gritty and grimy industrial image for culture, cafés, shopping and financial services. The changing cityscape does not go unnoticed by Banks, who in *Dry Bones that Dream* recalls the 'honest, slightly shabby charm' of the city and remains unconvinced by the makeover of this urban giant: 'Leeds was a scruff by nature; it wouldn't look comfortable in fancy dress, no matter what the price.' A harrowing detective thriller, *Aftermath* (2001) continues Robinson's rich vein of form, as Banks takes on the role of Acting Superintendent at **Millgarth** police station. Investigating the serial killing and sexual abuse of teenage girls, Banks and his team are shocked by their discoveries in a complex case with a surprising outcome.

Comfort is a long way from 'The Ripper Room – Millgarth, Leeds – Monday 22 December 1980: Standing room only – Smoke, sweat, and no smiles on 150 sad bloody faces' of **David Peace**'s (1967–) intensely bleak Yorkshire Ripper noir quartet. Having grown up in Yorkshire in the 1970s, Peace focuses his novels on the high-pressure box of Millgarth and on a force goaded by the real-life Ripper and hoaxers alike. Using terse, brutal prose, *Nineteen Seventy Four* (1999) opens the series in a monochromatic, rain-sodden Leeds with the story of a morally ambiguous crime correspondent who links the disappearance and subsequent murder of a nine-year-old with earlier, unsolved disappearances of schoolgirls. In the controversial *Nineteen Eighty* (2001), a Manchester ACC involved in the Ripper hunt finds himself ensnared in a nightmarish web of police brutality and corruption that is reflected by an uncompromising cityscape:

David Peace – chronicler of the dark Leeds years of the Yorkshire Ripper.

Back into the rain, back into the night, through deserted city streets, under broken Christmas lights swinging in the wind, along Boar Lane, the shopping centres and the vacant offices dark and huge, black canyon walls looming, up Market Street, the queues of empty buses all lit up with no place or passengers to go, through the Kirkgate stalls, past the mountains of rubbish, the rats and birds feeding, back to Millgarth, back underground… Two nights on and everything dead now…

An admirer of **Agatha Christie**'s effortless style, **Robert Barnard*** (1936–) has crafted a series of mysteries featuring sharp-eyed Charlie Peace and his superior Mike Oddie. Peace's skin colour and Brixton origins make him a double outsider in a series combining middle-England comedy with a keen eye for social and religious hypocrisy. The extensive **Beckett Park** in **Headingley**, to the north of the city centre, assumes a pivotal role in *The Bad Samaritan* (1995), while in *Unholy Dying* (2000), Charlie and Mike investigate allegations of sexual misconduct and misappropriation of church funds in a **Bradford** parish.

Reflections of **Leeds** landscapes new and old in the River Aire.

The Brontë Parsonage, **Haworth**, continues to exert its influence on the region's detective fiction.

The author of a York detective series, **Barbara Whitehead*** lives in The Brontë Birthplace at 72/74 Market Street in **Thornton**, a tiny village halfway between Haworth and Bradford (open to the public two days a week).

Some eight miles west of Bradford, the village of **Haworth** is most famously associated with the **Brontë** family, who lived at the grey Georgian Parsonage above the village. Close to the bleak high moors dotted with farmsteads and haunted by the restless ghosts of *Wuthering Heights*, Haworth still retains some of its atmosphere of serenity and seclusion despite the intrusion of literary tourism. Robert Barnard's work is sprinkled with affectionate tributes to the Brontë novels and the moors that inspired them. *The Missing Brontë* (1983) sees Barnard's first series detective, Perry Trethowan on the case of the mythical manuscript of **Emily Brontë**'s second novel.

In *The Corpse at the Haworth Tandoori* (1998), the owner of an Indian restaurant close to Haworth station alerts the police to the discovery of a young man's body in the boot of a waiter's car. Charlie Peace retraces the victim's steps to the home of a sinister painter, located between **Stanbury** and **Oakworth**, and very close to **The Old Silent**, a former Pub of the Year, which lends its name to **Martha Grimes**'* novel (1989). Set around the **Hebden Bridge** area south-west of Haworth, the attempts of a shady publisher to cash in on a twentieth-century Brontë rip-off go badly wrong in *A Hovering of Vultures* (1993), and Charlie mingles with the literary tourists to investigate.

The fresh air of Yorkshire brought **G K Chesterton*** to holiday here quite frequently, partly as a result of his wife's ill-health. In 1904 Chesterton was again based near **Ilkley** on the River Wharfe, when he met a Catholic parish priest who was to inspire his greatest creation: Father Brown. At that time, Father John O'Connor was curate at St Anne's in **Keighley**. In his *Autobiography* (1936), Chesterton describes O'Connor as 'a small man with a smooth face and a demure but elvish expression' and was struck by the 'tact and humour with which he mingled with his very Yorkshire and very Protestant company… Somebody gave me a very amusing account of how two gigantic

Robert Barnard walking up the Gill towards his **Leeds** home – close to the setting of *A City of Strangers* (1990), in which he contrasts life on a council estate with the defensiveness and class tensions of the adjoining middle-class houses.

'I think crime fiction has changed enormously, has become more serious, taken in a wider spectrum of characters and places, and issues,' says **Patricia Hall**. 'If you want to really find out what modern Britain is like, you'd do just as well reading crime fiction as you would "literary" fiction...'

Bradford, city of stone – 'When I was a child,' says **Patricia Hall**, 'Bradford was a very flourishing, prosperous place. Very dirty though, all the buildings were black. Since the textile industry has declined, they've cleaned up the buildings, and underneath is the most beautiful golden stone.'

Yorkshire farmers, of that district… wavered, with nameless terrors, before entering the little presbytery of the little priest.'

Born and bred in **J B Priestley**'s (1894–1984) hometown of **BRADFORD**, at one time the world's biggest producer of worsted cloth (made from closely twisted wool), former journalist **Patricia Hall** (pseud. Maureen O'Connor, 1940–) has created the West Yorkshire mill town of 'Bradfield' as a 'sort of shrunken replica' of Bradford. Detective Chief Inspector Michael Thackeray knows his way around Bradfield's curry houses, 'steep narrow shopping streets' and 'Wuthering Heights' high-rise estate. His lover, Laura Ackroyd, is a caring and unusually scrupulous reporter with the local newspaper, boldly going where police fear to tread. Hall's contemporary, well-paced, and spirited novels all reflect the landscape and society of inner-city Bradfield: *Dead on Arrival* (1999) charts changing attitudes towards race and gender, and the social realities of ethnic mix and immigration (Bradford is an important centre for British Muslims), while prostitution and drugs lie at the heart of *Perils of the Night* (1997). Hall tackles the emotive issue of abortion in *Deep Freeze* (2001) with Thackeray and Ackroyd clashing as they investigate the shooting of a young teenager outside a Bradfield clinic.

In The Bleak Midwinter (1995) allows Hall to contrast between the 'dark satanic mills – what's left of them – and the beautiful, absolutely wonderful moors just on the outskirts of Bradford'. Laura is seconded to prosperous 'Arnedale' (**Skipton**), an attractive market town 'surrounded by water-meadows' and strategically situated in the **Aire Gap**, the historic passageway into Lancashire, with its wild, rolling hills

and long snaking walls of rough limestone. This is the landscape of Thackeray's youth; his father still keeps Swaledale ewes by a low stone farmhouse on the high Pennine moors, though Thackeray, for reasons of his own, does not visit any more. Up on the wintry hills of the national park, an opportunistic farmer is selling off the stone from old walls and barns, and looking to reopen a nearby quarry. Locals are worried, some because it will alter the landscape, others because of the traffic and disruption – and there has already been one fatal accident… Hall convincingly describes the 'narrow, unforgiving quality' of a community lubricated by the 'dark, tannic brew' of Yorkshire tea and holding 'intractably to the absolute rightness of its prejudices.'

'The area around **Huddersfield** and **Halifax**, where my fictional town of Heckley is situated, is in the southern Pennines, where the limestone of the Dales gives way to millstone grit,' says **Stuart Pawson** (1940–), whose Charlie Priest procedurals are loaded with local lore, Yorkshire grit and dead-pan humour. 'It is this geological feature which has fashioned the area's history, providing the conditions which allowed the woollen industry, with all its iniquities, to burgeon here in the eighteenth and nineteenth centuries. It is a harsh landscape and it has produced some harsh people, including enough serial killers and hangmen to fill a waxworks.' Born in **Middleton**, in the south of Leeds, Pawson introduces quick-thinking renegade Inspector Charlie Priest of the 'East Pennine Police Force' in *The Picasso Scam* (1995). Charlie views Heckley (located very close to **Brighouse**) with a jaundiced eye, preferring the wilder surroundings of the evocatively named places such as **Scapegoat Hill** or **Blackmoorfoot**.

'I draw the circuits, make the connections, and wait for the sparks to fly,' says **Stuart Pawson**, whose background in electrical engineering at **Primrose Hill Colliery**, together with mediation experience in the probation service, has been useful in scheming the Charlie Priest series.

The **Sculpture Park**, near **Wakefield**, provides a surreal setting for a moonlit showdown in *Last Reminder* (1997), with shotgun pellets ricocheting off the Henry Moores.

A stretch of Roman road at **Blackstone Edge – Stuart Pawson**'s Charlie Priest loves to wander up here to watch the sun fall into **Morecambe Bay.**

Wildernesses have a way of helping you put things in perspective... The moors I live on the edge of have seen it all, heard it all. I love walking across them, the wind lashing my hair and the shadows of the clouds racing across the hillsides. They speak to me, too, in their way. There are ghosts up there. They tell of hardship and cruelty; vast wealth for a few, and indescribable poverty and degradation for the rest.

The Mushroom Man

In *The Mushroom Man* (1995), a serial killer appears determined to murder the local clergy, but Charlie has doubts and his investigations into the disappearance of a schoolgirl lead him into a child pornography ring and confrontation with the 'Mushroom Man'. Charlie enjoys walking on the moors, but his inquiries on the 'mean side' of Heckley recall a landscape where 'rows of terraced houses had stood two-up, two-down and back-to-back. No hot water, shared closets, and washing strung like bunting across the cobbled streets. But now people remembered them with affection, for there had been a sense of community that vanished when the bulldozers moved in. They'd been replaced by vertical warrens with unlit stairwells and cardboard walls.' A deep-thinking man beneath the wisecracks, Priest suffers a nervous breakdown after discovering the body of a missing schoolgirl, but returns older and wiser to continue his painstaking work. *Chill Factor* (2001) is a thought-provoking mystery focused on the murder of a murderer and a 'confession' that does not entirely convince Charlie.

Lying six miles south of Leeds, **Wakefield** is the birthplace of **Kay Mitchell**, who introduces Chief Inspector John Morrissey of hard-pressed 'Malminster' CID in *A Lively Form of Death* (1990) – a tale of seduction, poisoning and missing children in a tranquil village on the outskirts of town. In *A Strange Desire* (1994), the redevelopment experienced by many of Yorkshire's post-industrial landscapes comes under scrutiny as Morrissey discovers Malminster to be a hotbed of corruption and conspiracy. In Mitchell's hard-hitting series written as **Sarah Lacey**, the fictional Yorkshire town of 'Bramfield' is home to combative, caustic young tax inspector Leah Hunter. Leah is in big trouble in *File Under: Jeopardy* (1995) when an old school friend is rescued from the Aire and Calder Navigation Canal and Leah sets off on the trail of a dangerous syndicate involved in drugs, blackmail and extreme violence. Leah never knows when to back off, or when to accept help, though her stormy relationship with DI David Nicholls looks as if it could save her life.

Danuta Reah (1951–) views the changes in the industrial landscape of her native **SHEFFIELD** with the wary eye of someone who has stood on

Halifax 'without the building society' is the 'Cloughton' of **Pauline Bell**'s (1938–) detective novels with strong romantic subplots, where brash young DC Benedict 'Benny' Mitchell is a central character. In *No Pleasure in Death* (1992), a serial killer is targeting the sopranos of the choral society. While in *Sleeping Partners* (1995), a rich single mother is found in a bus shelter with her throat cut, and the police have to locate the father of her son.

Danuta Reah pictured in the **Dearne Valley**, close to the scene of the crime for *Only Darkness* (1999).

'Detective Inspector Steve McCarthy looked away, at the scene around him. The wheel was still and silent. There was a smell of damp stone and wood in the air, of weed and stagnant water. The yard was fading into shadows as the sun sank lower behind the trees. A breeze blew, and the trees sighed and rustled, sending the shadows chasing across the flagstones...' – **Shepherds' Wheel** provides the inspiration for the setting of *Silent Playgrounds*.

picket lines and taught redundant steelworkers and miners. In her page-turning police suspense thrillers Reah weaves a tapestry of fear around the lives of young female academics within the landscapes of industry and higher education. Detective Inspectors Lynne Jordan and Steve McCarthy need all their lateral thinking as they investigate in and around the 'city of steel'. 'In a way, the locations created the book,' says Reah of *Only Darkness* (1999). A serial killer is dumping the bodies of the women commuters he strangles by the railway line running through the **Dearne Valley** and into Sheffield's near-neighbour **Rotherham**. A young college lecturer has the misfortune to catch a glimpse of the 'Strangler' one night on the platform of 'Moreham' (Rotherham) station, which not only brings her to the attention of the killer, but also turns her into a pawn to a colleague's personal ambition – with terrifying consequences.

In *Night Angels* (2001), much of the action revolves around Sheffield's tallest building, the University's **Arts Tower**. Far from being an ivory tower, the linguistic research Danuta Reah's characters conduct here crosses too many vested interests.

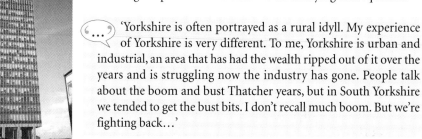

'Yorkshire is often portrayed as a rural idyll. My experience of Yorkshire is very different. To me, Yorkshire is urban and industrial, an area that has had the wealth ripped out of it over the years and is struggling now the industry has gone. People talk about the boom and bust Thatcher years, but in South Yorkshire we tended to get the bust bits. I don't recall much boom. But we're fighting back...'

The central location in *Silent Playgrounds* (2000) was inspired by **Shepherd's Wheel** in **Bingham Park**, 'one of the old mills on the River Porter. The water wheel and the grinding mill are still there, though falling into disrepair,' says Reah. When a little girl, Lucy, goes missing and the young woman looking after her is found murdered, Steve McCarthy must begin his search for the 'monsters' that appear on Lucy's drawings of the Park.

CHAPTER FOUR

The North-West

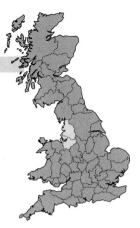

'In the nineties, the regions, particularly the North, really started to reassert themselves… and at the same time there was a development of regional fiction, particularly in the crime genre…'

Val McDermid

To the west of the Pennines the **LANCASHIRE** landscape takes in the remote, sparsely wooded expanse of **Bowland Forest** (an Area of Outstanding Natural Beauty), the famous north-west coastal resorts and an urban sprawl edging towards **Manchester** and **Merseyside**. Aside from the rigours of Northern life, there is a distance from the South that is more than geographic – shaped by a characteristic self-reliance, resilient humour and regional pride.

Its landmark tower still symbolizing the Great British Seaside Holiday, big brash **BLACKPOOL** has seven miles of sandy beaches, ice cream sellers, donkey rides, trams, bed and breakfasts and bars – and claims to have more hotel beds than Portugal. Using her local knowledge and journalistic background, **Barbara Crossley** (1952–) sets two lively

Blackpool Promenade – where other people find holidays, **Nick Oldham, Barbara Crossley**, and their detectives, watch out for trouble.

Opposite page:
The Big One, Blackpool – 'in the shadow of one of the world's hairiest roller-coaster rides' Detective Inspector Henry Christie stops to ponder his career in **Nick Oldham**'s *Nightmare City*.

Nick Oldham at the scene of the crime of his first detective thriller, *A Time for Justice* (1996), which features a bomb being dropped into the river from the bridge at the junction of the M6 and the A59.

In **Val McDermid's*** *Union Jack* (1993), reporter Lindsay Gordon comes to Blackpool to cover the Amalgamated Media Workers' conference. She finds herself in the right place for fish and chips, but cannot remember ordering vicious political manoeuvring and sudden, violent death.

mysteries in the amusements world of a 'Northport' resort closely resembling her home town. Fast-thinking, fast-talking journalist sleuth Anna Knight of the '*Northport News*' uncovers an incendiary mix of politics and murder in *Candyfloss Coast* (1991). The sparks continue to fly in *Rollercoaster* (1994), where Anna investigates the death of a fairground attraction director whose charred body is discovered on a Guy Fawkes' bonfire on the beach. With her personal life already on a roller coaster, Anna is encouraged by her editor to take a ride into the bizarre world of the 'Futures' funfair park: 'Futures shone on the horizon like a vision of the celestial city. Silver domes, golden towers, ivory spires grew out of the green and pleasant land… The site, on a flat plain where once a farmer eked out his set-aside subsidy, could be seen from miles…around. Signposts… billboards… its outer walls a continuous shopping-mall, its interior a fury of high-technology super-rides.'

'Looking out of the window of our end terrace house in **Belthorn**, a little village on the moors, you could see across to **Blackburn**, and, on a clear day, see right down to Blackpool Tower, forty miles away,' says police officer **Nick Oldham** (1956–) of his childhood landscapes. The Blackpool revealed by Oldham's tough and fast-moving police thrillers is unrecognizable from the boisterous, glitzy Golden Mile and packed promenades witnessed by most visitors. In *Nightmare City* (1997), Detective Inspector Henry Christie heads an investigation into the murder of a prostitute amid signs that organized crime is getting a firm grip on the north-west coast. Focused on seedy nightclubs and pubs, the novel describes a blurred, frightening world of racketeering, violence and corruption.

'Blackpool has a lot of faces, and that's what has always fascinated me. Eighteen million visitors a year, and 99% of them never see what goes on behind the seafront; they don't see the underbelly, a very seedy, drug-driven underside. Everything happens on this strip: behind, it's quite middle-class, with a few pockets of deprivation. I've worked there on a lot of occasions, it's an amazing place. With all that gloss and trash it knows what it's about, Blackpool, it knows what it has to do – and that is to make money.'

For many years Blackpool was the venue of choice for party political conferences, with the Labour Party in particular savouring the working-class flavour of the town. In *Backlash* (2001), Oldham recreates the frenzied media circus and fraught policing of a week-long party conference held in the huge **Winter Gardens** against a background of racism, feuds and riots on Blackpool's 'Shoreside Estate'. Demoted and back in uniform at the sharp end, a determined Henry Christie heads straight into action: disarming psychotic prisoners, organizing a rescue mission for his colleagues trapped on the estate and foiling attacks on members of the political establishment so temptingly displayed and corralled in one area.

Slaidburn's welcoming Hark To Bounty Inn could stand in for the 'Crofters Inn', where news arrives that the vicar is dead in **Elizabeth George**'s *Missing Joseph*.

For 'a cheap joke', **Burnley**-born **Peter Guttridge*** has his detective Nick Madrid grow up in **Ramsbottom** ('Tup's Arse' to locals), north of his home town and not far from Pendle Hill, an area he explores in *Foiled Again* (2001).

'The setting is absolutely crucial to my novels. Until I have the setting, I generally don't have the novel at all,' says **Elizabeth George*** (1949–), who places her favourite Inspector Lynley novel, *Missing Joseph* (1993), in the wilds of Lancashire, far-removed from seaside amusements. Drawing the intricacies of English custom, hierarchy and landscape in her own inimitable style, George develops the novel's central theme of parental love within a small parish setting. Surrounded by wide stretches of empty grouse moor, crisscrossed by old packhorse trails, the ancient stone cottages and cobblestones of 'Winslough' are inspired by the village of **Slaidburn** in the Bowland Forest. With Lancashire's skeletal winter hedges stark against the 'subdued blend of moorland russets and farmland sage', George taps into the historical account of the infamous **Pendle Hill** hangings in 1612, where ten 'witches' were convicted of holding diabolic rites, mainly on the evidence of one small child.

There is seldom a dull moment in the life of red-brick and terracotta metropolis **MANCHESTER**. From the factories and mills of 'Cottonopolis', the world's premier textile city, Manchester was transformed into 'Madchester', capital of an exhilarant club and drugs scene in the 1980s. From post-industrial despair, newly confident Manchester emerged as host to the 2002 Commonwealth Games. Long rows of terraces and empty shells of factories still vie for space with Victorian neo-Gothic architecture, while redevelopment of the commercial heart of the city, rent asunder by the huge IRA bomb blast in 1996, adds a contemporary sheen to the cityscape. With more than its fair share of urban crime, Manchester's hard edge and 'American' feel are major influences on the city's detective fiction.

Manchester's gritty urban scene inspired the novels of **Maurice Procter** (1906–73), widely credited as the pioneer of the British police procedural, whose *No Proud Chivalry* (1946) is a powerful semi-autobiographical debut charting the progress of an officer in the 'Otherburn Borough' police force. Born in **Nelson**, north of Burnley, Procter draws upon almost twenty years' experience as a police constable in **Halifax** ('I walked 5,000 miles a year and my weight fell to nine stone') in his novels, casting a grimly realistic eye on relationships within the force, and on the conflicts between policemen as individuals and their position in the community. In *Hell is a City* (1954) (US: *Somewhere in This City*), Procter introduces the formidable 'Granchester' Chief Inspector Harry Martineau, in an enthralling tale of police work and menacing urban metaphors.

Manchester – a city of towering ambition and rugged industry.

'The town had buttoned its lip' – *The Midnight Plumber* (1957) is considered to be Procter's masterpiece. The setting is again Granchester: a 'city of a million people in the centre of a close urban population of several millions', with gin palaces in dark back alleyways, 'United' and 'City' football grounds, 'Farways' prison (not to be confused with **Strangeways**), and a 'Northland Hotel' reminiscent of the massively ornate red-brick **Midland Hotel**. Procter lines up an array of villains against the backdrop of a metropolis with many faces. Away from the imposing homes of cotton magnates are the suburbs 'where many identical streets of blackened brick dwelling-houses' branch out from a road 'like the rungs of a single-stemmed burglar's ladder', and the

'You can see all these huge spaces under the viaducts, like cathedrals' – **Castlefield Basin** is scene of the crime in **Frank Lean**'s *Raised in Silence.*

'inner suburb of faded gentility which was still mainly inhabited by its original settlers or their relicts'. The 'Plumber' has his hands full, what with organizing the elimination of police informers and preparing for one last big job, the job to end all jobs…

'At the time that I started writing, Manchester was getting quite a reputation for crime; there was quite a lot of shooting and gang-fighting.' Born and raised in the 'mill-town atmosphere' of nearby **Bolton**, former teacher **Frank Lean** (pseud. Frank Leneghan, 1942–) is the creator of Manchester's maverick private eye Dave Cunane, whose body owes many bruises to 'the morally challenged elements of Manchester's citizenry'. Head of Pimpernel Investigations, Cunane has a deceptively 'honest open mush' and an unerring ability to land himself with femmes fatales as he dodges the local lowlife in pursuit of thieving supermarket employees.

'Dave is very gung-ho, doesn't stand on ceremony. This is a Manchester characteristic: very direct and in-your-face… This is a city with ambitions, and Dave is like that; he doesn't feel at all provincial' – Dave Cunane creator **Frank Lean**.

Tackling themes of disguise and mistaken identity, *Red for Rachel* (1994) is a hard-boiled tale focused on the disappearance of a banker's daughter. After uncovering more about his client than is good for him, Cunane finds himself trapped in Manchester's once notorious **Moss Side** district (currently being rejuvenated). Living in a block of flats adjacent to the **Meadows** nature reserve in the southern suburb of **Chorlton** along the banks of the **River Mersey**, Dave hopes to get away from it all. But any chances of an undisturbed cycle ride past the reed beds are a forlorn hope, as his work soon follows him home.

> When I hit the street the weather was playing one of those moody autumnal tricks for which Manchester is renowned. The sky was full of swiftly moving dark clouds threatening rain, but strong beams of light were breaking through the murk like probing rays. Little carousels of litter were gyrating along the pavement. Distant sunlight gleamed and then faded from office windows, highlighting first one building, then another.
> *The Reluctant Investigator* (1998)

With *Raised in Silence* (2002), a novel based around the canal basin at **Castlefield**, where the remnants of the Roman army occupation can still be seen, Lean has found a landscape close to his heart. When a girl's body is fished out of the canal, it seems to be a case of too much drink before a fall. But the girl's mother hires Dave to delve a bit deeper, and soon he's uncovering a shadowy and dangerous criminal network, and taking a dive into a deep section of the canal for his trouble. At the junction of the Rochdale and Bridgewater canals, with trains rumbling overhead, this is an echoing, atmospheric place of high, sooty black viaducts, heavy locks and iron bridges. The scene of great protests against the coming of the railways by weavers fearing for their liveli-hoods, the area remains an interface of Manchester's industrial past and redesigned present. Redundant red-brick warehouses have now become expensive loft apartments and trendy cafés.

'The city I write about is a real place, with imaginary additions' – **Val McDermid** guards the imaginary first-floor offices of Brannigan & Co: Investigations & Security at the corner of **Oxford Road** and **Hulme Street**.

One of Britain's most successful and versatile crime writers, **Val McDermid*** (1946–) has made Manchester her 'adopted home' – and the patch of resourceful Thai-boxing private eye Kate Brannigan. Setting out to portray a 'very centred' professional detective, McDermid lends a distinctive Northern feel to the Brannigan series, not only through the settings and Kate's resilient character, but also through her extensive network of contacts and supportive friends. Kate needs all the help she can get in *Kick Back* (1993), when a handsome visitor to the offices of Brannigan & Co sets her off on a bizarre trail of missing conservatories. What at first looks like a joke soon becomes something more sinister when Kate uncovers a complex scheme of financial and property fraud. Livewire Kate may enjoy wolfing down Chinese takeaways side by side with her lover Richard (they share adjacent bungalows) or playing computer games at the office, but there's nothing superficial in either plot or character as McDermid moves the action around labyrinthine **Warrington** housing estates, out to **Stockport** and back into central Manchester.

Manchester's **Canal Street** – at the centre of the city's high-profile gay culture.

'Kate has grown up with this sense that cities are places of hiddenness and dichotomy,' says McDermid. 'She's always had that notion that surfaces hide very different realities.' Kate certainly gets a good look behind the scenes in *Starstruck* (1998), when she takes on a spot of bodyguarding for an anxious star of the 'Northerners' TV soap. When a celebrity astrologer is murdered in her caravan on the studios site, Kate gets dragged into a deadly investigation. Continuing in her mapping of Manchester's progress through the 1990s, McDermid interweaves a sub-plot of 'shop-squatting' in the landmark **Arndale Centre** ('probably the ugliest building in central Manchester') that has tragic consequences.

Kate's feelings of vulnerability and unease ('anything could happen here') when she leaves the sanctuary of the city and heads across the moors point the way to a new direction in McDermid's writing. With chilling insight, the Gold Dagger-winning *The Mermaid's Singing* (1995) introduces psychological profiler Tony Hill, investigating a series of murders in 'Bradfield', an amalgam of Manchester, Bradford and Sheffield. Manchester's thriving gay scene around **Canal Street** and **Sackville Street** gardens comes under scrutiny as a crazed serial killer stalks Bradfield's gay venues around 'Temple Fields' and 'Crompton Gardens'.

'There's always been an attitude in Manchester, of confidence/cockiness, which I think is great. There's this spirit of, well, London might be the capital city, but we were the first industrial city… and Manchester has still got that legacy of success,' says **Cath Staincliffe** (1956–). Living on the working-class edge of **Didsbury**, Staincliffe uses her experience in community arts to bring out the character of the city beyond its central landmarks. Opening Staincliffe's engaging and very Mancunian series featuring Private Investigator Sal Kilkenny, *Looking for Trouble* (1994) explores 'the disparity between inner-city deprivation and the leafy Cheadle suburbs' as Sal enters the world of organized crime in the search for her client's missing son. Juggling childcare with crime investigation, as she heads towards a final confrontation in **Heaton Park**, to the north of the city, Sal is a wholly credible character whose day-to-day life reveals so much about multi-layered Manchester.

'This was real, this was savage' – against the emotionally charged background of the Arndale Centre bombing, *Dead Wrong* (1998) is a thrilling mystery edged with barely suppressed violence. Already investigating a stalker terrifying a young divorcee in cosmopolitan **Chorlton** (where she might even catch a glimpse of **Frank Lean**'s* Dave Cunane), Sal takes on the case of a teenage boy in custody accused of murdering his friend. Facing the grief and anger of a family determined to exact retribution, Sal realizes that the gap between truth and justice can be as wide as it is dangerous. With the Euro 96 Football Championships continuing in a shell-shocked city trying to come to terms with the scale of the bomb damage, a hoarding is erected: '*They went for the heart of Manchester but missed the soul*'.

Not much remains today of the famous **Hacienda Club** on Whitworth Street West. **Nicholas Blincoe** (1965–) draws on his Hacienda days and the explosion of the 'Madchester' club scene in *Acid Casuals* (1995). A 'chic-bombed' Manchester on the way to becoming a gay Mecca provides the backdrop to Blincoe's Silver Dagger-winning *Manchester Slingback* (1999).

Cath Staincliffe on **Wilmslow Road**, close to the home of Sal Kilkenny.

Symbolizing the city's resilient spirit, Manchester's **Arndale Centre** provides a backdrop for **Cath Staincliffe**'s *Dead Wrong* and is the site of some 'shop-squatting' in Val McDermid's *Starstruck*.

Merging Manchester and its western neighbour **Salford** into a fictional setting 'stuck between coastal Liverpool and the big inland conurbations', Lovejoy creator **Jonathan Gash*** creates an unusual pairing in his series featuring caring Dr Clare Burtonall, and Bonn, a high-class male prostitute. *Different Women Dancing* (1997) paints a city in thrall to an underworld inextricably linked with white-collar crime, focusing on the parallel universe of the criminal milieu around the decaying city square. 'I'm the sordid part of the city,' Bonn tells Clare, 'with me you'll only get gutter reasons, criminal logic, street chances. I can't change.' But he is still there in *Prey Dancing* (1998), when Clare's promise to a dying young drug addict leads to conflict with a violent gun-runner. Undeterred, idealistic Clare eyes the opportunity to establish an inner-city drugs centre, but realizes too late the price she has to pay in *Die Dancing* (2000).

LIVERPOOL displays its glorious mercantile past in the architecture of its waterfront, overseen by the soaring clock towers of the **Royal Liver Building** topped by the city's trademark 'Liver Birds'. With wharves sprawled seven miles along the **River Mersey**, this was once the Empire's second most important port. But just as the *Titanic* (which sailed on its fateful voyage from Liverpool) hit an iceberg, so the decline of its main trades and industries sounded the death knell for the docklands. Blighted by unemployment, Merseyside fell back on its innermost resources, its vital humour and its distinctive music. Home to the Beatles, Gerry and the Pacemakers, and the Merseybeat sound, Liverpool is strong on nostalgia, but through projects such as its dockland regeneration looks forward as much as back.

'During the sixties, everyone was in a Beat group,' says **Southport**-born **Ron Ellis** (1941–), 'and I couldn't play anything and I couldn't sing'. Undaunted, Ellis armed himself with an old Brownie Box camera and approached the stage door of his idols to enter a life in the music and entertainment business that inspired his PI Johnny Ace novels. Controversial DJ, entrepreneurial landlord and disheartened Everton FC supporter, wisecracking Ace lives in a luxury flat in a converted warehouse a short walk from the Royal Liver Building. His life is immersed in Liverpool's music and nightlife, and infused with an irrepressible 'Scouse' spirit: humour, unpretentiousness, and a warm heart. Ellis blends nostalgia with violence and intimidation in *Ears of the City* (1998). Ace

'I was glad to reach the bustle of Lord Street which had managed to retain some of its genteel Edwardian atmosphere with elegant shops beneath ornate glass verandahs down one side of the road and gardens and fountains along the other' – Johnny Ace visits **Ron Ellis**' home town of **Southport** in *Ears of the City*.

Liverpool's waterfront, viewed from **Albert Dock**.

'You can't get far away from the Beatles in Liverpool' – Johnny Ace creator **Ron Ellis** in Liverpool's **Cavern Walks**, in the shadow of the life-size statues of the Fab Four, which sadly exclude his favourite Beatle, Pete Best.

has so many contacts that Liverpool is like a village to him, but he is in the dark when an ex-band member asks him to investigate the death of his son – found at the bottom of a dock, with his ears chopped off and posted to his father.

It is impossible to keep the Mersey out of a Liverpool mystery, and Ellis' preferred title for *Mean Streets* (1998) would have been *Ferry to the Bottom of the Mersey*. When the body of a former Merseybeat star is found floating in the river's murky waters, Ace sets out to find out why. Blackmail seems to be the answer, but before long there is another murder, and Johnny himself is treading deep and dangerous waters. In *The Singing Dead* (2000), Ace turns his hobby into a career, setting up an investigations bureau in **Dale Street** with a former CID Detective Inspector as partner. Ace knows that the music business can be lucrative, and dirty, too, but even Ace cannot anticipate the danger he faces when he comes across an old John Lennon tape at an auction.

'Liverpool is a city with a tremendous resilience of spirit and character,' says **Martin Edwards** (1955–), who combines practising Employment Law in Liverpool's city centre with writing his Harry Devlin series, a blend of classic detection and urban *noir*. Liverpool solicitor and amateur detective Harry Devlin, a self-deprecating Scouser with a largely impoverished clientele and an outlook of humorous melancholy, is introduced in *All the Lonely People* (1991). Proud and protective of his city, Harry lives in a fictional part (currently a car park) of the restored early Victorian **Albert Dock**:

> The flat was on the river side of the Empire Dock building, a converted warehouse which had once stored tobacco and cotton, with walls built to withstand fire, tempest and flood. In the distance, he could hear teenage delinquents shouting unintelligibly. Joyriders, hooligans or petty thieves perhaps. Tomorrow's clients, anyway. A police car siren wailed and nearer by, the site security guard's Alsatian began to bark. Meanwhile, the Mersey below snaked away into the shadows. A string of lights gleamed along the water's edge, trailing beyond Empire Dock as far as Harry could see. On the opposite side of the river, he could make out the angular outlines of the shoreside cranes, looming like creatures on an alien landscape. It was a Liverpool night, like any other.

'The Mersey plays a part, at least in the background, in all the Harry Devlin books' – **Martin Edwards** by the **River Mersey**.

The bleaker tones of the early books, where Harry moves through a despairing inner-city Liverpool of boarded-up shops, litter and vandalism like 'a scar on the face of a friend', are superseded by the lighter tone and more complex plotting of later novels. Charting the city's social landscapes as the series develops, Edwards arrives on home ground in *First Cut is the Deepest* (1999). Harry knows he should not really get involved with the wife of a local villain, and he knows he should not tell lies. But he does both when he stumbles across the body

of a widely loathed colleague. This less than flattering portrayal of the legal world digs deep into what lies beneath – literally when Harry runs a suspect to ground in the incredible **Williamson Tunnels**, an early nineteenth-century network of tunnels honeycombing the area of **Edge Hill** and east Liverpool. Whether an egotist's dream or the ultimate job creation scheme, the tunnels were the brainchild of wealthy entre-preneur and philanthropist Joseph Williamson to alleviate mass unemployment and poverty after the end of the Napoleonic wars.

A place apart, the **Wirral Peninsula** has been home to wealthy nineteenth-century Liverpool merchants, as well as being a popular seaside resort. Lying between Liverpool and Wales, the Wirral today is a place of running tides, sand banks, cliffs and salt-marshes, and of contrasting settings between the former resort of **New Brighton** and affluent **West Kirby**. Martin Edwards explores the lie of the land here on a stormy night in *First Cut is the Deepest* and in a clash of professional loyalties in *Suspicious Minds* (1992). The peninsula also provides inspiration for Liverpool-born **Eileen Dewhurst***, who lives in **Oxton** and has spent much of her life on the Wirral. *There Was A Little Girl* (1984) and *Roundabout* (1998) both draw inspiration from the area, while the imaginary town of 'Linton' that features in *Curtain Fall* (1977) is an 'upwardly transmuted' version of New Brighton.

'The audacity of it simply takes your breath away. The tunnels go on for miles, you know. Nobody knows how far' – hidden from view for 170 years, the **Williamson Tunnels** feature in *First Cut is the Deepest* and are currently being excavated and restored by the Friends of the Williamson Tunnels.

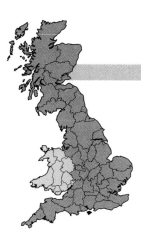

CHAPTER FIVE

Wales & The Marches

> Mr Lewker's heart did not, nowadays, leap up when he beheld
> a rainbow in the sky, but it never failed to perform that
> Wordsworthian feat when he saw the mountains of Wales.
>
> Glyn Carr, *Death Under Snowdon* (1954)

'The summit-cone of **Snowdon**, remote and dreaming' – at 3,560 feet, the highest mountain in Wales is at the heart of **Glyn Carr**'s *Death Under Snowdon.*

With miles of unspoilt coastline and the mountains of **Snowdonia**, the dramatic landscape of **NORTH WALES** guards some of the most authentic Welsh culture and heritage. The Welsh language is still widely spoken here, with a great oral tradition of storytelling, poetry and music since Celtic times. Though not widely represented, detective fiction certainly reflects the region's self-reliant spirit and respect for the natural landscape.

The jagged grey ridge of **Tryfan**, deep in the rugged beauty of **SNOWDONIA National Park**, is a Mecca for rock climbers and outdoor enthusiasts. It was on Tryfan's famous Milestone Buttress that explorer and climber **Glyn Carr** (pseud. Frank Showell Styles, 1908–) decided to begin a series of climbing mysteries. Heavyweight sleuth Sir Abercrombie Lewker first appears in *Traitor's Mountain* (1946), but the series really begins on the craggy site of Carr's first inspiration in *Death on Milestone Buttress* (1951), where Lewker confronts a killer who dares to use the mountains themselves as 'the means and mechanism of murder'.

The Welsh name for Snowdon is Yr Wyddfa Fawr, meaning 'great tomb', an appropriate description for Carr's breathtaking classic *Death Under Snowdon* (1952). The 'age-old peace of the valley' that Lewker feels embrace him at **Plas Mawr**, beneath the magnificent Snowdon Horseshoe, is soon shattered. Up in the 'scowling crags', high above the 'glittering waters' of **Llyn Llydaw**, a rock fall narrowly misses a climber. When a collapsing bridge later kills the man, Lewker knows that a murder has taken place – but can he prove it?

> Snowdon summit was hidden now behind the huge pointed peak of Crib Goch that reared its shadowed crags beyond the intervening glen. From that remote three-thousand-foot crest, as he knew from many a climb in the past, a knife-edge of bare rock flung its gigantic scallops across space to join the main Snowdon ridge, whence ambitious scramblers might cross Snowdon top and return along the twin ridge of Lliwedd, thus completing the famous traverse of the Snowdon Horseshoe. As he lit his short black pipe and stared, little eyes screwed up under bushy brows, at the immensity of the hills, Mr Lewker felt a resurgence of youth.

Following in Glyn Carr's footsteps – quite literally – **Gwen Moffat***** uses her own impressive climbing career (the first woman to become a professional rock-climbing guide) as the inspiration for her crime novels. Tryfan was the site of her first climb, and in her rereleased atobiography, *Space Below My Feet* (2001), Moffat recalls how the Welsh mountains changed her life: 'I liked the look of the big grey Buttress running down towards the lake… and as soon as I was off the ground… I knew that this was what I had been waiting for.' Much later, it was an article by Glyn Carr (writing under his real name of Showell Styles), about potholers near his **Porthmadog** home discovering explosives in a disused mine, which led Moffat to write her first mystery novel: *Lady with a Cool Eye* (1973). Introducing the formidable but caring Miss Pink, the book captures the essence of the dramatic Welsh landscape, with action on **Mynydd Mawr** mountain and down into the **Lleyn Peninsula**. Miss Pink returns to her beloved wild Welsh coast in *Persons Unknown* (1978) for a murder mystery set against a background of the nuclear industry. Both this and the subsequent novel, *Die Like a Dog* (1982), present Moffat's central motif of a precious natural environment under threat from outside interests.

Overleaf: Climbers' crime writer **Gwen Moffat** scaling the **Milestone Buttress** on Tryfan in the 1960s.

The focal point of a staunchly nationalist Welsh-speaking area, the university town of **Bangor** looks out over the **Menai Strait** to the island of **Anglesey**, where **Alison Taylor** (1944–) made many childhood visits and where her family roots go back generations. It is no accident that Taylor is drawn towards institutional environments: working as a senior social worker back in 1986, she uncovered systematic abuse of children in care homes in North Wales, informed the authorities – and lost her job. Fully vindicated by a major inquiry, Taylor wrote *Simeon's Bride* (1995), creating highly principled loner Detective Chief Inspector Michael James McKenna. Living in a run-down part of town, high on a hill overlooking the university tower, McKenna has 'never felt at home anywhere'. A Celt, though not a native Welshman, McKenna is aware of his dislocated cultural identity: 'I'm Welsh to the Irish, Irish to the Welsh, and trouble either way to the English.'

Alison Taylor's detective fiction is steeped in the atmosphere of **North Wales**.

In *The House of Women* (1998), Taylor presents the traditional elements of crime fiction – guilt, blackmail, deception, retribution – within a singularly Welsh world of old religion, strong taboos and long memories, interwoven with oral tradition, poetry and scholarship. On a sweltering summer's day, elderly Ned Jones dies at 'Glamorgan Place' – his home near the Menai Bridge – from what seems to be an extreme allergic reaction. A suspicious McKenna delves into the dynamics of the household, a strange ménage of three female generations, riddled with sins and veiled in secrets.

Industry, farming and tourism have all exacted their price from the Welsh countryside, and, in *The House of Women*, Taylor exposes a landscape of ravaged beauty: from the former explosives factory near Porthmadog so familiar to both Glyn Carr and Gwen Moffat, of which 'all that remained… were a few deep wounds in a hillside strewn with slivers of corrugated iron', and the contaminating 'cubic concrete edifice' of Trawsfynydd power station. Beyond is the timeless isolation of old Welsh territory – 'fields and sheep folds and dour granite buildings…

The House of Women was inspired by a long-running eighteenth-century feud between **Edward Jones** (1752–1824), a leading Welsh harpist, scholar and antiquarian, who accused poet **Edward Williams** (1747–1826) of faking a biography and poems of the most famous of Welsh poets: **Dafydd ap Gwilym** (*c*.1315–20 to *c*.1350–70).

'Menai Bridge seems like a tug of war between Anglesey and the mainland, something just balanced there, and not real or solid' – linking modern Wales with an ancient Druidic stronghold, **Menai Bridge** occupies a highly symbolic position in **Alison Taylor**'s *The House of Women*, while the muddy, tree-crowded foreshore of the **Menai Strait** is scene of the crime in *Child's Play* (2001).

Popular tourist resort **Llandudno** moves to the English South Coast to become 'Seaminster' in **Eileen Dewhurst**'s mysteries.

behind low stone walls and clipped hedgerows, a collage of land speckled with thousands of sheep', and a remote village (near **Bala**) – a 'tiny place of old cob and stone cottages and tapering lanes, with a church at its heart like the hub on the wheel of life'.

Eileen Dewhurst* bases her (ostensibly) South Coast resort of 'Seaminster' on the popular seaside town of **Llandudno**, endowing it with Llandudno's defining features: the hills of **Great Orme** and **Little Orme** (becoming 'Great Hill' and 'Little Hill') and its seafront 'lined with the elegant stuccoed early Victorian terraces'. Seaminster first appears in Dewhurst's favourite novel, *A Private Prosecution* (1986), which also introduces Detective Chief Superintendent Maurice Kendrick as the man leading the hunt for a strangler dubbed 'The Monster' by the local media. The south coast's 'colourless unmoving' autumnal sea provides few reassurances for Kendrick, but for Phyllida Moon, private eye and consummate actress, slipping from role to role, disguise to disguise, the landscape of Seaminster at least provides some sense of stability. Phyllida teams up with Kendrick in *Now You See Her* (1995).

Way out west, the seaside resort of **Aberystwyth** receives the hardboiled treatment from **Malcolm Pryce** (1960–) who explores the mean streets of his youth in his mad-cap detective thriller *Aberystwyth, Mon Amour* (2001). Aberystwyth's best – and only – private eye, Louie Knight, investigates the disappearance of schoolboys and the appearance of their body parts, dodging the hazards of Welsh heritage: Druids, language politics and religious conviction.

Despite some equally stunning natural scenery, detective fiction in **SOUTH WALES** focuses on the bleak nostalgia of the industrial heartland and great coalmining valleys driven deep into the craggy terrain between **Newport** and **Cardiff** in the eighteenth and nineteenth centuries and vividly described in the pages of **Richard Llewellyn**'s (1907–83) classic *How Green Was My Valley* (1939). Characterized by fierce religion and self-reliance, these staunchly working-class commu-

Ton Pentre, Rhondda Valley in the 1950s – childhood home of Roy Lewis.

nities were decimated by the demise of the old industries, forcing the area to rediscover itself.

The grim mines, impoverished terraces and austere chapels of the **Rhondda Valley** defined the landscape of **Roy Lewis'*** youth. Reflecting his 'memories and images' of the Rhondda, Lewis' Welsh-set mysteries move through a convincing, if slightly anachronistic, landscape. A man of few words, Inspector Crow investigates in the 'partly biographical' *A Question of Degree* (1974), set in the **Ton Pentre** area and based on an incident that occurred here during Lewis' teens. The brooding tale of a doctor who refuses to accept the police version of events when a local girl is murdered, *Witness my Death* (1976) unfolds a landscape that reveals 'the narrow tensions that can occur in small communities like the Rhondda'. Lewis' experiences at Margam Steel Works (just south of the heavily industrialized conurbation of **Port Talbot**) and the workmen he met on site there inspired *A Distant Banner* (1976).

Symbolic of the rebirth of the region is the dramatic dockland regeneration of **CARDIFF**, confident, cosmopolitan capital of Wales and home to the Welsh National Assembly. South of the city centre, tough **Tiger Bay** grew out of **Butetown** and the late Victorian docklands. Once a multicultural maritime mass lived here, but as the roar of the tiger grew more subdued, the docklands fell into disrepair and decay. Today, Cardiff Bay hosts some of Britain's brightest new architecture, a transformation that is a constant motif in **Bill James'** (pseud. James Tucker, 1929–) stylish, savagely humorous novels.

'It could be said that my novels are about a nowhere place, about a nowhere situation: you haven't got police and crooks living at two extremes; you have everybody living in the middle, and it's a kind of unspecific area where crime and policing operates' – **Bill James** at **Cardiff Bay**, with **Penarth Head** in the background.

Devious Assistant Chief Constable Desmond Iles works alongside his overburdened sidekick Detective Chief Superintendent Colin Harpur out of a fictitious police station in what might be **Bute Street** (close to the railway station). From *You'd Better Believe It* (1985), Harpur and Iles don't just bend the rules, they make them up as they go along in this series of interlinked snapshots providing a through-the-looking-glass perspective of a corrupt and cruel culture where the line between law-makers and law-breakers is often indistinguishable. The city is largely an atmospheric backdrop, though the Butetown architecture remains prominent, and is often reflected in the tide-less lagoon created by a barrage across the **Taff** and **Ely** rivers.

Panicking Ralph (1997) is the story of drug barons vying for position. The novel's eponymous anti-hero, Ralph Ember, is an emblematic series character striving for respectability in the quagmire of his inadequacy and inability to change. Upward mobility is an aspiration for most of James' underworld, with Cardiff's new housing an obvious attraction for ill-gotten gains. These themes continue into *Eton Crop* (1999) and *Kill Me* (2000), where the repercussions from a disastrous undercover operation on a floating restaurant continue to reverberate around the

The **Bethel Baptist Chapel**, which **James Tucker** attended as a child (and which temporarily became a night-club before falling into disrepair and being demolished) features in his **David Craig** novels as a watering hole for 'Tiger' villains keen to map out their misdemeanours.

docklands. There is a metaphor, too, in the mudflats of Cardiff Bay, now permanently covered by barraged waters: as old Cardiff is covered by new, old crime is covered by new as criminal players eagerly enter the regenerated landscape.

Cardiff's **Pierhead Building** and inner harbour – 'Was this once a working dock?' asks **Bill James** in his detective series.

> Brade liked the word Bay. This Bay – Cardiff Bay – was not just a patch of sea semicircled by cliffs and beaches, as, say, the famous Bay of Plenty in New Zealand is, or the possibly more famous Bay of Pigs in Cuba. This Bay was a concept, an advertisement slogan, a downtown redevelopment scheme, mostly land-based, although the sea lay there at the edge. It was industrial, commercial, had infrastructure, a barrage, streets, the Welsh Assembly buildings, cinemas, road tunnels, crime, a brilliant, architecturally vivid opera house (in drawing-board, dream form only), Harry Ramsden's fish and chip palace, crime, the ornamental dock and ornamental crane, a visitors' centre, crime and politics.
>
> David Craig, *Bay City* (2000)

Writing as **David Craig**, Tucker responds even more directly to the Big Future of Cardiff Bay, with paradoxical Dave Brade and black, Welsh-speaking, moral philosophy graduate Glyndwr Jenkins patrolling a Waterfront where criminal rivalry is rife and 'witnesses and sources are always scarce'.

As a child, James Tucker sailed with his father on the sand dredgers that were then a regular feature of Cardiff dock life. *Paydays* (2001), written as **Bill James**, features several maritime scenes alongside characteristic dialogue that James himself describes as 'a kind of elevated, pompous, pulpit language'.

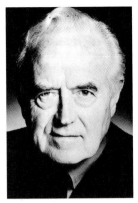

'Religion used to outmatch even coal as life's centrepiece for the mass of common people – making Wales a very unlikely setting for serious crime. And that's the besetting challenge that has faced Welsh crime fiction writers, and perhaps that's why there are so few of us in a highly literate country where almost every street has its quota of poets' – **David Williams.**

David Williams' hometown of **Bridgend,** a market town midway between Cardiff and **Swansea,** becomes 'Pontyglas', where a local man returning from Australia after forty years to claim his inheritance is stopped dead in his tracks in *Death of a Prodigal* (1995).

The 'bustling, dynamic thundering emporium' of Cardiff's Victorian **Covered Market,** '…stretching between two of its principal, and oldest, streets. The brashness of the market still balances the elegance of the arcades.' A murder victim's cry goes unheard here in **David Williams'** *Dead in the Market.*

The traditional whodunnits of **David Williams** (1926–) display an intimate knowledge of his native Wales. Williams' first detective, half-Welsh merchant banker Mark Treasure had already travelled to Wales (*Murder for Treasure*, 1980) to investigate in Britain's smallest city, **St David's,** but it falls to forceful DCI Merlin Parry and easygoing heavyweight DS Gomer Lloyd to fully explore the dynamic patch around Cardiff.

While Porsche-driving Parry is an enthusiastic choir member and occasional rugby-player, Lloyd – 'a lapsed Methodist… whose favourite tenet is that it's a sin to believe evil of others, but seldom a mistake' – represents a more reserved, Welsh-speaking generation. Parry and Lloyd often operate out of **Central Police Station** on the west side of **Cathay's Park,** the impressive neo-classical cluster of civic buildings and museums in white Portland stone. The distinctive wrought iron and high glazing of the **Covered Market** on **St Mary Street** is the scene of the crime in *Dead in the Market* (1996), where Parry is initially baffled by the lack of murder witnesses in a hall packed with hundreds of shoppers.

Ecclesiastical buildings and characters, with all their strictures and dilemmas, occupy a prime position in Williams' landscapes. Singing as a baritone with the church choir in 'Tawrbach' (the pretty town of **Cowbridge,** west of Cardiff), Parry is well-placed to investigate the death of the Rector of 'St Curig' in the first Parry mystery, *Last Seen Breathing* (1994). And there is no shortage of suspects in *A Terminal Case* (1997), when the parishioners of 'Bryntaf' (near **Llandaff** – the quiet suburb that is home to **Cardiff Cathedral**) are up in arms over their vicar's plans to divorce his wife and remarry an attractive young widow.

The insistent, lyrical voice of **Dylan Thomas** (1914–53) still echoes around the seven hills of **SWANSEA**, the 'ugly, lovely' place of his birth. Set along a wide, curving bay, Swansea sustained heavy bomb damage in World War II, resulting in a curious blend of architecture. Reflecting the city's social landscape and multicultural makeup, the detective chillers of **Katherine John** (pseud. Karo Nadolny, 1948–) brush parts of Swansea with the dark aesthetics of a **Stephen King** slasher. Gentle and perceptive Sergeant Trevor Joseph of the Serious Crimes Squad works his persuasive empathy alongside the less sensitive technique of Drug Squad colleague Sergeant Peter Collins. Both men are fond of breaking their shift for a walk along the nearby **Mumbles** seafront, whose sweeping coastline and pier feature in *Without Trace* (1989). When a young doctor disappears on his way to work, Joseph finds himself drawn towards the man's widow – and towards the Victorian pier (inspired by Mumbles Pier) at the centre of a terrible secret:

Katherine John's novels bring the chill of brutalized urban life to seaside **Swansea**.

> The lighthouse blinked steadily from the rocky promontory on his far left. In front of it, the moonlight picked out the ragged outline of the wired-off pier. Derelict, dangerous, it remained a testimony to the unpalatable fact that the town didn't have enough money to clear up all the rotting ruins left over from its past. He walked on slowly. What was it about waves, water, the eternal movement of the sea, that cast a primitive, calming spell on men? Made them thoughtful, quieter? He stepped down to the shoreline, his footsteps mingling with the thick, sucking noises of the water swirling amongst the pebbles.

Mumbles Pier, near **Swansea** – 'I've always been fascinated by piers,' says **Katherine John**, whose detectives investigate a wired-off, barricaded pier in *Without Trace*.

Badly injured, Joseph ends up in the Victorian psychiatric hospital with 'masses of old corridors, disused mortuaries' that John uses as the focus for the sequel *Six Foot Under* (1993). The hospital becomes a nightmare world of looming Gothic silhouettes, where the wind rattles 'the skeletons of the dead leaves that had escaped the gardener's rake by piling deep in the undergrowth'. *Murder of a Dead Man* (1994) stems from John's experiences working next door to a hostel for the homeless near the docks, in **Gloucester Place** ('Jubilee Street'), where she and her colleagues would hand out cups of coffee in the morning.

If the past is indeed a foreign country, then it could well resemble the forested and rolling green borderland of **THE MARCHES** between Wales and England. Defined by the great eighth-century earthen rampart of **Offa's Dyke**, the borders are a neither-nor world of their own. Referring to the Middle March of Wales, **Ellis Peters*** (1913–95) wrote: 'no ground in the kingdom has been more tramped over by armies, coveted by chieftains, ravaged by battles, sung by poets and celebrated in epics of legend and tragedy'. Not only does the past refuse to lie down here, its literary crime chroniclers actively encourage it not to.

'It is no mere inventory. Its inquiries have been so thorough and its scope so wide that it is a veritable Domesday Book. All our earthly deeds are entered neatly in abbreviated Latin… our deeds – and our misdeeds,' says a character from **Edward Marston**'s* (pseud. Keith Miles, 1940–) dramatic eleventh-century crime series. Using actual land disputes recorded in the Domesday Book, Marston's series features King's commissioners Ralph Delchard and Gervase Bret. Cardiff-born Marston cycled around The Marches in his youth – but in the Domesday series this is a highly volatile area. In *The Dragons Of Archenfield* (1995), headstrong Norman soldier Delchard and more contemplative monastery-educated Bret ride into the strategic earldom of **Hereford**. It was the Bishop of Hereford who remarked of the Domesday Survey 'and there was much misery and terror as a result', and Delchard and Bret soon find themselves embroiled in much more than mere land disputes. Today, Hereford is a small market city of some 50,000 inhabitants, home to the county administration and the cider industry. In 1086 this compact, cosmopolitan garrison town of some 1000 people was dominated by its impressive castle, a 'massive stone building… perched on the River Wye' (of which, sadly, nothing now remains). Some twenty miles to the south-east, at the head of the River Severn, the cathedral city of **Gloucester** provides the setting for *The Owls of Gloucester* (2000): Delchard and Bret arrive at **Gloucester Abbey** to investigate the murder of a monk, using a combination of inspiration and perspiration that Brother Cadfael would no doubt find admirable.

Marston's historical landscapes are dominated by the key buildings of the period: the castles 'sophisticated' by the Normans, and the monasteries and abbeys that acted as 'university and hospital combined'.

'I'm a great believer in primary sources… and the primary source for me is place' – **Edward Marston** at home with history in his eleventh-century Domesday series.

As well as giving shelter to travellers of Delchard and Bret's importance, these places are central sources of gossip and information essential to detectives operating without any real forensic evidence. In *The Hawks of Delamere* (1998), a much-mellowed Delchard and more self-assured Bret are called to the castle and abbey of **Chester** on the northern Welsh borders. Leading a hunting party through the densely canopied tracks of **Delamere Forest**, north-east of Chester, the capricious and brutal Earl of Chester is shocked to witness his favourite hawk being struck by an arrow. The Earl extracts swift and bloody retribution, but is there a wider plot to challenge his control of the borderland?

The Domesday Survey of 1086 recorded that **Shrewsbury** had some 250 houses, held protectively in the watery grip of Britain's longest river, the **Severn**. With a wealth of old buildings and narrow, winding cobbled streets, central Shrewsbury today retains much of its medieval character. Apart from the Norman gateway, little remains of the original castle, although a short walk across the **English Bridge** leads to the impressive red sandstone abbey of **St Peter and St Paul**. It is here that **Ellis Peters** (pseud. Edith Pargeter, 1913–95) based her twelfth-century series

'So many of the places I've visited are still exactly as they were… you can get a feel for the kind of people who lived there. Landscapes shape the way people think and behave, and in the Domesday books my characters are all shaped by their individual environments. We're talking about a society where people rarely moved more than five miles from where they were born, and some people in their entire lives would never move more than a couple of miles from the house in which they were born' – **Edward Marston**.

The Abbey of **St Peter and St Paul, Shrewsbury** – 'He doubted if there was a finer Benedictine garden in the whole kingdom, or one better supplied with herbs both good for spicing meats, and also invaluable as medicine… Here, in the enclosed garden within the walls, close to the abbot's fish-ponds and the brook that worked the abbey mill, Brother Cadfael ruled unchallenged.'

featuring worldly detective monk Brother Cadfael. Using 'an amalgam of stark fact and derived fiction', Peters traces the unfolding history of the Shropshire and Marches area she loved and knew intimately.

Based upon a documented expedition, *A Morbid Taste for Bones* (1977), opens one sunny May morning in 1137 with fifty-seven-year-old Brother Cadfael flexing his green fingers in the herb garden of Shrewsbury's Benedictine Abbey. After a 'roving youth of... battle and adventure', Cadfael has arrived at the 'quietude' of abbey life, 'like a battered ship settling at last for a quiet harbour'. His proven skills as a herbalist are matched by a keen understanding of human nature and an inquisitive mind – so when his ambitious Prior decides to lay claim to the bones of a lesser-known saint from a distant Welsh village, Cadfael is keen to join the party. A Gwynedd man of 'antique Welsh stock', whose first language is Welsh, Cadfael is the ideal interpreter for the expedition to **Gwytherin** (lying just a few miles from the beautiful **Vale of Conway**, which today marks the eastern boundary of Snowdonia National Park). He is also an ideal peacemaker when things start to go badly wrong, and his skill with herbs, and their medicinal qualities, plays a major role in uncovering the truth in this intriguing first mystery.

Through her Welsh grandmother, Ellis Peters had a 'toehold over the border', and displays strong cultural empathy in her descriptions of communities struggling to co-exist in the tensions and strife of the borderland. In one of Peters' most powerful novels, *The Virgin in the Ice* (1982), Cadfael's past and present collide as he seeks the killer of a young nun. Clearly aware of her own mortality, Peters carefully paced Cadfael's life and ageing alongside her own, culminating in the final Chronicle, *Brother Cadfael's Penance* (1994), in which Cadfael contemplates leaving the order to go in search of his missing son. All of the ancient backstreets and passages mentioned in the Chronicles exist: the steep, winding uphill road of the **Wyle**, the **High Cross**, **High Street** and **Butcher Row**, whilst in the abbey church it is quite possible to imagine the cowled figure of Cadfael, peacefully propped upright in semi-sleep behind one of the stone pillars to the rear of this 'vast stone ship'.

In **David Armstrong**'s* (1946–) *Thought for the Day* (1997), Detective Inspector Frank Kavanagh passes through Shrewsbury en route to the scene of the crime under the honeycombed limestone cliffs and 2,000-year-old mines of **Llanymynech Hill**. With Offa's Dyke nearby and buzzards keening over the fields, this beautiful and atmospheric Roman site now forms part of the **Llanymynech Heritage Area**. The lonely brick chimney of the **Hoffman Limekiln** stands as a stark reminder that this was once one of the busiest industrial areas in Shropshire. The discovery of a body has Kavanagh and DC Jane Salt journeying between 'cheek-by-jowl' London and sleepy rural Shropshire on the trail of a brutal kidnapper and killer. When the ransom money is thrown from a train window into a damp field beside the Severn river, the killer appears to have escaped. But in these parts nothing much goes unnoticed ('If you're looking at hedges and sky and sheep all day long, a car down the lane's

From his **Oswestry** home, **David Armstrong** explores the borders in *Thought for the Day*.

an event') and a local farmer notes the car registration. But just as Kavanagh seems to be making progress, another corpse surfaces in a bunker on a Shropshire golf course. Armstrong, who lives just north of Llanymynech in **Oswestry**, paints contrasting landscapes in this intense, compelling piece of detective *noir*.

'"In Lydmouth", Williamson said, waving his fork for emphasis, "there's no such thing as a coincidence. Or rather, it's *all* coincidence. Everyone knows everyone else."' Rooted firmly in the southern Anglo-Welsh borderland of the 1950s, **Andrew Taylor**'s* (1951–) powerful 'Lydmouth' series opens with *An Air That Kills* (1994). In a post-World War II climate this remote part of rural Britain is grappling with the unwelcome, invasive force of modernity, as Taylor evokes a 'self-

contained, provincial, strangely claustrophobic society in transition'. Lydmouth and its hinterland are modelled on the **Forest of Dean** and east Monmouthshire area that has been home to Taylor for over twenty years. Lydmouth most closely resembles the ancient Welsh market town of **Monmouth**, where the rivers **Wye** and **Monnow** loop gently around three sides of its elegant Georgian buildings and eleventh-century castle ruins. Monmouth's **Wye Bridge** is the model for Lydmouth's 'New Bridge', while Taylor's home town of **Coleford** donates its old coaching inn, **The Angel**, to become the High Street 'Bull Hotel', 'a large white building, rather older than its eighteenth-century façade suggested' and the **Angus Buchanan VC Recreation Ground** becomes Lydmouth's 'Jubilee Park'.

'I wanted to describe a relatively enclosed society struggling to come to terms with a world in the throes of enormous changes. There's no nostalgia in Lydmouth. Change of any kind is suspect; outsiders are by definition suspicious, agents of change' – **Andrew Taylor**, pictured overlooking the **Forest of Dean**, describes his Lydmouth series.

An Air That Kills sets the Lydmouth scene: under a grey November sky, themes of temptation, guilt and remembrance unfold. Journalist Jill Francis arrives in town, fleeing painful London memories; her hurt translated into a coldness that both repulses and attracts Detective Inspector Richard Thornhill. When the bones of a baby are found on the site of an old inn, Jill and Richard become drawn towards each other and into a mystery that impacts on the lives of the whole community. In an age of afternoon tea and Spam sandwiches, where class delineation remains rigid and social placement paramount, Lydmouth's past has a habit of intruding uncomfortably into the present. Hence the Forest Freeminers play a role in *The Suffocating Night* (1998) and the old Monmouth slaughterhouse that 'made the river run with blood' influences *Where Roses Fade* (2000). The 1830s Forest of Dean enclosure riots suggested an important element of *Death's Own Door* (2001), which continues the series from the perspective of Thornhill's wife Edith. Along a long chain of local connections, an investigation into an apparent suicide leads directly to Edith Thornhill's door. While Richard and Jill try to establish their futures, Edith finds herself on an unwelcome voyage back to her past as memories of another death come thundering into the present like a train down the track.

The titles of **Andrew Taylor**'s Lydmouth novels are taken from the poems of **A E Housman** (1859–1936), notably from *A Shropshire Lad* (1896) – a collection much-admired by **Ellis Peters** and **Colin Dexter*** – which describes a 'land of lost content'.

Opposite: The **Forest of Dean** close to **Monmouth** – for **Andrew Taylor** this is an 'enigmatic and very beautiful strip of land which isn't quite England and isn't quite Wales, but is wholly itself.'

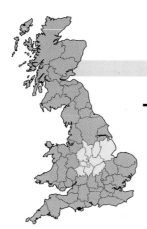

CHAPTER SIX

The Midlands

As he walked, he noticed *en passant* that yet another of the old factories had disappeared under the demolition hammer, revealing open spaces and an ancestral view of distant hills…

Marjorie Eccles, *Requiem for a Dove* (1990)

A broad belt across the belly of Britain, from the Lincolnshire coast to the Welsh border, the Midlands buckles together the industrial heartland of the country with hugely varied natural scenery. From the fertile flatness of farmlands and fens to the limestone and grit of the Peaks, from multicultural urban sprawl to regenerated warehouses and canals, this is an area alive with contradictions and contrasts of character and landscape.

Trapped between the conurbations of Manchester and Sheffield at the southern tip of the Pennines, the **PEAK DISTRICT** is a largely self-contained region of craggy dales, dark moors, scattered farms and market towns. Britain's first national park, this is an area of extremes, from the brooding, high moorland tops of the **Dark Peak**, with their

'A wisp of steam trailed over the furrow of the cutting' – the **Cromford and High Peak Railway** is at the centre of **John Buxton Hilton**'s Sergeant Brunt mystery *Gamekeeper's Gallows*. The railway operated between 1830 and 1967; its tracks now form part of the **High Peak Trail**.

wind-sculpted gritstone, to the gentler limestone hills and streams of the **White Peak**.

Alive with hill-country folklore, customs and social history, the immediate prose of **Buxton**-born **John Buxton Hilton** (1921–86) captures the area's unique atmosphere. Set around the turn of the twentieth century, the Detective Sergeant Brunt mysteries are particularly rich in lore and landscape. Even reaching the isolated **High Peak** community of 'Piper's Fold' proves a challenge in *Gamekeeper's Gallows* (1976), where Brunt encounters the **Cromford and High Peak Railway** and its enigmatic train driver Thomas Beresford. Brunt is struck by 'a powerful and bewildering feeling of unreality' as he enters the 'wild moors and empty hills, under the even wilder and emptier skies of the High Peak Hundred' to investigate the case of a missing girl. The thirty-three mile journey on the Cromford and High Peak Railway takes an incredible five and a half hours, but it is the traffic in young girls through the community that most concerns Brunt. He faces an uphill task, too, trying to uncover the link between Beresford's neglected animal traps and the missing girl. In *Dead-Nettle* (1977), Brunt switches to the **Low Peak** to investigate a murder in the 'organic grey stone huddle' of the abandoned Dead-Nettle lead-mine. Buxton Hilton again recreates the timeless aspects of hill life and the narrowly defined lives of 'unforthcoming' communities still fighting the same feuds and following the same ancient codes.

Exploring similar themes within a contemporary setting, Hilton sends London-based Superintendent Simon Kenworthy on holiday in limestone country in *The Anathema Stone* (1980). When a young woman's body is discovered on an ancient monument, Kenworthy's holiday is quickly forgotten as he investigates modern motives and ancient rivalries in a timeless landscape:

> They walked miles over hilltops and across the heads of cloughs that fed ice-cold rivulets down into the dales. The air was clean. They had immense tracts of country to themselves. Except for the white rubble walls, parcelling the middle distance into tiny, irregular, unviable fields, there was nothing on the skyline that would have seemed alien to Neolithic man… even the rectangular enclosures had something that was primeval in spirit.

A testimony to 'the sort of people I have lived among all my life', **Stephen Booth**'s (1952–) brooding detective debut *Black Dog* (1999) is the first of a series exploring the changing seasons of the Peak District. Investigations into the death of a schoolgirl focus on the inscrutable figure of retired miner Harry Dickinson, and Booth's polarized pairing of police detectives Ben Cooper and Diane Fry. The headquarters of the fictional 'E Division' (largely based on the **Buxton**-based B Division) are in 'Edendale', at the meeting point of Dark and White peaks:

Writing as **John Greenwood**, Buxton Hilton created distinctive Detective Inspector Mosley in a satirical look at detection alive with landscape. In *Mosley by Moonlight* (1984), Mosley finds himself up in the **Pennines**, 'the vertebrae of England', looking across a 'living map, in an infinity of greens and browns, extending to a blue blur of distant trees'.

'I was born in Derbyshire, in a remote spot, from where visits to seaside or city were a rarity,' says **Frances Fyfield***. 'We were half a mile from the nearest house, two miles from a bus stop, seven miles to a town… I was one of four children in what felt like a crowded house, but was, in real life, big and utterly remote, full of laughter and drama and quarrels, tears and debts, and latterly, madness. To be honest, that house influences what I write more than anything else. I have translated it into other houses and places more times than I can record.'

Stephen Booth pictured above
Hope Valley – where the
limestone hills of the White
Peak meet the peat and
gritstone moors of the
Dark Peak – a 'source of
endless inspiration' for his
detective fiction.

The patchwork of farmland and tree-covered slopes to the
south looked welcoming and approachable lit by the sun, but
was full of hidden depths and unseen corners. It was criss-crossed
by a pattern of dry-stone walls and erupted here and there in steep
limestone cliffs or the ripples and pockmarks of abandoned mine
workings. It was, above all, a human landscape, settled and shaped
by people, and still a place where thousands of years of history
might be expected to come to the surface, if you cared to look…
To the north, the moors of the Dark Peak looked remote and
forbidding, an uncompromising landscape that was anything but
human. The bare faces of hardened gritstone seemed to absorb
the sun instead of reflecting it as the limestone did. They seemed
to stand aloof and brooding, untouched by humanity and
therefore offering a challenge that many took up, to conquer their
peaks.

In the heat of summer, the personal dramas of *Black Dog* are played
out against a background of wider conflicts in a national park with
some 22 million visitors a year. Tensions between tourism and preserva-
tion, between public access and farmers' and landowners' interests, and
between natural scenery and local industry, are deeply embedded.
'Derbyshire's landscape has that sort of character,' says Stephen Booth,
'its history is etched on it like the familiar lines on the face of a friend.'

Symbolizing 'guilt and
innocence and punishment',
the **Nine Ladies** stone circle
stands on **Stanton Moor**, near
Matlock. For *Dancing with the
Virgins*, **Stephen Booth**
merged this location and a
different – incomplete – stone
circle nearby.

With the distinctive red jackets of the Peak Park Ranger service bold
against an autumn background, *Dancing With The Virgins* (2001) taps
a rich vein of folklore and superstition in an area where ancient rituals
such as well-dressing continue to this day. When the body of a woman
is found in an ancient stone circle, Cooper and Fry have to set aside their
differences to tackle a vicious murderer. Continuing Booth's hugely

evocative series in the snow-bound moors of the Dark Peak, *Blood on the Tongue* (2002) explores the links between a World War II plane crash, modern murder and Derbyshire's Polish communities.

Perched just outside the south-western edge of the Peak District, the old mill town of **Leek**, 'Queen of the Moorlands', has more in common with the Derbyshire dales and moors than with the clay-rich Staffordshire Potteries that claim its affiliation. With its eighteenth-century Brindley Mill, brick and gritstone farms and churches, Leek is every inch a moorland town. Cycling the hilly, four-mile journey to Leek Police Station from her cottage in **Cheddleton**, 'feminine feminist' Detective Inspector Joanna Piercy is the creation of **Priscilla Masters** (1952–), in a series rich in local character.

'The location was more important than for any other book I've written,' says **Val McDermid*** of her powerful detective thriller *A Place of Execution* (1999), which moves around the **Buxton** and **Bakewell** area. 'I was trying to draw out the hiddenness, the mysteriousness of a very beautiful landscape… there's always been for me a sense, in the White Peak particularly, that there are things hidden here, that strange things could happen, and nobody would know.'

Priscilla Masters atop the **Winking Man** – 'The dark, menacing moor guarded by the craggy outcrop… a fitting setting for a violent crime, a graveyard of nature's making'.

'I love Staffordshire figures and have always collected them,' says **Priscilla Masters**, whose interest in the stories that lie behind the figures inspires her novels. DI Joanna Piercy has inherited her aunt's collection of Victorian figures and, as in *Embroidering Shrouds* (2001), uses them to meditate on her investigations.

'Looking around at the wide expanse of moors Joanna shivered and thought she knew no lonelier place on God's earth. It seemed cut off from civilization, towns and streets. And yet there was a raw beauty up here – a sense of truth and purity.' Fleece-clad visitors often head the five miles out of Leek on the A53 Buxton Road to the distinctive rocky outcrop of the **Roaches**. Exposed to brutal, chilling moorland winds, one rock formation in particular stands out from this popular climbing spot: the **Winking Man**. Shaped like a man's head, this gritstone curiosity appears to wink at passers-by through a trick of the open sky and rock behind. In *Catch the Fallen Sparrow* (1996), a boy's burnt body is discovered under the Winking Man's impassive, stony gaze. Contrasting the wild, elemental moorland with the sedate shelter of the town, Masters weaves the tragic life and death of a neglected young boy into an engaging and deeply moving mystery.

It would be impossible to represent the Leek landscape without reference to the farming community. With a strong sense of rural life, *Scaring Crows* (1999) focuses on Joanna's investigations into the deaths of a farmer and son in their stone farmhouse. *Endangering Innocents* (2002) tackles the rural blight of foot and mouth disease, footpath closures and the terrible consequences for a strange, mute schoolgirl who goes missing.

Six miles to the south-west of Leek, the conurbation of **STOKE-ON-TRENT**, one-time pottery capital of the world, is the location for **Mary Kelly**'s (pseud. Elizabeth Kendal, 1927–) Gold Dagger-winning *The Spoilt Kill* (1961). Guided by eighteenth-century pioneers such as Josiah Wedgwood towards the peak of its fame, mass-production meshed Stoke and surrounding towns into the giant industrial region of the 'Potteries':

> Our Town! That grey haphazard sprawl, that welter of shallow hills and twisting roads netted with little streets; six towns that had split outwards and run into each other as their native industry swelled. Burselm, Tunstall, Longton, Fenton, Hanley, Stoke. Later I could see differences between their centres, at least, assign characteristics. On that day I saw only the confused legacy of past opportunism and nineteenth-century industrial expansion. Houses, factories, chapels, laundries, shops, and potteries, built as needed, sprouting along the roads that linked the six, till they touched; no plan, no architectural consistency, only on all sides the unity of dark red brick blackened with soot, more or less, according to its age.

With success came squalor and grime: until its recent post-industrial facelift Stoke was known as the pollution capital of Britain. Kelly's stylish mystery, in which private investigator Nicholson infiltrates a family firm to investigate the passing of designs to foreign imitators, is a walking,

Stoke-on-Trent – '…a row of bottle kilns blocking the gap between blackened brick buildings, and beyond them a factory chimney and the peak of a slag heap, wraiths even in the middle distance. There was no far distance, only a grey blankness of cleaned smoke mixed with the drizzle that seeped from low-lying clouds.'

Mary Kelly, *The Spoilt Kill*

talking guide to the history of pottery. Its title derived from the local pronunciation of kiln as 'kill', the novel depicts Stoke on the cusp of change, a smoke-smudged landscape of old bottle kilns and proud heritage with a whiff of 'faintly sulphurous air'. Nicholson is irresistibly drawn towards a purposeful people 'alive and conscious of where they were living', and to the factory's attractive designer in particular. But everything changes when a dead body is pulled from a tank of liquid clay.

Like Stoke, the large East Midlands city of **NOTTINGHAM** offers a landscape rich in industrial heritage. Reputed for the manufacturing of bikes, cigarettes, pharmaceuticals and lace, and for its outlying coal-mining areas, Nottingham's enduring fame is as the land of Robin Hood. The scant remains of the once-great **Sherwood Forest** lie to the north of the city, while the swirling waters of the **River Trent** loop around the south. The famous old **Trent Bridge** cricket ground lies close to the river crossing, while the grounds of Nottingham's major football clubs face each other over the water.

From his home near **Alexandra Park**, in the north of the city, **John Harvey**'s (1938–) Detective Inspector Charlie Resnick can see the **Meadow Lane** floodlights of his favoured team, Notts County FC. Born into a Polish family in the industrial Midlands, Resnick likes nothing more than ambling down from his base at **Canning Circus** Police Station to the various delicatessens in the city centre market, eating substantial sandwiches and drinking strong Italian coffee. Appropriately enough for the divorced and often melancholy Resnick, his first appearance, in *Lonely Hearts* (1989), involves investigating a series of attacks on women who have been using the Lonely Hearts column of a local paper. The novel sets the scene for a series clearly influenced by American writers such as **Elmore Leonard** (1925–) and merging Harvey's strong social conscience and passion for jazz and blues with the very real social problems of a large urban community. From the cemetery off **Canning Circus** to the poorer, largely working-class area of **Radford**, from the more affluent semi-private estate of **The Park** to the student flats of **Lenton**, and out west to the 'burgeoning clubs and pubs', Resnick's patch has it all.

A poet and scriptwriter with the ghosts of local literary giants **D H Lawrence** (1885–1930) and **Alan Sillitoe** (1928–) peering over his shoulder, Harvey spent seventeen years in Nottingham, taking every opportunity to absorb the city's atmosphere: 'I would stroll around the city most days, sit on buses, walk the walk that Resnick took down through the centre to the Italian coffee stall in the market and sit there, never making notes, but watching and listening, occasionally chatting, feeling – if never quite rightly – that I belonged.'

The result is a series of acutely observed, multi-stranded urban narratives with a touch of street blues, wrapped around the rather shabbily dressed figure of Charlie Resnick. In the gripping *Cutting Edge* (1991), Resnick investigates a series of gruesome attacks on staff at a city hospital. As Resnick's team finally juggle the clues into place, the scene is set for a breathtaking climax. The final Resnick mystery is *Last Rites* (1998), in which a convicted murderer returns to the city to attend his mother's funeral, and is soon on the run. Resnick already has his hands full contemplating a possible promotion when a drugs war looks like erupting…

Long-serving journalist **Frank Palmer** (1933–2000) lived in **Keyworth**, to the south of Nottingham, but used his two main detective series to explore traditional landscapes and industries along the length and breadth of the East Midlands area. Hard-bitten, would-be crime novelist Detective Inspector 'Jacko' Jackson of the 'East Midland Combined Constabulary' investigates the murder of a former colleague in *Testimony* (1992). A complex case exploring police corruption, racism, and the unsolved case of a drowned teenage girl, Jacko's inquiries

'There were new covers over the stools, fresh red and green paint on the counter, the cappuccino machine had been moved from one side to the other' – DI Charlie Resnick's favourite Italian coffee stall in Nottingham's indoor **Victoria Market.**

Frank Palmer explored the character of the East Midlands from his Nottingham base.

The lonely brick chimney of the Hoffman limekiln at **Llanymynech Hill** stands as a stark reminder of the industrial heritage of the Welsh border region explored in **David Armstrong**'s *Thought for the Day*, (1997).

The mysterious landscape of **Middle Fen** near **Ely**.

'At last the violet rim of the German Ocean appeared over the green edge of the Norfolk coast…' – the view from **Happisburgh Church**, with the **Hill House** from **Arthur Conan Doyle**'s 'The Dancing Men' (1903) below left. The headland is also at the centre of **P D James**' *Devices and Desires* (1989).

Nottingham – home of the modern British police novel.

Operating with the real Nottinghamshire Constabulary, CID detective **Keith Wright** won wide acclaim for his police procedurals featuring no-nonsense DI Dave Stark. Christmas is cancelled for Stark and his team in *Addressed to Kill* (1993), when a brutal rapist brings terror close to the Stark family home. *Fair Means or Foul* (1995) visits one of Nottingham's oldest traditions, The Goose Fair, as Stark pursues the killer of a teenage girl in a riveting, desperate whodunnit with a neat twist in the tail.

are further complicated by the fact that his main witness is a blind man. *Dead Man's Handle* (1995) moves in and around a chilly, fog-shrouded Nottingham, as Jacko comes face to face with a shotgun-wielding killer. With Jacko heading for retirement, the novel introduces a new series character in Chief Superintendent Phil 'Sweeney' Todd, who steps in to rescue Jacko at great risk to himself. The changeover of characters is intriguingly manoeuvred in *Dark Forest* (1997), ostensibly written by Jacko himself as a debut novel, in which Todd investigates against the backdrop of the miner's strike and Nottingham's pharmaceutical industry. A keen football and cricket fan, Palmer explored the big-money world of professional football in *Final Score* (1998). With a fugitive on the loose, Todd's investigations take him from Nottingham to nearby **Pride Park, Derby**, home to the 'Rams' of Derby County FC.

In *Over My Dead Body* (2000), Detective Chief Inspector Robert Graham contemplates a return to his home city of **Nottingham**. Focused on the city's **Waverly Street/Portland Road** area, the Forest Road red-light district and **Nottingham Central Police Station**, the novel features familiar territory for Flynn, who served many years as a police officer with the Nottingham Central Division.

Former Nottingham police officer **Raymond Flynn** (1940–) exiles his sardonic Detective Inspector Robert Graham to **LINCOLNSHIRE**, the same fenland county where Frank Palmer began his journalistic career. Another Todd family member is at the centre of Graham's investigations in the debut *Seascape with Body* (1995), set in a Lincolnshire coastal resort festering with murderous intent. Conceived as a form of 'Nottingham-on-Sea', 'Eddathorpe-on-Sea' is a transient place with a winter population more than doubled by seasonal visitors and bears more than a passing resemblance to the popular resorts of **Skegness** and **Mablethorpe**. However, Flynn's landscape is largely one of the procedures and routines of daily policing: the cautioning and questioning, the scheming, swearing, joking, friendship and friction in the offices and cells of Eddathorpe Police Station. In *A Fine Body of Men* (1997), a 'bucket and spade day; cans of lager and fish and chips' on a sunny August Bank Holiday weekend is ruined when a man's body is found dumped on the beach. DI Graham faces a gruelling and often baffling investigation into the death of a local small-time criminal. Off-duty, away from his investigations into seedy pubs and a local caravan site, Graham finds time for a quiet evening walk with his dog along the Esplanade and onto the beach:

The 'gentle swish and suck of the sea' by **Skegness Pier**.

> We plunged down the steps on to the beach; it was quiet,
> silent except for the gentle swish and suck of the sea. The tide
> was almost out and the moon defined a deceptive, shimmering
> silver line where foam met sand at the edge of the beach. By
> daylight the brownish, sluggish surge of tide against beach was
> fairly unattractive… At night, under a full moon and with a little
> help from the glow of the sodium lights on the Esp above, even
> cynical, reluctant dog-walkers could manage the ghost of a
> romantic stroll…

Deep in the 'Utilitarian, arable flatness' of a bleak and marshy Lincolnshire coast, the mysterious town of 'Flaxborough' is the creation of **Colin Watson** (1920–82). Behind the façade of olde worlde shops and prim, net-curtained houses, lurk the less-than-respectable, lecherous Flaxburghians. Their misdemeanours are investigated by polite but persevering Inspector Purbright and Sergeant Love, under the watchful eye of pompous Chief Constable Harcourt Chubb. A blend of social satire with the macabre, Watson's dollop of erotic farcery in 'a high-spirited town… like Gomorrah', is a world away from the cosily regimented communities that he describes in his acclaimed critique of the Golden Age of crime fiction, *Snobbery With Violence* (1971).

Watson coined the term 'Mayhem Parva' to describe the nostalgic hybrid of traditional English village and commuter town used by writers of detective fiction for reassuringly formulaic settings. In *Coffin, Scarcely Used* (1958), a local newspaper owner is found in a field, below a pylon, electrocuted. Purbright is puzzled by the 'uncharacteristic' cleverness of the crime for 'a town of earthy misdemeanours'. His trail leads, via an antiques front for good citizens' peccadilloes, to devious murder in a forgotten landscape:

> It was still light enough to see Clee Hill crouching like a lonely
> old sheep dog in the mist away to the left. On the near side of
> it, a small forest of skeletal trees held tapering, motionless fingers
> against the slate-coloured sky. The occasional roadside cottage,
> withdrawn against a leafless, dripping orchard or standing amidst
> a forlorn garden of soured, broken potato plants and stripped
> brussel stalks, showed no sign of occupancy. Here was a landscape
> gone to seed and bedded down to rot quietly until spring.

At the centre of *Lonelyheart 4122* (1967) is the mystery of disappearing Flaxborough ladies, whose only common link is their wealth and eligibility for marriage. Purbright heads for Handclasp House, a marriage bureau, and straight into some murderous skul-duggery. Purbright is led a merry dance by Miss Lucilla Edith Cavell, who, in *The Flaxborough Crab* (1969), is seen selling aphrodisiac dande-lion salads and complaining about the lack of sexual action in the town.

The city of **Lincoln** provides the inspiration for Inspector Proby's 'Hampton'.

Rising high into the wide sky of the flatlands, the ancient cathedral city of **LINCOLN** provides the inspiration for **John Gano**'s (pseud. Freddie Stockdale, 1947–) 'Hampton'. Gano adds some docks and an estuary to make it more of a 'Lincoln-by-Sea', and in a final flourish gives the town a canal modelled on **Basingstoke Canal** and woods from **Great Park** in Hampshire where he grew up.

First seen in *Inspector Proby's Christmas* (1994), open-minded, straight-talking Proby is under pressure as he hunts for a shotgun killer while his wife is having an affair with the prime suspect. The case is complicated by the fact that the countryside surrounding Hampton is littered with woodland, small farms and lots of legally held shotguns. In a wintry landscape familiar to Gano through his own farming in Lincolnshire, anticipation hangs in the air as Proby looks for a way to trap his man:

> The mud was frozen, making the ruts hard to walk on. The small shoots of winter wheat that punctuated the field seemed dwarfed by the great clods of solid clay. Everywhere the frost had outlined even the most fragile tendrils with silver, repainting the dun-coloured landscape of winter with a glittering palette… He paused and sniffed the air. Snow was coming. He could sense Nature's anticipation of the approaching change. The whole wood seemed tensed and silent, waiting for its magical transformation.

With Hampton hit by flooding from the 'River Ham' ('a dark deceptive river born from a thousand small tributaries', modelled on the **River Witham**), police investigations in *Inspector Proby's Weekend* (1996) are hampered by chaos. A murder leads Proby into the nearby ancestral home of an eccentric landowner, where a real-life game of Cluedo is underway, and nobody is quite sure who will be killed next.

The farming community of the **Lincolnshire Wolds** and the village of **Thoresway**, where her father grew up, provide an atmospheric landscape for **Jane Adams**'* (1960–) ghostly novel *Bird* (1997). In her Detective Inspector Ray Flowers series, Adams draws the action into the thriving, multicultural city of **LEICESTER** where she was born and now lives. In *The Angel Gateway* (2000) (inspired by an actual alleyway in the centre of Leicester close to The Angel pub), much of the town of 'Middleton' is inspired by Leicester's cityscape, including its Victorian **Town Hall Square**, with its fountain and landmark clock tower.

Jane Adams sets an original, haunting mystery series in her native **Leicester**.

It is here that Flowers is the victim of a horrific petrol bomb attack outside the courthouse that changes the course of his life. While Flowers contemplates his future in his late aunt's cottage, a body is being pulled out of the canal close to 'North Gate Bridge' in Middleton. As Flowers gets drawn into the life of a woman burnt at the stake in the seventeenth century, his past, present and future collide as this intriguing mystery moves towards its dramatic conclusion.

It is a freezing February in *Like Angels Falling* (2001), as Flowers takes up a friend's offer of partnership in a new security and detection business. Investigating the killings of young boys, which appear to be linked to a dead cult leader, Flowers finds that his home town of 'Mallingham' is in the process of 'having the heart ripped out of it, physically and now emotionally' as 'development by destruction' continues unabated and the community struggles to face up to the children's deaths. Adams pays homage to parts of a 1970s Leicester 'set on reinventing itself by destroying its past' as she draws **St Leonard's Church** ('the final outpost of what had once been a community') and her local **Fosse** cinema (taking its name from the **Fosse Way** military road linking Lincoln with **Cirencester**) into the scene of the crime.

Leicester City Square, where the life of **Jane Adams**' DI Flowers is changed forever.

Bordering Leicestershire to the south, the county of **NORTHAMPTON-SHIRE** becomes the fictional 'Bartonshire' of **Jill McGown**'s (1947–) Lloyd and Hill series. One of the area's main industrial towns is **Corby** – a village in Elizabethan times which developed into a town courtesy of the massive steelworks that employed McGown until its closure in the early 1980s. British Steel's loss was crime fiction's gain, as McGown went on to write *Perfect Match* (1983), in which Corby becomes 'Stansfield' and Welshman Detective Inspector Lloyd and Detective Sergeant Judy Hill investigate a murder that appears to be a 'perfect crime'. Stansfield inherits Corby's 'frontier mentality', aligned with a 'classless, non-judgmental, generous-spirited society' owing much to the multicultural workforce that shaped the town. 'Most of its inhabitants actually regard

Jill McGown attended Corby Grammar School, where she was taught Latin by a certain **Colin Dexter**[*].

home as somewhere else altogether,' says McGown, 'and there is no sense of collective pride in its achievements or dismay at its failures; everything is someone else's business.'

For Lloyd and Hill, of course, what goes on in the town is very much their business, and McGown applies landscape sparingly and fittingly to create a believable environment for her detectives. A Stansfield shrouded in thick blankets of fog not seen since the 1950s provides an apt setting for *The Other Woman* (1992), with Lloyd and Hill becoming enveloped in a shocking tale of adultery, rape, police brutality and murder. Based upon the village of **Rockingham** and its eleventh-century castle close to McGown's home, a snowbound 'Byford' provides the setting for McGown's own 'Murder at the Vicarage' in *Redemption* (1988). A short walk across the icy fields from Byford's 'dark, forbidding fortress', the vicarage at the centre of the investigations offers little in the way of Christmas cheer. The deep-running passions and taut relationships they discover here extend to Lloyd and Hill's own partnership, as Lloyd journeys into a Byford 'rendered utterly monotonous by the snow... the snow deadened everything; no colour, no sound'.

Set in the Northamptonshire village of 'Long Piddleton', *The Man with a Load of Mischief* (1981) was the debut of US mystery writer and Inspector Richard Jury creator **Martha Grimes**. Setting the scene for future novels featuring Jury and his aristocratic friend Melrose Plant, the novel intrduces a range of eccentric characters and also begins Grimes' custom of using real-life English pub names for her book titles. 'Pubs are a very specific way to get a variety of characters in a book,' says Grimes. 'Plus, they are so symbolic of Britain.'

Founded on steel – the Midlands town of **Corby** provides the light and darkness for Jill McGown's 'Stansfield'.

Powerhouse of the West Midlands, sprawling multicultural conurbation and Britain's second city, **BIRMINGHAM** offers plenty of colour and culture, with a renewed vigour since the major regeneration of its post-industrial areas. The city's magnificent architecture, new canal development of **Brindley Square**, and demolition of its notorious Bull Ring leave no doubt that 'Brum' is back in business. Surprisingly, 'the city of 1001 trades' where the pioneers of the Industrial Revolution forged their ideas has attracted very few writers of detective fiction.

Birmingham – 'city of 1001 trades', and almost as many architectural styles.

Criminal lawyer and Sherlock Holmes mystery writer **Barrie Roberts** (1939–) models his fictional 'Belston' on the **Black Country** (so-called for its industrial pollution and a remark attributed to Queen Victoria: 'What a Black Country') boroughs north-west of Birmingham. Belston is home to unconventional lawyer Chris Tyroll and his Australian fiancée Sheila McKenna. In *The Victory Snapshot* (1997), Tyroll investigates the death of Shelia's last surviving relative, murdered in a West Midland park. *Bad Penny Blues* (2000) continues the theme of hidden pasts, as social historian Sheila sets off on the dangerous trail of a Victorian convict's family history.

Born in the Black Country borough of **Oldbury**, to the west of Birmingham, **Judith Cutler** (1946–) has pioneered two distinctive Birmingham detective series, rooted firmly in the culture and landscape of the city. Lecturing at a college of further education reminiscent of the institution where Cutler herself taught for many years, Sophie Rivers

'I hope I convey Birmingham and the Black Country in everything I write' – Brum author **Judith Cutler** in Kate Power's **King's Heath** garden.

Part of Matthew Boulton's 'vast, cathedral-like' **Soho Foundry**, which becomes scene of the crime in **Judith** Cutler's *Dying in Discord* (2002).

After a hard day at work in *Staying Power*, **Judith Cutler's** DS Kate Power 'thought she'd stop off at her favourite chippie. Not for fish and chips: for a wonderful concoction, chicken tikka in a naan bread, with salad and spicy mint sauce… and just to round it off, a cup of that milky drink full of sweet noodles they'd started to sell. Faluda, that was it. Yes, there were a lot of good things about Brum.'

is a young amateur detective prone to diving in at the deep end. Sharing her creator's passion for classical music, Sophie first appears in *Dying Fall* (1995), in which one of her students is murdered and a body is discovered in the 'Music Centre' (inspired by the impressive **Symphony Hall** on King Alfred's Place/Broad Street). From her home in the 'couth' suburb of **Harborne**, where Cutler once lived, Sophie has to juggle a complicated love life, problems at work, and, in *Dying to Score* (1999), her passion for the game of cricket with the fact that her boyfriend is prime suspect in the murder of a rival cricketer.

There is a satisfying depth to Cutler's writing, and the landscapes she creates are founded as much on human experience as they are created by plot. So when her soft-centred young Detective Sergeant Kate Power first arrives in 'Worksop Road', **King's Heath**, in *Power on Her Own* (1998), she has to contend with the nightmares of home improvements on a shoestring alongside a growing conviction that a paedophile ring is operating close to home. Gradually easing into Birmingham's multicultural buzz, Kate soon enjoys weaving her way around the 'Balti Triangle' of Asian restaurants at **Balsall Heath**. She can usually hold her own, but Kate needs all her *Staying Power* (1999) to ward off memories of a lost lover, fend off bullies who consider her and a young Muslim colleague fair game, and to distinguish friend from foe. For sense of place, *Dying in Discord* (2002) is Cutler's favourite – 'I had one of the most moving experiences of my life being taken into Matthew Boulton's vast, cathedral-like Soho Foundry'.

Having lived in the Midlands for over thirty years, **Marjorie Eccles** (1927–) had a ready-made landscape for her series of traditional police mysteries. Largely inspired by the towns of **Brierley Hill** and **Stourbridge**, the fictional market town of 'Lavenstock' is located 'on the very edge of the Black Country, between Staffordshire and Worcestershire'. Lavenstock is home to Detective Inspector Gil Mayo, who, like his creator, is Yorkshire-born and bred. Mayo is a keen walker in the high land surrounding Lavenstock, and his house on one of the hills offers extensive views over the town towards the urban sprawl of Birmingham.

When living in Stourbridge, Eccles researched into the area's history of glassmaking, resulting in the intriguing *Requiem for a Dove* (1990). Marion Dove, wealthy widow and reclusive owner of a glass factory, lives a simple life in a lonely lock-keeper's cottage. When her body is found in the weed-choked waters of the adjacent canal, Mayo is tempted to look for the obvious motive: money. But the shards of her life story point to the past. *More Deaths Than One* (1991) picks up the transformation of the area, as Mayo, investigating what appears to be a fake suicide, visits the smart new warehouse conversion flats overlooking the **Stockwell** river – 'Down by the river, it was as cold as charity'. Eccles emphasizes the Black Country's industrial heritage but also explores the surrounding 'areas of great natural beauty', notably **Bridgnorth**, which she uses in *Late of this Parish* (1992).

'This place of silence and secrets' – **Stourbridge** canal and glass kiln evoking the landscape of **Marjorie Eccles**' *Requiem for a Dove* (1990).

Birmingham-born **David Armstrong**[*] uses the atmospheric settings of the Midlands & North-West canals in the 1930s for his debut novel *Night's Black Agents* (1993). With the help of a brutal bargeman, a hotel landlord arranges the death of his wife's lover. DI John Hammond of Birmingham City Police investigates. Armstrong revisits the area with *Small Vices* (2001), in which DI Kavanagh investigates a serial killer of Midlands prostitutes.

CHAPTER SEVEN

Cambridge & The Fens

But in Cambridge, I never allow myself to forget that
appearances can oh so easily deceive.

Michelle Spring, *Nights in White Satin* (1999)

Grouped around tranquil courts and trimmed lawns, the colleges of **CAMBRIDGE** were established in the early thirteenth century after a number of students fled from Oxford to what was then a small town on the edge of the mysterious watery flatness of the **Fens**. Despite the profusion of wheels spinning along the streets of Britain's cycling capital, Cambridge still retains an intimate feel. Its ancient colleges are gathered around **King's Parade** and punts glide past the spacious green **Backs** on the waters of the **River Cam**. Thematically and stylistically, Cambridge detective fiction has a more scientific, less exuberant and less literary slant than the Oxford variety, but punts, port and privilege still figure heavily. Women writers and sleuths dominate the scene, and favourite

Cambridge skyline, viewed from **St Mary's the Great** church.

seasons are autumn and winter, when the colleges are bathed in low golden light or glazed with a frosty sheen.

After the first Cambridge college, **Peterhouse**, was established here in 1248, murder and mayhem were never far behind, as **Susanna Gregory** (pseud., 1958–), a Yorkshire policewoman turned Cambridge research scientist, knows well. Gregory has long been interested in the medieval origins of the city, in particular the fourteenth century, 'a period of change, massive fluctuation and growing public unrest', where Cambridge was experiencing the unprecedented social upheaval of 'land starvation' and the Black Death. Setting is vital to Gregory's atmospheric series featuring college physician Matthew Bartholomew of Michaelhouse College:

> '…' 'I try my very hardest to make the streets come alive, to describe the roads – how they smell, the people that walk along them, the sounds of footsteps and hooves on the thick layer of manure that comprised the streets, the colours of the clothes the people wore. The spirit of the place, I think, would have been busy, bustling, noisy, odorous, crowded, filthy and perhaps a little desperate.'

Independent-minded Bartholomew is considered an outsider for his work with the poor and for his unorthodox methods. While caring for victims of the bubonic plague in the first Chronicle, *A Plague on Both Your Houses* (1996), Bartholomew uncovers a conspiracy among the town's traders to close the university down. The real Michaelhouse, looking on to the Backs, was founded in 1324 by a rich cleric and by the sixteenth century was a fairly wealthy college – 'at which point', says

Susanna Gregory cooks most of the medieval meals her characters eat in her Cambridge kitchen.
V C Clinton-Baddeley* gives a recipe for the Oxbridge speciality of crème brulée in *My Foe Outstrech'd Beneath the Tree* (1968). His don detective Dr Davie habitually walks round the Fellows' Garden, and in *Death's Bright Dart* contemplates the gnarled mulberry tree from which all the fellows receive a jar of jam: 'Special privileges. Of course, when the reformers get to know of it mulberry jam will be doomed.'

Pythagoras Hall, the oldest building in Cambridge (part of St John's College).

St John's Gateway – 'This jibe about the red-brick university has always bewildered me,' says Dr Davie, in **V C Clinton-Baddeley**'s *My Foe Outstrech'd Beneath a Tree* (1968), a tad disingenuously. 'My college at Cambridge is red brick. So is St John's. So is Trinity great gate. Half Cambridge is red brick. What's the matter with red brick?'

St John's is the college that first challenged Oxford to a boat race on the Thames in 1829, starting the venerable tradition of light blue versus dark blue vests rowing for victory, which continues to this day, inspiring a few detective novels along the way.

Only a few stones in the walls of Trinity College and some foundations buried under the grass remain of Bartholomew's Michaelhouse. However, as **Jill Paton Walsh*** points out in *A Piece of Justice* (1995): 'Cambridge colleges are immortal… though a few have been born and nearly all have been metamorphosised in harmony with modern ideas like the equality of sexes, none have died. None have died, and therefore none have paid death duties. The custodianship of their buildings, and their traditions, like the music in King's College and Trinity chapels, is a burden lovingly discharged'.

Gregory, 'Henry VIII decided to take it and a few other academic institutions and combine them into a grand new college called Trinity'. In the annals of detective fiction, **Trinity College** on Trinity Street, the largest Oxbridge college, and home to over thirty Nobel Prize winners, shares with **St John's** the honour of most popular mystery setting.

In *A Bone of Contention* (1997), Bartholomew's investigations into the discovery of human remains take place against a vivid backdrop of Cambridge struggling with the legacy of the Black Death. There are violent clashes between students and townsfolk, who object, amongst other things, to the presence of so many clerics in Cambridge. As Gregory describes how medieval Cambridge's 'myriad of waterways' were used as rubbish dumps, the stench virtually wafts off the page. Bartholomew, embroiled in college rivalry between Michaelhouse and the Hall of Valence Marie (now **Pembroke**, off **Trumpington Street**, featuring the oldest surviving Gatehouse in Cambridge), is too busy to notice, and when the bones he is examining turn out to be hailed as relics, fragile relations between Town and Gown are on the brink again.

Cambridge detective fiction begins with **T H White**'s *Darkness at Pemberley* (1932). Inspector Buller is unable to find enough evidence to arrest the murderous fellow of 'St Bernard's College' who has shot an undergraduate and a history don and decapitated a porter. Buller then finds himself pursued by his suspect and in grave danger of permanently losing the plot.

With its succession of differently styled courts – such as the New Court, or 'Wedding Cake', built across the Cam – **St John's**, Cambridge's second largest, is also one of its most impressive colleges. St John's was the inspiration behind **Dilwyn Rees'** (pseud. Glyn Daniel, 1914–1986) meticulously detailed 'Fisher College', squeezed into the gap between St John's and Trinity, where archaeologist and amateur detective Sir Richard Cherrington is Vice-President. On a cold day, when 'raw sharp winds' blow 'from off the dank fens and the grey-cold North Sea', the gamely Cherrington enjoys a 'King's Evil' special brew 'to keep away the Fen ague'. *The Cambridge Murders* (1945) accurately recreates the atmosphere and landscape the author knew from his time as an undergraduate, and later don, at St John's. A keen reader of detective fiction, Cherrington assists the police in solving the murder of a college

With its breathtaking fan-vault roof the largest in the world, **King's College Chapel** is a Cambridge landmark. **Nora Kelly**'s *In the Shadow of King's* (1984) introduces Newnham-educated historian sleuth Gillian Adams, who, on a year's sabbatical in Cambridge, becomes entangled in the suspicious death of a Professor of Modern History at King's.

'How indeed, she thought, could the heart be indifferent to such a city where stone and stained glass, water and green lawns, trees and flowers were arranged in such ordered beauty for the service of learning' – **P D James*** returns to the city where she attended school in *An Unsuitable Job for a Woman* (1972), sending Cordelia Gray, a Cambridge student *manqué*, to investigate the suicide of a Cambridge micro-biologist's son, a mystery in the spirit of **Margery Allingham's*** *Police at the Funeral* (1931).

porter found in the screens (open passageways) between the two Tudor brickwork courts, and with the disappearance of an unpopular Dean. With all this on his hands, Cherrington still finds time to marvel at Cambridge in Spring:

> [Cherrington] …stepped briskly across the College lawns, let himself out by the River Gate and crossed the Backs to Queen's Road. He glanced from side to side admiringly at the flower-decked lawns of Trinity and St. John's. The crocuses were in their early glory, and the Backs were triumphant in their stretches of blue and yellow. There were few crocuses on the Fisher lawns, but there were daffodils under the trees in the Fellows' garden. The glory of the Fisher College Backs was earlier, when in late January and February, they were a mass of aconites and snowdrops, harbingers of the spring, when the Trinity and John's Backs were still winterly barren.

The splendid seclusion of **Jesus College** on Jesus Green inspired **V C Clinton-Baddeley**'s (1900–70) 'St Nicholas' College, which 'stands back from the world, at the end of an open paved corridor'. Clinton-Baddeley's witty and cleverly constructed detective novels feature elderly donnish detective Dr R V Davie. Davie's rooms are in 'Baxter's Court, an eighteenth-century building exactly fitted to his mind' and overlook the college close, the park bordered by clipped yews, and 'St Nicholas Piece' stretching down to the river. In *Death's Bright Dart* (1967), amidst the jostling for college posts, and the popular undergraduate sport of roof climbing (back into college after curfew), Davie investigates the murder of a handsome but arrogant professor. Primed by reading three detective novels a week, Dr Davie browses for murder weapons in an exhibition in a side street behind Cambridge's (modern) **Guildhall** but the solution lies closer to home, right under his nose in the beautiful roses of Baxter's Court.

Effectively the only hill in Cambridge, **Castle Mound** is the chosen location of **Jill Paton Walsh*** (pseud. Gillian Bliss, 1937–) for 'St Agatha's' beautiful Jacobean brick court of Barnack stone, surrounding a turf maze. This is the fictitious workplace of Cambridge-born and bred college nurse and amateur sleuth Imogen Quy, who probes criminal minds with empathy, a distrust of coincidences and a 'long training in teasing out of people what they dreaded to tell you'. Just as Imogen hides personal disappointment beneath her calm, efficient exterior, St Agatha's splendour masks financial problems. Benefactors like to tie outlandish conditions to their bequests, of which the obligation for rose water to be dabbed behind dons' ears after dinner is a harmless variety. *The Wyndham Case* (1993) revolves around the condition of one such bequest: that the college's vaulted 'Wyndham Library', containing a famous oak bookcase, is always kept locked, and that an audit and book-count be carried out once every century, at a random date. When the

Imogen Quy creator **Jill Paton Walsh** completed **Dorothy L Sayers'*** *Thrones, Dominations* (1998) on the strength of six draft chapters and a plot diagram.

Imogen Quy 'climbed the castle mound, on the zigzagging path. She loved to see it as it was now, lined with crocuses and aconites naturalised in the grass' – Cambridge's **Castle Mound** as described in *The Wyndham Case* (1993).

body of a bright young first-year is found in the Wyndham Library, his fellow students clam up, which proves to be just the beginning of St Agatha's troubles.

In *A Piece of Justice* (1995), Imogen's efforts to help her lodger, Fran, put her on the trail of a killer. Excited by the prospect of researching a biography on Cambridge mathematician Gideon Summerfield, Fran soon finds herself in direct conflict with his widow, and senses something deeper and darker back in Summerfield's past. Like all good biographers, she refuses to be deflected from her task. Intelligently crafted and humorous, with the central premise of seeking order and patterns in life when so often people ignore the evidence in front of their very noses, the mystery digs beneath the veneer of academia to expose a framework of paranoia, pressure and envy.

In contrast to St Agatha's beauty, the architectural merits of **Ruth Dudley Edwards'*** (1944–) 'St Martha's' College, featured in *Matricide at St Martha's* (1994), verge on zero. St Martha's is 'the least well-known of the Cambridge colleges' and unappealing 'unless one happened to have a penchant for neo-Gothic piles with overhanging turrets and lots of narrow windows peering out of the scarlet brick'. When a millionaire leaves an enormous bequest to the former women-only college, the various factions all have their own ideas as to how to spend it. Some will fight for it, some will even murder for it. Dudley Edwards is herself a former undergraduate of red-brick-built **Girton**, Cambridge's first women's college. In this entertaining, often scathing satire of sexual politics and academic infighting, she subverts Cambridge stereotypes and takes the humanity of college folk to hilarious extremes. Domineering Baroness Troutbeck, outrageous Mistress of St Martha's, rears her fearsome head again to embroil ex-civil servant Robert Amiss in a murder enquiry and a web of incompetence of Inspector Romford's own making.

In *For the Sake of Elena*, **Trinity Hall** provides the inspiration for the architecture of 'St Stephen's College', which is squeezed into the space between the Hall and **Trinity College**.

'...ten iron steps climbed up to Crusoe's Bridge and descended to Coe Fen on the east bank of the river... The bridge itself looked suspended over nothing...' – the bridge over the River Cam leads to tragedy in **Elizabeth George**'s *For the Sake of Elena*.

Only minutes away from the colleges, walking through the meadows along the River Cam where cows graze peacefully, visitors can truly appreciate the rural feel of Cambridge, while the towpath is a popular route for runners and joggers. In *For the Sake of Elena* (1992), **Elizabeth George*** subverts this tranquillity when pretty, intelligent and deaf undergraduate Elena Weaver is bludgeoned to death on her morning run. In an intelligent and poignant mystery, George uses the grassy riverbanks and foggy autumnal meadows to chilling effect, and explores an academic landscape where sexism is still rife. Behind the façade of intellectual excellence, respectability, and unconcealed ambition, Detective Inspector Lynley and Detective Sergeant Barbara Havers must uncover the real Elena, and the passions, desires and obsessions of those around her. Against the backdrop of a thriving, traffic-clogged tourist city, there is the claustrophobia of a privileged, self-absorbed and secretive college system shielding all-too human passions.

Autumn is also the scene for *Dirk Gently's Holistic Detective Agency* (1987), where detective fiction forges improbable links with disappearing cats and quantum mechanics, as it descends into the kind of mayhem that only **Douglas Adams*** (1952–2001) could produce. Having left Cambridge in disgrace for predicting exam results a tad too accurately, Dirk Gently, private investigator, shuffles back through the twelfth-century gates of 'St Cedd's' in search of the extremely ancient Professor 'Reg' Urban Chronitis, Regius Professor of Chronology. Named after 'one of the duller Northumbrian Saints', St Cedd's is a composite of architectural splendour, ancient tradition and low academic profile – with a lonely, haunted air:

'These lonely stretches of glistening mud and water with their huge skies fascinated me' – the ancient Essex port of **Maldon** is an inspiration for **June Thomson**'s detective fiction.

One of Europe's busiest container ports, **Felixstowe** provides a contrast to the mainly rural Suffolk beat of **Ann Quinton**'s Detective Inspector James Roland.

'There are few sights more pleasant than the sails of a mill… against the wide Norfolk sky' –
Cley-next-the-Sea Mill is a constant on the landscape of **Brian Cooper**'s retired DCI Lubbock.

It was a chill November evening of the old-fashioned type. The moon looked pale and wan, as if it shouldn't be up on a night like this. It rose unwillingly and hung like an ill spectre. Silhouetted against it, dim and hazy through the dampness which rose from the unwholesome fens, stood the assorted towers and turrets of St Cedd's Cambridge, a ghostly profusion of buildings thrown up over the centuries, medieval next to Victorian, Odeon next to Tudor. Only rising through the mist did they seem remotely to belong to one another.

Born and educated in Cambridge, the scientist and science-fiction writer **Douglas Adams** revisits the city with his eccentric detective fiction.

Here to elucidate the killing of a Cambridgeshire computer wizard by an electric monk, Gently discovers that one of the city's greatest mysteries is finding an escape from its dreaded one-way system. Fondly remembered at St Cedd's as a 'rounder than average undergraduate', Gently fortunately knows his old professor like he does his pizza, and is eventually able to fathom the mystery of the Cambridge 'Time Machine'.

The splendour of the colleges holds great appeal for forensic pathologist Doctor Samantha Ryan, although her line of duty sees her just as easily tramping across graveyards or investigating at an American airbase. Her creator, **Nigel McCrery** (1953–), investigated several murders during his earlier police career. Sam herself, fully committed, is the total antithesis of the archetypal pathologists seen grumbling away in many British detective novels. Ambitious to the point of sacrificing her love life, Sam relaxes from the rivalry and banter of the police force in her cottage with views across Cambridgeshire fields. In *Faceless Strangers* (1998), Sam's curiosity combines with helping out a disgraced colleague and leads her into a high-profile murder case in which she enlists the help of a Trinity undergraduate to reconstruct the victim's face. From a dreary council estate, contrasting sharply with the opulence of the colleges, to a house in **Grantchester**, and out to the crumbly heat-baked soil of a sugar-beet field, Sam stays on the trail – though sometimes distracted by her surroundings:

A former coaching inn, **The Eagle** in Bene't Street, with its famous ceiling decorated by Air Force soldiers and associations with the Double Helix scientists Crick and Watson, is forensic pathologist Dr Sam Ryan's favourite pub.

As they drove slowly over Trinity Bridge towards the Backs, Sam looked to her left and the wonderful view of St John's College. From this angle Sam had often thought it was the most beautiful college in Cambridge… But then, she thought, most of the Cambridge colleges had at least some small part which could not be described without the use of superlatives. All were beautiful and evocative in their own way. As she continued to admire John's through the tree-lined lane, Sharman's penetrating voice cut short her thoughts. 'Did you believe him?'

The author staking a leading claim to the 'Chair in Cambridge Detective Fiction' is Canadian-born writer and sociology professor **Michelle Spring** (pseud. Michelle Stanworth, 1947–). Spring's Laura

'For some reason I've had extraordinary brushes with violence in my life,' says **Michelle Spring**, who through her Cambridge series likes to put 'all my fears onto my readers'.

Principal, introduced in *Every Breath You Take* (1994), is a convincingly drawn private investigator and dynamic first-person narrator of cases spanning contemporary Cambridge, town and gown. 'In a way I feel like I am documenting Cambridge *now*,' says Spring, 'providing a lens into the city, an alternative to the picture-postcard image... that more reflects the living city and is less locked into the commercial view of Cambridge.' Spring appreciates the beauty of Cambridge, which 'mixes city and country in a way very few places do', but still remembers her first impressions of 'a very small town dominated too much by the university... Cambridge seemed very dark to me; the college buildings seemed rather oppressive, rather claustrophobic.' Laura Principal read history at **Newnham** College, but through her working-class background always remained somewhat on the outside. Spring's particular interest in issues of gender, society and education is reflected in the social landscape of her seductive and lively novels, a landscape increasingly marred by violence.

'The ball had taken place, as May Balls should always do, on a warm night in the middle of June – a champagne and oysters kind of night, following a strawberries and cream kind of day. By the early evening, even a stranger to the city could sense that something extraordinary was about to occur. There was a low sun glazing the spires of King's College Chapel, and a pulse of excitement in the air.' *Nights in White Satin* (1999) contrasts the carefree joy of the May Ball with the dark side of venerable colleges closing ranks to protect their own. Laura Principal is hired to oversee security in St John's 'ten green acres', securing 'the mock-Gothic portals of New Building' and the weak link of the river running through the college, where students might try to dodge the steep admission fee. The disappearance of a young woman from the ball leads Laura to uncover the sordid reality of student prostitution as she enters the frighteningly misogynistic world of 'St Bartholomew's College' overlooking **Midsummer Common**.

Chesterton towpath – scene of a dramatic climax in *Standing in the Shadows* (1998). The proximity of the river to the city is very important to **Michelle Spring** who uses watery imagery throughout the Laura Principal series. Laura used to row for Newnham and still takes her boat to the Cam to clear her mind and think her cases over.

The growing technology corridor around Cambridge is often dubbed 'Silicon Fen', but beyond the glare of the offices and industrial units, the unrelieved flatness of the **FENS** holds sway across a 12,000 square-mile region that recognizes no district or county boundaries. Criss-crossed by drains and dykes, this is reclaimed, rich agricultural land and as mysterious a territory as anywhere in Britain.

St Peter and St Paul's Church, Upwell – 'Thank God. Where there is a church, there's civilization,' says Lord Peter Wimsey in *The Nine Tailors*, although he is soon wishing that 'everything wasn't so rectangular in this part of the world.'

'Flat as a chess-board, and squared like a chess-board with inter-secting dyke and hedge, the fens went flashing past them.' In *The Nine Tailors* (1934), **Dorothy L Sayers*** returns to the landscapes of her childhood. Developed around the very English tradition of bellringing, this Fenland mystery brings Lord Peter Wimsey into the wintry parish of 'Fenchurch St Paul'. Lending a hand with the ropes for a nine-hour session of change ringing, Lord Peter unwittingly becomes an agent of violent death. From 1898, Sayers grew up in the large Georgian vicarage at **Bluntisham** on the southern edge of the Cambridgeshire Fens. This was an area still redolent with memories of the spring flood of 1713, when the bursting of **Denver Sluice** had led to catastrophic flooding – which Sayers adapts for a dramatic climax to her tale. Situated between **Sixteen Foot Drain** ('Thirty Foot Drain') and **Christchurch** (in 1917 her father transferred to the red-brick Victorian rectory here), the magnificent church of 'Fenchurch St Paul' provides the focus of the mystery. An amalgam of churches in the northern Fens such as **Walpole St Peter** or **Terrington St Clement**, the superb angel roof of St Paul's is similar to those in **Upwell St Peter** or **St Wendreda's** in **March**.

Padnal Fen, near **Ely** – 'In its own limited, austere and almost grudging fashion, the Fen acknowledged the return of the sun' – the Fens cause Lord Peter Wimsey problems from the outset in *The Nine Tailors*.

In *Death of an Expert Witness* (1977), **P D James*** uses the experience of her first, 'disastrous' Home Office job in the Fens to develop an institutional landscape around a fictional forensic science laboratory located on the edge of the **Black Fens** some ten miles from **Ely**. From the opening images of a woman's body in the 'clunch' field of the soft chalk mined here from the Middle Ages, James picks up on the 'rich loamy smell' and brooding isolation of the Fens. In his search for a murderer, Adam Dalgliesh witnesses the gradual unravelling of personal vendettas, ambitions and passions that emerge from a landscape where folk can be 'superstitious, unforgetting and unforgiving'. The Fens are by turns hostile and sheltering, frequently bleak and empty, sometimes secure, but seldom comforting: the living here is not easily won.

The vast flatness of the **Black Fens** appears to offer few hiding places.

Ely Cathedral and the rooftops of 'Rosington' are significant features in the real-life and fictional landscapes of **Andrew Taylor.**

'In the dark flatness of the Fens, you could never quite escape the towers of the cathedral,' says **Andrew Taylor***. 'The place was, and probably still is, fundamental to my becoming a novelist.' The son of a clergyman, Taylor spent his formative years in Ely, attending the **King's School** in the old monastic buldings close to the cathedral's famous castellated west tower. Ely appears as 'Rosington' in Taylor's John Creasey Award-winning, *Caroline Minuscule* (1982), which introduces the morally ambiguous sleuth-cum-criminal William Dougal, who returns to the area in *An Old School Tie* (1986). Set mainly in Rosington's cathedral close in 1958, *The Office of the Dead* (2000), is the chilling third novel in Taylor's acclaimed 'Roth Trilogy', which gradually unravels the interlinked histories of two families. In a strongly autobiographical setting, Rosington is revealed as 'an island set in the black sea of the Fens, a place apart, a place of refuge', but also a focus of ancient conflict and inner turmoil:

> Below me was the great encrusted hull of the cathedral and the tiled and slated roofs of Rosington. Around them as far as the eye could see were the grey winter Fens. They stretched towards the invisible point where they became one with the grey winter sky. For an instant I was more terrified than I had ever been in my life. I was adrift between the sky and the earth. All my significance had been stolen from me.

The gritty police novels of **Jo Bannister** (1951–) focus on the Fenland town of 'Castlemere', which she locates west of Cambridge and close to **Bedford** and **St Neots**. Castlemere features a crumbling castle on the hill, with Georgian houses below, but it is the many waterways running through and around the town that serve as the arteries of the plots.

'The location is a member of the cast: just as people can only behave true to their own characters, so some events can only happen convincingly in certain places' – **Jo Bannister** finds her 'Castlemere' series at home in the Fens.

Individualistic and impulsive Detective Sergeant Cal Donovan lives on a houseboat to the east of town. When he tracks a garage robber through the fields using a Fenland parish church spire for orientation in *Broken Lines* (1988), Donovan gets involved with a notorious and violent family from a Castlemere estate, and quickly finds his credibility on the line. *No Birds Sing* (1996) references the four canals meeting in the heart of Castlemere and the redevelopment of the old Victorian warehouses beside the 'peaty water and gaily-painted boats'. But away from the sunshine and smiles, the town is in the grip of ram-raiders, train robbers, pit bull terrier fights and a serial rapist. Detective Inspector Liz Graham has a strong intuition respected by thoughtful, bulky Detective Superintendent Frank Shapiro, but feels the frustration of operating in a man's world. *The Hireling's Tale* (1999) involves a prostitute found dead on a narrowboat on the Castlemere Canal, and never far in the background are the 'Castlemere Levels' (inspired by the **Bedford Levels**) where Donovan has his houseboat, and on which Bannister maps the troubled crimescape of her series:

> '…' 'It's a remote, bleak, in some lights almost alien landscape, a sort of wet desert. Like much of East Anglia, it has the feeling of being further from the population centres of England than geographically it is. That sense of remoteness is a positive advantage to a crime writer. Things could happen in the Fens that you couldn't imagine happening in more domestic kinds of scenery… For *Changelings* (2000), for example, I envisaged a fenland village so small and isolated that it operated on the level of an extended family, keeping family secrets in a way that would not have been possible in a more open society. There's nothing cosy about the Castlemere Levels. For a couple of months in the middle of summer the hire-boats on the canals may make it look quite jolly, but the bones of the land are hard, ancient and implacable. People can die in the Fens and never be found; and never be missed.'

Caught between the Midlands, Fenlands and London, the Bedford-shire town of **Luton** is perhaps best known for its 'London' airport serving budget airlines. 'In *The Lost Traveller's Guide*, a page and a half of Luton's ten-page entry is deservedly set aside for the Central Police Station', writes **Reginald Hill*** of the setting for his second series featuring black, balding lathe-operator turned private eye Joe Sixsmith. In *Born Guilty* (1999), Joe, a keen singer, manages to escape his pushy aunt by slipping out the side door of St Monkey's Church, only to stumble across the dead body of a young man.

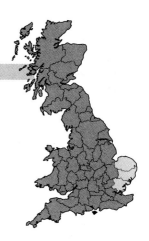

CHAPTER EIGHT

East Anglia

Let me first say that our fabled East Anglia of historic renown
has a lurid past. Sinister stories abound.

Jonathan Gash, *The Grace in Older Women* (1995)

Comprising the counties of **Norfolk, Suffolk** and **Essex, EAST ANGLIA**
is a land of big skies and embattled coasts, with a quiet resilience and
understated rural charm. Its agricultural centres and ports have a proud
trading past, while its isolated shores and eerie waterways make the
region a rich source of legend and superstition.

The most visited and varied coastline belongs to **NORFOLK**, a county
as durable as the flint that defines its architecture, and often as
impenetrable: isolated geographically, independent spiritually, Norfolk
is good at hiding secrets. From the eerie **Broads** and empty **Brecklands**,
to the frayed edge of half-land, half-sea of the north coast, Norfolk
provides ideal landscapes for detective fiction, while its long history of
non-conformism inspires a number of religious mysteries.

The **North Norfolk Coast** offers an intriguing combination of
unspoilt sandy stretches, flinty strands, cliff-top walks and frayed edges
of salt marsh and creeks. The mysterious marshes and muddy inlets of
the saltings around **Burnham Overy Staithe** and Wells-next-the-Sea
are explored by one of the great Golden Age writers, **Henry Wade**
(pseud. Henry Lancelot Aubrey-Fletcher, 6th Baronet, 1887–1969), in
his atmospheric classic *Mist on the Saltings* (1933). Attracted by the
unique light of the area, a painter arrives in the coastal village of 'Bryde-
by-the-Sea' to make a fresh start. The timeless tranquillity of the coast
is shattered when a writer living on the nearby sand dunes is found
dead, and Chief Inspector Poole discovers that the victim was having
an affair with the painter's wife. While Inspector Lamming struggles
with the 'leisurely speech and apparent dullness of the seaboard folk',
the mystery arrives at a profound and powerful climax.

It is hard to believe that the small village of **Cley-next-the-Sea**,
perched a mile inland and surrounded by marshes and scrubland, was
once a thriving port. But this is just one of the many aspects of
Norfolk history referenced by retired history teacher **Brian Cooper**
(1919–), who has been visiting Norfolk for over thirty years. 'Most of
my plots begin with seeing a place that intrigues me, and linking it

'The sea keeps working its way
into the things that I write,'
says **Michelle Spring***, whose
Cambridge sleuth Laura
Principal shares 'Wildfell
Cottage' close to the North
Norfolk coast. *In the Midnight
Hour* (2001) is the tale of a
child who disappeared without
trace on the untamed stretch
of shoreline at nearby
'Cleybourne' (an amalgam of
Weybourne and **Cley**) and
miraculously turns up near
Cambridge, many years later.
But is this the same person?

'It stirred something inside me… the marshes and the mists and the windmills and the running tides' – **Brian Cooper** on his first impressions of the North Norfolk coast. Thirty years later, this landscape continues to inspire in *The Murders Column* (2003).

with either a legend or historical fact,' says Cooper, whose long-running Tench & Lubbock series is largely set along a post-World War II North Norfolk coast. Detective Chief Inspector John Spencer Lubbock retires to the solitude of a cottage at the foot of Cley Church in the first novel, *The Cross of San Vincente* (1991), but just cannot keep his nose out of subsequent police investigations. Lubbock's assistance is a mixed blessing for DS Mike Tench, who has to tolerate the fact that his ruminative and condescending old boss is usually right. Happily engaged in recording each and every one of the county's many windmills, Lubbock is the perfect man to help Tench investigate a mysterious fire in *The Singing Stones* (1993). Cooper juggles with the area's topography by moving **Kettle Hill** (close to **Blakeney**) inland a mile or so, and places a fictional, fully functioning mill here as the scene of a crime that leaves Tench in some confusion.

Blakeney saltmarsh – 'Dreary and desolate though they are, the Saltings have for those who love them a fascination which no written word can describe, a beauty which defies the most skilful brush' – **Henry Wade**'s *Mist on the Saltings* enters the atmospheric salt marshes of Norfolk's north coast, which also inspire **Brian Cooper**'s *The Blacknock Woman*.

Immersed in the sticky marsh mud around Blakeney, *The Blacknock Woman* (1999) is a complex and rewarding mystery. The 'dull patch of mud' of Blacknock conceals a wealth of cockles, but is a dangerous place of swift-running tides, where the legend of cockle woman Mary Bunn, trapped by the incoming tide and tragically drowned, lives on to this day. When the tide washes a woman's body onto the mud, Mike Tench leads his team into a community as tightly closed as a cockle-shell ('Medford' is an amalgam of coastal villages). In a mystery as impenetrable as the local dialect greeting the investigating 'furriners' of the Norwich police, Tench views the scenery with a mixture of admiration and apprehension:

> The landscape was one of flat desolation stretching away beyond the range of his vision: just a tangle of dull brown saltmarsh grass intersected by twisting, watery channels that merged with the grass and then lost themselves out in the featureless waste. It wasn't land, it wasn't sea, but an indeterminate mixture of both, lonely and sullen as the light began to fade.

With its faded grandeur, long promenade, chip shops and crabs, the tourist resort of **Cromer** provides an unlikely setting for a classic murder mystery – *Death Walks in Eastrepps* (1931), by **Francis Beeding** (pseud. John Leslie Palmer, 1885–1944, and Hilary Aidan St George Saunders, 1898–1951). Visitors to this part of Norfolk may be familiar with the outlying villages of **Northrepps** and **Southrepps**, but to find the model for the 'Eastrepps' at the heart of this thrilling tale need look no further than the landmarks of Cromer itself: its pier, church, lighthouse and former Cromer High station. With 'the salt tang of the

An ideal habitat for waders and rare migrating birds, the coastal marshes of the North Norfolk coast are famous for their bird watching. **Ann Cleeves*** weaves the findings of her study of 'twitchers' at university into her debut novel, *A Bird in the Hand* (1986). Cley becomes 'Rushy', and its bird reserve a scene of the crime, with keen ornithologist and detective George Palmer-Jones at his eagle-eyed best spotting rare avocets and well-concealed clues.

'Oi hev seen the mairderer… On the cliff naire the loighthouse' – an important witness helps Inspector Protheroe as he investigates in *Death Walks in Eastrepps* around **Cromer** lighthouse, pictured here with the town in the distance.

sea wind' in the air and the 'dark, unharvested waters' of the North Sea close to hand, a credible cast of characters is assembled for Inspector Protheroe to contemplate as he seeks the identity and motives of a multiple murderer. Full of local flavour, the suspense is palpable as the action moves around the town and clifftop, and from the Coroner's inquest (usually dealing with drowned fishermen rather than murders) to a dramatic courtroom scene.

Local lore has it that Black Shuck, the dreaded giant spirit dog with eyes glowing like coals, still roams along a track that today forms part of **Mill Lane** and **Sandy Lane**. When **Arthur Conan Doyle***** arrived at Cromer's fashionable **Royal Links Hotel** (where today's Links Country Park holiday complex stands) in 1901, this was a deep, narrow, sandy track running past the hotel and into the grounds of nearby **Cromer Hall**. Conan Doyle was soon submitting the outline for a 'real creeper' of a story to his publishers, and when *The Hound of the Baskervilles* (1901) appeared, it became clear that the Gothic architecture of Cromer Hall had provided the model for 'Baskerville Hall', and that Norfolk had played a pivotal role in one of detective fiction's most famous tales.

Cromer was by no means the only Norfolk location familiar to Conan Doyle – in 1903 he was staying some twelve miles further down the coast at the **Hill House** (today's pub has a corner dedicated to Sherlock Holmes) in **Happisburgh**. The lonely, much eroded headland here provides the backdrop for one of Conan Doyle's favourite short stories, 'The Dancing Men' (1903). In this cryptic mystery Holmes is lost in 'a blank melancholy' as he and Watson travel through 'as singular a countryside as any in England', where 'on every hand enormous square-towered churches bristled up from the flat, green landscape'.

'The whole front was draped in ivy, with a patch clipped bare here and there where a window or a coat of arms broke through the dark veil. From this central block rose the twin towers, ancient, crenellated, and pierced with many loopholes… A dull light shone through heavy mullioned windows' – **Cromer Hall**, pictured *c.*1900, around the time **Arthur Conan Doyle***** was outlining ideas for *The Hound of the Baskervilles.*

In her atmospheric and complex mystery *Devices and Desires* (1989), **P D James**⋆ lends the Happisburgh area a real sense of foreboding, as Commander Adam Dalgliesh, taking a break at his aunt's Norfolk mill to top-up his poetry portfolio, ends up on the trail of the sinister 'Norfolk Whistler'. Referencing the coast's tragic maritime history, **Happisburgh Church** appears as the 'embattled symbol of man's precarious defences against this most dangerous of seas', while the headland itself has 'the desolate look of an old battlefield'. **Jane Adams**⋆ uses an ancient Norfolk pathway to access Happisburgh's ghostly past in *The Greenaway* (1995). Introducing DI Mike Croft, this chilling mystery is set in a landscape 'full of memories' and focuses on the eponymous high-hedged lane between Norfolk fields where twenty years previously a young girl vanished. 'The Greenaway is a place that I knew well as a child when I stayed in Happisburgh,' Adams recalls. 'It scared me. It was dark and silent and filled with ghosts.'

County capital and cathedral city, **NORWICH** has a history of cultural and religious tolerance that epitomizes Norfolk's refreshing 'du different' attitude. Journeying between London and Norfolk in **Francis Beeding**'s⋆ *The Norwich Victims* (1935), Inspector George Martin of Scotland Yard bases himself at the **Maid's Head Hotel** (on the corner of Wensum Street). Martin's murder investigations lead him around the chilly autumnal backstreets of Dickensian old Norwich and out to the countryside beyond as the mystery heads towards a startling conclusion.

Only in her mid-sixties did Norwich-born journalist **S T Haymon** (pseud. Sylvia Haymon, 1918–95) begin writing the detective novels that secured her critical acclaim. Introducing tall, darkly handsome Detective Inspector Ben 'Valentino' Jurnet (who takes his name from a real-life medieval Norwich Jew, Isaac de Jurnet) of Norfolk CID, *Ritual Murder* (1982) won the Silver Dagger and pointed to the themes that would drive successive mysteries. When Jurnet investigates the murder of a choirboy, apparently ritually sacrificed outside 'Angleby' (Norwich) Cathedral, he is drawn back to the twelfth-century massacre of local Jews and questions about his own identity and religiosity. Jurnet's character is symbolic of Haymon's Angleby: independent, tolerant, shaped strongly by the past, but less certain of the present.

Revelling in her home city's 'completeness', **S T Haymon** created the first **Norwich** detective series.

Haymon continued to draw deep on the city's distinctive non-conformism and rich cultural background, often shaping her modern-day murders around historical atrocities. Perhaps the strongest parallels are drawn in Haymon's eighth and final detective novel, *Death of a Hero* (1996). The square bulk of **Norwich Castle** takes on a more menacing significance in a mystery based upon the life of rebel leader Robert Kett, hanged here in 1549 'like a ham hung up for winter store'. Norwich's history of dissent comes knocking on the city's door in the form of 10,000 men assembling on 'Monkenheath' (**Mousehold Heath**) to protest against soaring unemployment. In scenes reminiscent of Kett's march against land enclosure some 450 years earlier, the charismatic

Norwich Cathedral is a scene
of calm in **Francis Beeding**'s
The Norwich Victims, but scene
of the crime (as 'Angleby'
Cathedral) in **S T Haymon**'s
Ritual Murder.

figurehead of Charlie Appleyard leads his men towards conflict with
the authorities. When he meets an untimely end in Norwich's red-light
district, Appleyard's followers move menacingly towards the market
place, and Jurnet needs to find some answers quickly.

'The landscape of my imagination was England,' says **Kate Charles**
(pseud. Carol Chase, 1950–), who grew up in the 'very flat and featureless'
American Midwest. Her ecclesiastical mysteries are infused with English
architecture and Church history, providing a powerful contrast between
spiritual tranquillity and violent death in religion's very human
institutions. Sharing Charles' love of 'church crawling', amateur sleuth
David Middleton-Brown is a solicitor working in Norwich but living in
the attractive market town of **Wymondham** to the south-west of the city.
Together with his lover and fellow sleuth Lucy Kingsley, David gets drawn

into the controversial issue of the ordination of women in *A Dead Man Out of Mind* (1994), and enters 'the extremes of emotion, and the extremes of conviction' of the renowned annual pilgrimage to **Walsingham** in *The Snares of Death* (1992). When the controversial new incumbent of the Anglo-Catholic parish of 'South Barsham' is murdered, there is no shortage of suspects. But another death during the pilgrimage alerts David to the real motives behind the case, while Lucy is left speechless by the garishness of the religious imagery at the shrine.

Nothing is quite what it seems in the ancient Norfolk village of 'Walston', with its historical connections to Ann Boleyn, in *Evil Angels Among Them* (1995). The arrival of a lesbian couple bringing up a six-year-old girl sets the curtains twitching, while a malicious caller is

'I found in the Church of England the fertile ground of inspiration for writing the books I'd always wanted to write,' says **Kate Charles**. 'The church is an institution that represents an ideal, but it's made up of human beings, of various degrees of fallibility, of goodness, of badness, of mixed motives.'

Sheila Radley's* exciting Tudor mystery *New Blood from Old Bones* (1998) draws inspiration from the turbulent times of Henry VIII and the murky morality surrounding **Blickling**-born Ann Boleyn. This historical feast of seduction, manipulation and murder is set in a fictional 'Castleacre', but uses the topography, history and ruined castle and abbey remains of **Castle Acre**, some twenty miles west of Norwich.

'It's a monastic abbey church, it has two towers, one of which was built by the abbey, and one was built by the town, because they didn't speak to each other...' – **Wymondham Abbey** symbolizes the conflict inherent in **Kate Charles**' ecclesiastical mysteries.

making the life of the vicar's wife a misery. When violent death strikes, David and Lucy are left with little time to admire the spectacular angel roof and medieval Doom painting of 'St Michael and All Angels', a composite of Norfolk churches but drawing upon two of Charles' favourites, **Salle** and **Cawston**:

> St Michael and All Angels was not the sort of church one might have expected to find in a small, rather undistinguished Norfolk village like Walston; its size bespoke past glories of which scarcely a trace remained. Built in the Perpendicular style, its exterior, crowned by a massive square tower, was a marvel of flushwork in Norfolk flint, and the interior, with its vast expanses of clear glass in the side aisles and the deep clerestory, was irradiated with the sort of light that is only found in East Anglia, as if the sky had somehow found a way to invade the church.

Alan Hunter, whose amiable and imperturbable Chief Inspector Gently continues to sift red herrings almost fifty years since his first appearance.

The eerie atmosphere of the Broads has inspired numerous ghost stories, and in *Wraiths and Changelings* (1978), **Gladys Mitchell*** brings an unlikely party of ghost-hunters and fake phantoms to Norfolk. Only at the end of her spine-chilling and murderously funny mystery does the genuinely haunting presence of Brother Pacificus raise his spectral head at **Ranworth**.

Sentinel wind-pumps and mills stark against huge skies, **THE BROADS** represent the most unique and disquieting area of Norfolk – a lonely reed-covered flatness offering concealment and exposure in equal measure. Even the origin of these interconnected waterways remained a secret until 1960, when tests revealed that the Broads were actually formed by medieval peat digging. A few miles east of Norwich, the riverside village of **Brundall** is home to **Alan Hunter** (1922–) and the perfect base from which to launch a series of mysteries featuring Chief Inspector Gently, whose dedication and painstaking probing are combined with the flashes of intuition characteristic of all great fictional detectives. With locales all 'sketched from life', widely travelled Gently seems most at home sagely puffing at his pipe in this watery landscape close to 'Norchester' (Norwich):

> The broad at this end had an air of exclusiveness contributed to by a number of rush and reed islands. These not only served as a screen but also deterred the near approach of the thronging holiday-craft. In the secret waterways between them flourished superb water-lilies, while there was an air of tameness about the population of coots, water-hens and great-crested grebes. Gently surveyed these fastnesses with a jaundiced eye. He was suddenly struck with the size of the task of finding one particular human being, even on a medium size broad...

Born in **Hoveton St John** on the River Bure, close to the bustling boating village of **Wroxham**, Hunter puts his knowledge of the area's boatyards to good use in *Gently Down the Stream* (1957). Forced to abandon a planned fishing holiday, Gently arrives in 'Wrackstead' (covering both Wroxham and Hoveton) to investigate the mysterious death of a businessman discovered in a burnt-out Broads yacht. In a

'The towers of forgotten windmills stood out like castles of Faery. It was a strange land, a poetic land, a land burgeoning with fable and supernatural story' – the **Norfolk Broads** present Inspector Gently with a complex investigation in *Gently Down the Stream.*

complex case of numerous leads and too many lies, Gently bases himself at 'Wrackstead Dyke', modelled on upstream **Belaugh**. *Gently Floating* (1963) is a Gently classic in which Hunter's self-deprecating detective investigates the murder of a boat-builder and fleet owner around the **Potter Heigham** area. Combining precise description and strong sense of place with an effortless stream of consciousness, this timeless mystery epitomizes Hunter's distinctively gentle approach to mystery writing.

A land of sandy, flint-strewn fields and oak, pine and birch woods, the forlorn beauty of **BRECKLAND** stands aloof from the ordered plantations of modern Forestry Commission trees. Born on Christmas Day 1885, in the then primitive confines of **Great Hockham** village, north-east of **Thetford**, **Christopher Bush** (pseud. Charlie Christmas Bush, 1885–1973) describes his 'neglected corner' of south-west Norfolk as 'something unique and curiously intimate'. A prolific writer, Bush penned more than sixty traditional detective novels featuring Ludovic Travers over a forty-year period. Bush's third novel, *Murder at Fenwold* (1930) (US: *The Death of Cosmo Revere*), brings Travers to the isolated village of 'Fenwold', deep in the Norfolk countryside. When the body of the local landlord, presumed to be away on 'some flint grubbing

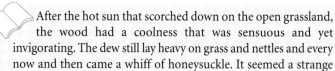

The bracken, silver birch and pines of **Breckland** near **Rushford** and **Euston** – home ground for **Christopher Bush** and distinctive backdrop to **Sheila Radley**'s border mysteries.

'In writing about the ingrained attitudes of country people I made considerable use of my own rural background' – **Sheila Radley**'s village upbringing and fourteen years behind the counter of a Norfolk post office inform her Chief Inspector Quantrill series.

expedition or other', is found in a nearby wood, Travers applies his considerable intellect to an intriguing mystery:

> After the hot sun that scorched down on the open grassland, the wood had a coolness that was sensuous and yet invigorating. The dew still lay heavy on grass and nettles and every now and then came a whiff of honeysuckle. It seemed a strange thing to be going in search of death in a spot where the hand of man was scarcely to be discerned.

In this, as in many of his mysteries, Bush points to the 'strange, holding sort of appeal' exerted by 'feudal survival' here in rural Norfolk, with its brooding seclusion and hostility towards strangers. The enigmatic Travers blends perfectly into this landscape and it is with some regret that he departs 'Fenwold Hall' with its 'evocation of the past; of the times when life was stately and men had time to pause and look on beauty'.

An old saying holds that, when crossing the border, the first town in Norfolk 'Diss-appears'. **Sheila Radley*** (pseud. Sheila Robinson, 1928–) nominally places the 'Breckham Market' at the centre of her Chief Inspector Douglas Quantrill series in Suffolk, but finds the essence of the town on her doorstep in the Norfolk market town of **Diss**. The distinctive mere, market place and church high on the hill of her home town are merged with the town hall, police headquarters, river, bridges and industrial estates of nearby Thetford, to form this wholly credible Breckland border town in which Quantrill lives and works.

Radley's first novel, *Death and the Maiden* (1978), sets the tone for the series, occupying the borderland where detective mystery meets psychological whydunnit. *A Talent for Destruction* (1982) is a realistic portrayal of the wicked and the vulnerable aspects of human nature. Quantrill investigates the discovery of a body in the meadow behind the rectory of 'St Botolph's Church' and finds himself up against an obstructive silence unable to disguise obvious emotional distress. While the bleak winter landscape reflects the inner chill of the rectory, Quantrill lets DC Ian Wigby loose on the warm, smoky pub trail in the hunt for information. As the closely confined lives of the rector and his wife come under increasing scrutiny, the sordid and tragic past gradually emerges.

Fair Game (1994) brings the series to a close as Quantrill enters the 'Chalcot' country house estate – 'a time warp, a small piece of leafy, traditional England, hidden away behind its high enclosing walls' – to investigate a pheasant shoot that appears to have gone horribly wrong. 'The countryside glowed with the last of the autumn colours – hawthorn berries crimson, bramble leaves rose-pink, oak leaves buff as chamois leather, field maples incandescent.' The changing seasons in the novel reflect the changes in British rural life: away from the traditional rural patchwork of the Chalcot estate towards intensive farming, away from rigid social structures into a brave new world of broadening equality – and Quantrill's life is changing too.

Dominated by 'St Botolph's Church' (**St Mary's**) the 'centuries-old juxtaposition' of church, (former) pub and market place of **Diss** town centre forms the nucleus of **Sheila Radley**'s 'Breckham Market'.

'I'm so intrigued by East Anglia… the sea, the marshes, the birds, the emptiness, the great skies, the churches which are particularly magnificent, and the sense of being a place rather alien and totally apart' – **P D James** pictured at the Suffolk coast.

'…a familiar, ordinary, primitive hut… on the brink of nothingness' – **Minsmere** bird reserve provides the inspiration for 'Monksmere', where an observation hide becomes scene of the crime in *Unnatural Causes.*

The mellow rural beauty of **SUFFOLK** also offers wide skies and a ravaged coast, while an abundance of church towers, leafy lanes and hidden villages punctuates the gently undulating farmlands. Often cited as one of the founders of the crime genre, anarchist **William Godwin** (1756–1836) was a preacher at **Lowestoft** on the east coast, and a minister further south in inland **Stowmarket** until he was expelled from Suffolk in 1780 over a theological dispute. His thrilling novel *Caleb Williams* (1794) depicts largely a political landscape, but through its detection, psychology and pursuit foreshadows the modern crime novel.

One of the finest exponents of landscape in detective fiction, **P D James*** (1920–) enjoys the relative solitude of her Suffolk home in stylish and austere **Southwold**, located some ten miles south of **Lowestoft**, where James spent childhood camping holidays perched on Pakefield Cliffs. Southwold's exclusivity has earned it the nickname of 'London-on-Sea', but the area is dominated by the restless, invasive force of the North Sea which over the centuries has forced the boundaries of human settlement to retreat further and further inland. This contributes to the atmosphere of loss underlain by history, and of solitude tinged with danger, that defines James' fictional landscapes strung along the beleaguered East Anglian coast.

The loneliness and raw natural beauty of the Suffolk coast near **Minsmere** and **Dunwich** is fully exposed in *Unnatural Causes* (1967), a traditional, tightly bound whodunnit set at 'Monksmere Head'. With the dome of Sizewell power station hazy on the horizon, a walk around Dunwich today speaks mainly of what is lost – this was once a major Saxon port with a Benedictine abbey and several churches before the sea continued its relentless advance.

The landscape is well suited to Scotland Yard detective Adam Dalgliesh, a solitary and very private man who arrives to visit his aunt at Monksmere. With an assembled cast of objectionable local literati awaiting him, Dalgliesh's planned holiday was always doomed to failure, and when the corpse of a local crime writer is found floating in a wooden dinghy, he reluctantly enters the fray. Dalgliesh's involvement ruffles the feathers of local Inspector Reckless, and even a spot of birdwatching is tainted by the reek of death as Dalgliesh reassesses his view of the brooding shoreline:

'It's safe enough… if you don't walk too close to the cliffs' – **Covehithe** provides the inspiration for 'Ballard's Mere' in *Death in Holy Orders*, where a cliff fall precipitates tragic events.

It was a lonely shore, empty and desolate, like the last fringes of the world. It evoked no memories, cosily nostalgic, of the enchantments of childhood holidays by the sea. Here were no rockpools to explore, no exotic shells, no breakwaters festooned with sea weed, no long stretches of yellow sand sliced by innumerable spades. Here was nothing but sea, sky and marshland, an empty beach with little to mark the miles of outspate shingle but the occasional tangle of tar-splotched driftwood and the rusting spikes of old fortifications. Dalgliesh loved this emptiness, this fusion of sea and sky. But today the place held no peace for him. He saw it suddenly with new eyes, a shore alien, eerie, utterly desolate.

Alan Hunter's Chief Inspector Gently explores Suffolk in several mysteries, and with his wife Gabrielle moves into their beautiful 'Heatherings' home three miles inland from Dunwich at 'Welbourne' – a village 'suggested by **Westleton** and situated at the site formerly occupied by Ralph's Mill'.

'*Devices and Desires* began when I was visiting Suffolk, standing on the shingle and looking out over the North Sea. It was very empty… just some fishing boats drawn up, nets drying in the wind, and I was thinking that it must have looked the same a thousand years ago – with the same smells, the same sounds. Then I turned my eyes and saw this great stark outline of Sizewell nuclear power station' – **P D James** explains the origins of *Devices and Desires* (1989) and 'Larksoken' power station.

Ann Quinton's detective fiction often begins in the seclusion of her lovingly restored gypsy caravan.

A church within a church without a village, mysterious **Covehithe** lies on a road to nowhere along the sandy clifftop midway between Southwold and Lowestoft. This lost settlement provides the atmospheric setting for *Death in Holy Orders* (2001), a poignant mystery in which place, character and plot are integrated to perfection. Dalgliesh returns to Suffolk for a visit to 'St Anselm's Theological College' (imaginary, but influenced by the impressive church ruins at Covehithe) to appease the wealthy father of a student found smothered by a fall of sand from the friable, eroded cliffs. Within the deep tranquillity of the college, Dalgliesh finds a community whose values, and very existence, are as besieged as the coast. From the 'oily surface hinting at unfathomable depths' of the mere (**Benacre Broad**) to the comfort of the nearby 'Crown' in Southwold, from the medieval magnificence of the Doom painting (inspired by the Doom at nearby **Wenhaston Church**) to the spartan pig-farming cottages, James distils the very essence of coastal Suffolk.

Further down the Suffolk coast, **Ann Quinton** (1934–) has mapped out her detecting territory in and around her home village of **Kirton**, north-west of **Felixstowe**. Mercurial Detective Inspector James Roland and stolid local Sergeant Patrick Mansfield travel past the distinctive 'Suffolk Pink' façades and thatched roofs of small villages, through the floral charm of market towns such as 'Woodford' (**Woodbridge**) and into larger towns such as Quinton's birthplace of **Ipswich** (here reverting to its old name of 'Gippeswyk'). Both detectives live in the village of 'Wallingford' (**Walton**), due north of 'Felstone' (Felixstowe), one of Europe's busiest container ports.

Under wide skies, Quinton's novels are firmly rooted in Suffolk's landscape, history and characters, with the reed-fringed marshes around Kirton Creek capturing the mood of the series. The first of Quinton's Suffolk mysteries, *To Mourn a Mischief* (1989), is based upon a true story.

'The tide crept silently along the creek' – **Kirton Creek**, painted by **Ann Quinton** epitomizes the timelessness of the Suffolk landscape and is a favourite setting for both her painting and writing.

The excavation of a German World War II plane by a historical research society throws the village of 'Croxton' (loosely modelled on Kirton) into turmoil. When a more recent skeleton is disturbed from its resting place in the river mud, the secret past and present of this creek community are pushed into the light too. Another personal favourite of Quinton's, with a strong sense of place, *A Little Grave* (1994) sees Inspector Roland investigating the disappearance of small children in the Felstone area. Mental illness, the yearning to have children, and the responsibility for them, are central issues in this mystery set deep in a wintry Suffolk. As tensions rise, the investigation draws towards the 'vast acres' of 'Pendleton' (**Rendlesham**) Forest also encountered in *To Mourn a Mischief* and devastated by the 1987 hurricane, when the trees here 'could have been cardboard cutouts, scenery from the Babes in the Wood'.

Out to the west of the county, a short distance from Cambridge and the Fens, Britain's horse-racing capital of **Newmarket** is reined into Suffolk by a quirk of the county boundary looping around the town like a bridle. Suffolk's gain is some 3,000 horses and 15,000 people in a town that lives, eats and breathes racing. A former champion steeple-chase jockey, detective thriller writer **Dick Francis** (1920–) may never have turned to a life of crime writing had his horse, Devon Loch, not collapsed inexplicably whilst leading the 1956 Grand National down the home strait. It was an enormous blow to Francis, but assisted by his wife Mary he turned to a new and even more successful career.

One way or another, Newmarket features in many of Francis' fast-moving racing novels. In the Gold Dagger-winning *Whip Hand* (1979), jockey turned private detective Sid Halley, who lost his hand in a terrible riding accident, turns up in town on the trail of a powerful syndicate of owners who will stop at nothing to win. Bookmaking plays a crucial role in horseracing and the perfect formula for predicting winners remains a gamblers' dream. A teacher finds himself in possession of a computer programme that can do just that in *Twice Shy* (1981), a tense Newmarket thriller with a typical Francis setting:

> I loved the Heath in the early mornings with the manes blowing under the wide skies. My affection for horses was so deep and went back so far that I couldn't imagine life without them. They were a friendly foreign nation living in our land, letting their human neighbours tend them and feed them, accepting them as servants as much as masters. Fast, fascinating, essentially untamed, they were my landscape, my old shoes, the place to where my heart returned, as necessary to me as the sea to sailors.

In *Wild Horses* (1994), movie director and former amateur jockey Thomas Lyon comes to Newmarket to make a controversial racing film and is soon raking over the ashes of a past Jockey Club scandal. The action moves from the suites of the **Bedford Lodge Hotel** to the **Jockey**

'Moving everywhere simultaneously in two different worlds – horses and books – has given me perhaps wider understandings of humanity than either might have done on its own' – **Dick Francis** pictured in the saddle.

Newmarket has been a favourite with royalty since James I, and in **Peter Lovesey**'s* *Bertie and the Tinman* (1987), amateur sleuth Bertie (Albert, Prince of Wales) arrives in Newmarket in a 'Victorian Dick Francis' based upon the suspicious real-life death of famous jockey Fred Archer, whose ghost is still said to haunt the tracks.

Vet and anaesthetist **Manda Scott*** lives near Newmarket and uses her experience working with horses in her equine detective thriller *Night Mares* (1998). Her sleuth, Kellen Stewart, also runs a horse farm with a gnarled ex-jockey who joins her in Scotland as an escape from 'the endless fens of East Anglia where the closest things to a mountain is the half-mile of one-in-ten slope that makes up the training run of Newmarket Heath'.

Newmarket – 'the town long held to be the home and heart of the horseracing industry worldwide,' says **Dick Francis.**

Club offices in Newmarket's High Street, and across to the Heath where horses are trained every day – and where a knife-wielding assailant waits to strike.

For many years, the border village of **Polstead** was home to **Ruth Rendell***, who uses the area's forgotten lanes and villages to enhance the psychological suspense in one of her favourite novels, *A Judgement in Stone* (1977).

Some of East Anglia's most unspoilt and undiscovered rural beauty lies along the hedgerows, fields and woods of the gently winding **Stour Valley** that defines the Suffolk/Essex border. Painted many times by the artist John Constable, this landscape is a strong feature in the highly evocative detective novels of **J R L Anderson*** (1911–81), which weave together various strands of Suffolk's historic, naval and artistic heritage. The Dutch ancestry of contemplative and caring high-flyer Chief Constable Piet Deventer reflects the historic trade links between Suffolk and the flatlands of Holland across the water, and having curtailed his painting career as a potential 'Dutch Master', Deventer is now in charge of the 'Fine Art Squad' at Scotland Yard.

Investigations in *A Sprig of Sea Lavender* (1978) focus initially on **Sudbury** station, where a female passenger joins the train with her outsize art portfolio, on her way to London. When the young woman ends up murdered, the portfolio is found to contain four oil paintings, one of them possibly a landscape by John Constable – a painter whom Deventer strongly admires. His enquiries lead Deventer up through 'the soft-hued, unemphatic beauty of the Suffolk countryside' to the 'indescribably lovely' seascape of the Dunwich coast and into the historic surroundings of the old wool town of **Lavenham**:

Having played the lead role in Agatha Christie's *The Mousetrap* for two years, **Anthony Oliver** (1922–95) went on to write a series of four crime mysteries set in the Suffolk town of 'Flaxfield'. In the often farcical *The Pew Group* (1980) and the more insinuating *The Elberg Collection* (1985), Mrs Lizzie Thomas joins forces with former police detective Inspector John Webber to tackle crimes in the East Anglian antiques world.

Lavenham has come well into the twentieth century, preserving a fairy-story quality from the past without looking consciously pretty. Its overhanging timbered buildings seem to have grown there, the twisting lanes between them seeming to remain just as they were trodden by the first footsteps making from cottage door to well or cabbage patch. The wealth from wool that went into the great church and merchants' houses seems somehow to have lasted from the Middle Ages, paying each new generation a dividend of gracious surroundings.

With family homes either side of the border, the early detective fiction of **Margery Allingham*** (1904–66) is characterized by archetypal East Anglian landscapes. The first Albert Campion novel (in which her detective actually appears as a minor villain), *The Crime at Black Dudley* (1929) (US: *The Black Dudley Murder*), uses scenery around her parents' Suffolk home in picturesque **Letheringham**. In the summer of 1931 Allingham moved with her husband Philip 'Pip' Youngman Carter just over the county boundary to **Chappel**, which inspired the settings for *Sweet Danger* (1933) (US: *Kingdom of Death/The Fear Sign*) and the village of 'Pontisbright' in *The Beckoning Lady* (1955) (US: *The Estate of the Beckoning Lady*).

'How beautiful it was in its forlorn way' – the little branch line of **Sudbury** where once 'drays, pulled by great Suffolk Punches, would have carted produce to the t ains' features prominently in the opening scenes of **J R L Anderson**'s *A Sprig of Sea-Lavender*.

The inscrutable marshland and snaking creeks of the **ESSEX** coast, home to rare wildlife and countless wading birds, are a world away from the loud urban vulgarity usually attributed to the buffer towns between London and rural East Anglia. The spacious Georgian Old Rectory at **Layer Breton** was the Allingham family home that provided young Margery with her first glimpse of the austere insularity characterizing classic English detective fiction. The solitude of the large garden was a joy to the young writer, but it was the lure of nearby **Mersea Island**, where the family regularly returned for holidays at **West Mersea**, that inspired some of her strongest landscapes. The ancient Roman causeway across the muddy **River Colne** estuary, and the tidal straits of the **Blackwater** estuary looking out to sea to the south of the island, make it easy to imagine an inhospitable, treacherous terrain concealing smugglers and villains. Campion meets his old adversary from Black

'On the grey marshy coast… the village of Mystery Mile lay surrounded by impassable mud flats and grey-white saltings' – *Mystery Mile* shows how the mud creeks of **Mersea Island** inspired some of **Margery Allingham**'s most atmospheric settings.

Margery Allingham – a major figure from the Golden Age of detective fiction whose East Anglian connections inspired a number of mysteries.

Dudley again in *Mystery Mile* (1930), which is firmly immersed in the mists and marshes of Mersea (although Allingham twists the topography by placing the island of 'Mystery Mile' in Suffolk, surrounded by the waters of the **River Orwell**). As Campion challenges a master criminal to reveal himself, the thrilling climax takes place amidst the 'ominous clucking' of the saltmarsh and the mud 'squelching and gurgling as the sea came nearer and nearer'.

When Margery and her husband Pip moved to the imposing red-brick D'Arcy House in the centre of **Tolleshunt D'Arcy** in 1934, it was still within easy reach of the coast. It is fitting that her final novel, *Cargo of Eagles* (1968), completed after Allingham's death by her husband, should be set in the defining marshes and mudflats of the Essex coast. With its silted-up harbour, 'Saltey' is believed to be an old smuggling route into East London, and Campion has to brave local hostility and ghostly happenings on the trail of some valuable modern booty: a cargo of eagles.

As a child, Margery Allingham holidayed in the more working-class resort of **Clacton-on-Sea**. Further north along the peninsula, **Elizabeth George*** sets her incendiary murder mystery *Deception on his Mind* (1997) in the Essex seaside town of 'Balford-le-Nez', an amalgam of middle-class **Walton-on-the-Naze** and upper-class refuge **Frinton-on-Sea**. DS Barbara Havers, still bearing the scars of her previous case, spends a less than restful 'holiday' in Balford.

There are plenty of Constables, and other valuable works of art and antiquity, in **Jonathan Gash**'s* (pseud. John Grant, 1933–) Lovejoy series, though sadly most of them are forgeries. Soft-centred Lovejoy is a 'divvy', able to divine the authenticity of an antique by sense alone. He is also a scruffy, incorrigible rogue who consorts with low life and aristocracy alike whilst wheedling his way into East Anglia's antiques

'A great crime writer I used to know lived right in the village' – **D'Arcy House**, **Margery Allingham**'s former home in the centre of Tolleshunt D'Arcy. In an affectionate tribute, **Jonathan Gash** uses the house as the model for Dame Millicent's manor house in *The Grace of Older Women*, and for Sir Jasper Haux's home, which Lovejoy burgles in *Every Last Cent*.

shops, country homes and auction houses in search of priceless artefacts. Irresistible to women, Lovejoy's inseparable addictions of sex ('making smiles') and antiques frequently lead him into sleuthing – and into deep water.

From his home in **West Bergholt**, Gash is perfectly placed to explore the antiques strongholds along the Essex border, as well as the ancient arcades of England's oldest recorded town and first Roman capital, **Colchester**. Thinly disguised as 'St Edmundsbury', Colchester provides locations for many of the Lovejoy novels, including the scene of the crime in *The Grace in Older Women* (1995). With 'Lovejoy Antiques' – run from Lovejoy's lonely, decrepit cottage in a 'straggling' border village bearing an uncanny resemblance to West Bergholt – hitting rock bottom, Lovejoy is distracted by the murder of an old acquaintance in the River Colne boating pond. In a thrilling romp moving from **Spring Wood** (close to **St Mary the Virgin Church** in West Bergholt), through the streets of Colchester and into border country, Lovejoy needs to be at his most resourceful to find the killer – and to stay alive.

Lovejoy creator **Jonathan Gash** – a great admirer of Margery Allingham* and Ellis Peters*.

Every Last Cent (2001) is packed to the hilt with the lore and laws of antiques ('It's not the money, it's the price'), as Lovejoy's son Mortimer displays an uncharacteristic honesty in his dealings that has other antique traders up in arms. Lovejoy traipses around Colchester's **North Hill** teashops and **St Peter's** churchyard, but when his burglary accomplice turns up dead, he realizes that he has crossed some very powerful and dangerous people.

June Thomson (1920–) lovingly recreates the 'gentle calm landscape of ploughed fields and woodland, of hedgerows and leafy lanes' of her Essex childhood in the Detective Chief Inspector Jack Finch (Rudd in the US) mysteries. Combining ingenious puzzles with thoughtful character analysis, Thomson's unhurried prose reflects the rural

The thatched cottage near **Great Dunmow**, where **June Thomson** went to live as a child. 'The open green in front of the cottage was thick with harebells and campions, meadowsweet and ladies' bedstraw,' says Thomson. 'In most of my books, there are references to wild flowers and the joy they can bring'.

Opposite: The author of Victorian novels of sensation, **M(ary) E(lizabeth) Braddon** (1835–1915) created one of the earliest fictional amateur detectives, with sharp-eyed Robert Audley unravelling tangled clues pointing to his aunt's crimes in *Lady Audley's Secret* (1862). The mansion of 'Audley End' is inspired not by the famous domain of that name near Saffron Walden, but by **Ingatestone Hall**, located some six miles south-west of **Chelmsford**. The distinguished home of the Petre family for many years, the hall retains the avenue of limes and distinctive stable clock Braddon describes.

The Blackwater town of **Maldon** – where **June Thomson** finds inspiration for her rural Essex mysteries and **Phil Lovesey** opens *Death Duties*.

environment of her mysteries, where village life can 'breed intense and potentially dangerous relationships, veritable hot-beds of emotion where crime flourishes in the dark'. Finch's deceptively bland Campion-esque features conceal a 'watchful, alert, perceptive' character first seen in *Not One of Us* (1971). In this tale of a local recluse living in an isolated cottage, Finch uses his laconic, low-key manner to win over the recalcitrant Essex folk.

'Another type of Essex countryside which I later grew to love was the marshes and creeks along the river Crouch and, more particularly, the Blackwater. These lonely stretches of glistening mud and water with their huge skies fascinated me. They had a sinister, dangerous reputation and stories were told about them, one of a farmer and his horse, who disappeared one night and whose bones were later found picked clean by the crabs. I loved the isolation and the air of melancholy about these mudflats, the smell of salt, the sounds of the wind whistling through reeds and the cry of sea-birds.'

In *Past Reckoning* (1990), Thomson's 'Selhaven' is firmly based on the ancient Blackwater port of **Maldon**, site of a legendary Viking battle and long famous for its salt. Nina Gifford, who is first encountered in *To*

'Tiny coffin-like sheds, smoking compost heaps, bird-scarers... A scene frozen in time from the mid-thirties' – Chelmsford's **Avenues Allotments**, where a fire ignites a trail of terror in *When The Ashes Burn.*

Make a Killing (1982) (US: *Portrait of Lilith*), makes an emotional return to Essex haunts but becomes embroiled in the murder of a woman who runs a museum devoted to the memory of her writer brother. The obsessive, verging on incestuous, nature of Thomson's claustrophobic communities, coupled with themes of exile and exclusion, add elements of tragic realism and suspense to her convincing whodunnits.

The gently staid commercial centre of **Chelmsford**, where June Thomson's Chief Inspector Finch and Sergeant Tom Boyce are stationed, has few cultural or historical attractions to evidence its rise to county town. There is certainly little remaining of the small Elizabethan town described by US writer **Leonard Tourney** (1942–) in his Matthew Stock series. Respected clothier and businessman Stock, who is also town constable, is drawn into a number of mysteries by Lord Burghley, one of the Queen's most important advisers.

During the nine years **Phil Lovesey** (1963–) spent in Chelmsford he discovered that, with its law courts, police headquarters and prison all in easy reach of each other, the town was well-suited to detective fiction. *Death Duties* (1998) marks a chilling debut linking events from Maldon in 1969, when a young girl kills her father, to modern Chelmsford, where Christmas is fast-approaching and the young girl is now a grown woman intent on a mission of 'mercy'. The season of goodwill in Chelmsford is dark, cold and unforgiving, with the courts and police station overworked, a killer on the streets and shoppers looking over their shoulders. Merging compassion, madness and violence, Lovesey brings the investigation to its climax in the huge atrium of the County

Hall offices, where death waits beside the carp pool. The landscapes of Lovesey's second novel, *Ploughing Potter's Field* (1999), are largely institutional: the prison, police headquarters, central library and university. When a PhD student in Forensic Psychiatry gets too close to the life and crimes of a psychopathic killer, his research and amateur sleuthing begin to spiral dangerously out of control.

The unfashionable patchwork of scruffy grass, turned soil and small sheds of the **Avenues Allotments** a short walk from Lovesey's former home in **Rectory Lane** provides the unlikely flashpoint for the clash of Chelmsford's older and younger generations in *When The Ashes Burn* (2000). Lovesey's despairing tale takes freelance reporter Jack Latimer out from his kebab shop offices and into the nightmarish world of doomed George Picket. As Picket struggles to maintain his illusion of dignity and respectability, the vandalized allotments become a battleground pushing him to the brink. With the help of Detective Sergeant Sampson of Chelmsford's **New Street** Police Station (who shares an office with Alan Mason from *Death Duties*), Latimer sniffs a big story in this 'undistinguished little town', especially when he discovers that Picket is the son of a former hangman.

'The longer I looked at the town, strived to find some kind of identity for it beyond the corporate shop-fronts, the less I got to know the place, the less it yielded to me' – **Phil Lovesey** on the difficulties of bringing crime fiction home to Chelmsford.

CHAPTER NINE

London

CENTRAL LONDON

It didn't happen in London? He grinned at the thought. Didn't it!
Everything happened in London... Every night and every day.

Peter Cheyney, *The Urgent Hangman* (1938)

Capital of England, capital of crime and detection, **LONDON** is in a constant state of flux. Around its historic landmarks the city is dismantled and reassembled as the landscape adapts to change – though remaining distinctively, uniquely London. For decades, the capital was *the* setting for detective fiction, but often used only as a backdrop for the cerebral challenges of murder mystery. London's detective fiction may be inexorably linked with the quiet hiss of gas lamps in the shadows and fog of Victorian alleyways, but its variety of form and setting through the years reflects the multi-textured hues of a metropolis. While London's fringes celebrate the city's more contemporary, multicultural form, central London remains largely the preserve of Classic and Golden Age mysteries – perhaps awaiting a new generation of writers?

Contrast, the backbone of many convincing detective fiction settings, is amply played out in the sprawling cityscape of **London**.

For centuries, the dank stone walls of the **Tower of London**, the sometime palace, prison, and place of execution begun under William the Conqueror, were a symbol of fear. Protected from the river's edge by a wharf beside **Tower Bridge**, the towers and turrets of today's more benign tourist attraction still retain a haunted air of distant despair – none more so than the squat **Bloody Tower** behind **Traitor's Gate**, scene of one of history's great unsolved mysteries. In **Josephine Tey**'s* acclaimed *The Daughter of Time* (1951), Inspector Alan Grant, ill in hospital, applies his razor-sharp mind to the disappearance of the sons and heirs of Edward IV from the Tower in 1483 and to challenge the role played by their uncle, Richard of Gloucester, the much vilified Richard III.

The 'grim old building seemed at that moment to hold for him in one graspable whole all the past centuries of this noble, sea-girt isle' – the **Tower of London**, scene of many gruesome crimes and mysteries, makes an impression on Inspector Ghote when he arrives from Bombay in **H R F Keating**'s* *Inspector Ghote Hunts the Peacock* (1968).

'It was full of evil suggestion…
a long, flattened arch of stone,
like the hood of an unholy
fireplace' – **Traitor's Gate**,
through which condemned
prisoners were brought to the
Tower, is scene of the crime in
John Dickson Carr's *The Mad
Hatter Mystery* (1933).

'Medieval London is never far away. Skyscrapers, concrete and tarmac
cannot hide the lanes and runnels which once ran like needles through
the ancient city,' says headmaster and historical crime writer **P(aul)
C Doherty*** (1946–). A favourite location, and focal point of medieval
London, is the churchyard of **St Paul's Cathedral**. 'Here all the great
events of the period were first proclaimed,' says Doherty, 'the fall of
kings, invasions, the outcome of battles.' In *Satan in St Mary's* (1986),
Doherty conjures up late thirteenth-century city life, introducing his
medieval detective Hugh Corbett as a clerk at the court of Edward I.
Corbett's status improves in direct proportion to his prowess in solving
mysteries, and he is soon ferrying the choppy waters of the Thames
between the Tower and **Westminster** to gain the ear of the King. For
the time being, a young and less experienced Corbett has to watch his
step in the dangerous bustle of St Paul's:

> Corbett, however, was cautious, securing his purse and
> keeping his hand on his dagger as he passed through the great
> west gate into the church of St Paul's. The area was a well-known
> haunt of 'Wolfheads', outlaws and members of the city's murky
> underworld, who lived in and around the church ready to bolt for
> sanctuary should the forces of the law appear. Corbett walked
> through the main door of St Paul's into the main meeting place
> under its vaulting nave. It was still busy. At the west end sat twelve
> scribes ready to prepare documents, indentures, letters, bonds for
> anyone willing to hire their services. Serjeants-at-law in their
> ermine-lined robes stood in the aisles, meeting clients or
> discussing the finer points of law with each other, while around
> one pillar, anxious serving-men waited to be hired.

To historical mystery writer
P C Doherty, **St Paul's Cross**
in the cathedral churchyard
embodies London's medieval
history.

'We gets a fair few dead uns in
the Acre and all around
there…' – **Anne Perry**'s*
Death in the Devil's Acre
(1991) enters the appalling
Victorian slums of 'The Devil's
Acre' in the shadow of
St Paul's. Thomas Pitt dons a
disguise to head into an
insalubrious environment of
slaughterhouse yards, foul
drains and sparse gaslights to
investigate a multiple murder.

The distinctive dome of St Paul's was designed by Christopher Wren
in the aftermath of the Great Fire of 1666, which destroyed four-fifths
of medieval London. Inspired by Wren, rising young architect
Christopher Redmayne takes centre stage in **Edward Marston**'s*
mystery series exploring the skin-deep gentility and hedonistic upper
crust of Restoration society. In *The King's Evil* (1999), Redmayne joins
forces with dutiful Puritan constable Jonathan Bale, who lives close to
St Paul's, to investigate thievery and murder at the London townhouse
Redmayne is designing.

London's commercial artery for hundreds of years, the **River Thames** carries a good number of murder mysteries.

'One place does inspire me: standing on one of the bridges overlooking the Thames. The city may change but the river doesn't. It's still violent, treacherous, capable of producing a surprise as well as hiding the swollen corpse of a murder victim. The bridges are clean and swept but, if you close your eyes, you can recall these packed thoroughfares of medieval London and the awful, blood-spattered poles fixed over the edge of the bridge bearing the severed heads of traitors.'

P C Doherty

On the opposite bank to St Paul's, across the swirling waters of the Thames, the ancient borough of **SOUTHWARK** was once detached from the jurisdiction of the city of London and synonymous with brothels, bear-pits and theatres. Today the enormous shell of Sir Giles Gilbert Scott's Bankside Power Station is dominated by the brick tower of the **Tate Modern**, overlooking the river and revitalizing an area that in the sixteenth century housed five prisons, amongst them the notorious 'Clink'. **Paul Harding** (pseud. P C Doherty*) recreates Southwark's foul-smelling fourteenth-century slums in his vivid and entertaining 'Sorrowful Mysteries' featuring Dominican friar Brother Athelstan, who lives very close to the Tabard Inn (**Talbot Yard**, at the rear of Guy's Hospital). It is from here that **Geoffrey Chaucer**'s (*c.*1343–1400) pilgrims depart for Canterbury in April 1387, and *The Canterbury Tales* are recreated by P C Doherty in a separate series of historical mysteries.

'If I could live in one period of history, it would be Elizabethan because of the theatre,' says **Edward Marston***, whose Elizabethan sleuth Nicholas Bracewell, book holder (stage manager) of Lord Westfield's Men, has learned to 'live and work in the shadow' of the city authorities' disapproval. 'London was the capital of noise, a vibrant, volatile place, surging with life and clamorous with purpose.' Not far from **William Shakespeare**'s (1564–1616) fully restored and working **Globe Theatre** lie the semi-excavated remains of **Bankside**'s first theatre, **The Rose** (56 Park Street). 'Theatre back then was much closer to a football match than it is these days,' says sports enthusiast Marston, 'you had to be good to survive.' **Judith Cook**'s (1933–) Bankside physician Dr Simon Forman also investigates dark deeds here in *Murder at the Rose* (1998).

Some five centuries later the much-changed face of Southwark forms the backdrop to **Alison Joseph**'s mysteries featuring the engaging amateur detective Sister Agnes Bourdillon. In a landscape scarred by work on the Jubilee Line extension, Southwark's older housing and dingy pubs compete with trendy bars and luxury flats in 'a brave new world of glass and steel'. Agnes, a nun of English/French extraction who belongs to an order involved in the running of a Southwark hostel, carries her family problems, her faith and her doubts into a string of intelligent murder mysteries with a strong human touch. In *The Dying Light* (1999), Agnes is on secondment to the chaplaincy in a Southwark women's prison where an inmate's dream about the death of her father comes eerily true.

Occupying an elevated position in Southwark's regenerated housing, Trish McGuire is a smart, successful and idealistic barrister introduced by **Natasha Cooper*** (pseud. Daphne Wright, 1951–) in *Creeping Ivy* (1998). High up on the top floor of a converted engineering works in a small side street off **Blackfriars Bridge Road**, Trish lives in a spacious flat full of modern art that reflects the new self-assurance of this part of London. Specializing in cases involving children, Trish knows full well the vulnerability of the young. But when her cousin's four-year-old daughter goes missing, Trish herself begins to look increasingly vulnerable as she becomes a suspect in the case. Smart new Southwark is still juxtaposed with increasingly forlorn-looking parts of Old London and extreme poverty. Cooper exploits the 'edgy atmosphere' here to the full in the moving *Out of the Dark* (2002), when Trish has a rare opportunity to discover 'the most depressing housing estate she had ever seen' only a few streets away from her own flat:

Natasha **Cooper** with her favourite London view from **Blackfriars Bridge** – Cooper's barrister sleuth Trish McGuire often pauses here on her daily walk to chambers at the **Courts of Justice**, 'to look back over the muddle of Puddle Dock and the Mermaid Theatre to the dome of St Paul's sitting magnificently solid above them'.

Built of dirty redbrick, probably between the wars, it looked cramped as well as broken down. Each of the four long blocks was six storeys high… There was no grass anywhere, or trees, only cracked concrete. The area between the blocks was half-filled with rusty cars. Weeds grew in the cracks, and muddy puddles showed how bad the ground drainage must be. A group of small children were throwing stones at the worst of the cars. It had only one tyre left and the windscreen was smashed. Above them a skein of geese flew in arrow-straight formation across the gold-and-blue sky, as though to show the inhabitants of this desolate place just how firmly shackled they were.

Temple Bar – where **Fleet Street** meets the **Strand**. Traitors' heads once lined the gate where today traffic clogs the busy roadway.

'Jury studied the paving stones at his feet as he walked up Ludgate Hill.' In *The Blue Last* (2001), **Martha Grimes** takes Inspector Richard Jury back to his tragic past in World War II London. When excavations at the site of a former pub on **Blackfriars Lane** near **Ludgate Circus** unearth two skeletons, Jury joins forces with DCI Mickey Haggerty to discover the links with the murder of a city stockbroker and the secrets of 'The Blue Last'.

Trish Maguire's extensive network of female friends includes Willow King, a trained mathematician, civil servant and romantic novelist who features in Cooper's early novels. From the refined air of **Belgravia**, Willow applies her logical mind to a series of dangerous mysteries, much to the annoyance of her Scotland Yard superintendent husband. In Cooper's personal favourite, *Rotten Apples* (1995), Willow sets out to investigate the suicide of a beautiful art historian and enters a world of vengeful bureaucracy and jealously guarded hierarchies in a fictional Inland Revenue building on the 'broad, thunderous artery' of **Vauxhall Bridge Road**.

At eleven o'clock at night, Fleet Street is near its busiest. Windows are lit up in all the great cliffs of building, motor vans dash westwards to the main railway stations, headlamps blazing and horns blaring, and the pavement vibrates with the thump of printing presses. On good nights the walk from the Temple Bar to Ludgate Hill, with all that life and urgency in the air, is as exhilarating as a ride on a fast horse or a windy day by the sea.

Gillian Linscott*, *Dance on Blood* (1998)

A short journey westwards from St Paul's leads to **Ludgate Circus** and into **FLEET STREET**. From the opening of a printing workshop here in the late fifteenth century right up until the 1980s, this pulsating canyon of newspaper office blocks, old-fashioned taverns and small winding lanes was the centre of the British news industry. Many crime writers cut their journalistic teeth here, and before *The Times*, the newspaper of choice for classic fictional detectives, was evicted east to **Wapping**, it had been published here since 1785. US writer **Lilian de la Torre**'s* atmospheric 'histo-detector' mysteries fictionalize the real-life partnership of Fleet Street *habitué* **Dr Samuel Johnson** and his Scottish biographer, advocate **James Boswell**. Lodging by **Inner Temple Gate**, in *Dr Sam: Johnson, Detector* (1946), Dr Sam casts his short-sighted gaze over London's villainy as he and Boswell track down 'The Flying Highwayman' terrorizing North London, hunt ghosts in a **Fenchurch Street** churchyard and brave scary shadows in the Wax-Works (based on Mrs Salmon's famous eighteenth-century wax works) in a narrow house next to the early Gothic revival **St Dunstan in the West** on Fleet Street. With wooden street-signs creaking ominously on their irons, the two detectives pass the stone arch of Wren's **Temple Bar** spanning Fleet Street, with the 'shapeless black lumps' of the heads of Jacobite rebels 'affixed on poles above it' (these were the last traitor's heads to be displayed on Temple Bar).

The **Edgar Wallace*** **Pub** at 40 Essex Street – one of the meeting places of the Edgar Wallace Society – close to Fleet Street, where the prolific author plied his trade, and **Ludgate Circus**, where Wallace first sold newspapers aged eleven, and which has a memorial tablet to him on its north-west side.

Based in a cellar below another cellar somewhere off Fleet Street, *The Club of Queer Trades* (1905) was the intriguing creation of **G K Chesterton*** – a collection of interlinked short stories, in which detection is all about proving that no crime has actually been committed. Former judge and Holmesian sleuth Basil Grant's 'genuine romantic interest in the life of London' enables him to penetrate the myth of a club whose members have each invented a unique way of earning a living. Following the course of the **River Fleet**, rising at Hampstead Heath, flowing under today's **Farringdon Road** and into the Thames at Blackfriars Bridge, Chesterton's old school friend **E C Bentley** (1875–1956) thought up the plot for *Trent's Last Case* (1913) walking between his Hampstead home and the offices of the *Daily News*. Intended as 'an exposure of detective stories' featuring a fallible Fleet Street hero, *Trent's Last Case* deservedly ended up as one of the most famous detective stories of all time.

In *Wild Justice* (1987), former *Guardian* journalist **Lesley Grant-Adamson*** evokes life in a bustling newspaper office and outlines the reality of Fleet Street in the 1980s: tycoons vying to buy newspapers lock, stock and barrel – influencing editorial, dumbing down and starting the exodus to Wapping. Celebrity gossip columnist and amateur detective Rain Morgan investigates the all-too literal back-stabbing of the unpopular new proprietor of the '*Daily Post*' – who has his last meal in the wedge-shaped **Black Friar** (**174 Queen Victoria Street**): 'one of London's unlikelier pubs, an *art nouveau* collision between the ecclesiastical and the most secular'.

El Vino wine bar, a veritable institution with journalists and lawyers, and an old favourite of **G K Chesterton**'s*. For many years unaccompanied women were not served at the bar, until a successful legal challenge brought in change – ushering in the custom of **Natasha Cooper**'s* female detectives, amongst others.

The **Old Bailey Central Criminal Court**, which opened in 1907 on the site of the notorious Newgate prison, is the symbol of Britain's criminal justice system.

'Defend the children of the poor & punish the wrongdoer' – the inscription above the imposing entrance to the copper-domed **Old Bailey** leaves no doubt that **LEGAL LONDON** means business. Numerous dramas, both real and fictional, have been played out within the intimidating grandeur of London's Central Criminal Court, where **John Mortimer**'s (1923–) *Rumpole of the Bailey* commands centre stage. In **Cyril Hare**'s (pseud. Alexander Gordon Clark, 1900–1958) unorthodox masterpiece, *Tragedy at Law* (1942), a judge gets involved in a drink-driving incident and is later knifed outside the Old Bailey, a place whose 'synthetic atmosphere' he'd never liked anyway. In their own inimitable style, ageing and unsuccessful lawyer Francis Pettigrew and Inspector Mallett step in to investigate.

Off-stage from the daily drama of the Old Bailey and Fleet Street's **Royal Courts of Justice**, the elegant courts and hushed gardens of the **Inns of Court** spread gracefully between the **Embankment** and **Clerkenwell Road**. Deep within this oasis of calm, forensic medic Dr John Evelyn Thorndyke sets about solving crime in his laboratory on the third floor of a (fictional) seventeenth-century building at **5A King's Bench Walk, Inner Temple**. Created by London-born **R(ichard) Austin Freeman** (1862–1943), who reputedly carried out all his detective's experiments himself, the impassive Thorndyke first appears in *The Red Thumbmark* (1907). When a haul of diamonds is stolen from a safe, a blood-stained thumbprint nearby appears to make it an open-and-shut case – until Thorndyke gets his scientific mind and apparatus into gear. 'You never know…,' says Thorndyke, as he goes quietly about his business in the short stories of *The Singing Bone* (1912) (US: *The Adventures of*

Temple Church – modelled on the Holy Sepulchre in Jerusalem, the former Templar church was taken over by the legal profession in the fourteenth century and hugely restored after the 1941 Blitz. Reputedly haunted by the ghost of a lawyer unwilling to leave, the church features in **P D James'*** *A Certain Justice* (1997) as Adam Dalgliesh hunts the killer of a successful female barrister.

'They aren't fields as such, of course. Fields are big green things which wave in the wind and live beyond the M25 motorway and are eligible for European Community subsidies. **Lincoln's Inn Fields** is really a big lawn with a crisscross path and iron railings round the perimeter' –

Mike Ripley, *Angel City*

Dr Thorndyke), in which Freeman conjures the 'inverted' detective story: the reader knows from the outset who commits the crime, whilst the detective has to follow clues to the guilty party. The Inner Temple also holds the fictitious chambers of eminent if choleric ('Marshal your facts, boy, marshal your facts') Sir Nicholas Harding QC and his nephew and junior partner Antony Maitland. Paving the way for **Sara Woods**' (pseud. Sara Hutton Bowen-Judd, 1922–85) long-running series of legal procedurals, *Bloody Instructions* (1962) involves the stabbing of an elderly partner in an established solicitors' firm near the Inner Temple. Maitland was enjoying a cup of tea and slab of fruitcake at the time, but this risk-taking, rhetorically brilliant barrister with the calmly insistent grey gaze and expression of permanent amusement suddenly finds himself to be both principal witness and potential suspect.

Solicitor **Michael Gilbert***, who drafted **Raymond Chandler**'s (1888–1959) will, worked from an office in the seventeenth-century **New Square, Lincoln's Inn**. His masterpiece, the satirical legal mystery *Smallbone Deceased* (1950), evokes the atmosphere of the old-fashioned offices here as Chief Inspector Hazelrigg investigates the case of a client found dead in one of the hermetically sealed deed-boxes. In *The Shortest Way to Hades* (1984), **Sarah Caudwell**'s (pseud. Sarah Cockburn, 1939–2000) characters move inside a 'dark, old-fashioned office, its walls lined with Law Reports and Encyclopaedias of Conveyancing Precedents; the window looking out on the green rectangle of Lincoln's

Inn Fields' and often need to be rescued from trouble by larger-than-life law professor Hilary Tamar. The prevailing atmosphere of witty banter, sexual innuendo and hilarious exaggeration makes Legal London sound a fun place to be – especially for those clutching an Oxford degree.

Fitzroy Angel is by now used to no-questions-asked delivery jobs around some of the poorer parts of London, but nothing has prepared **Mike Ripley**'s* comic hero for the cynical cheek-by-jowl of dignity and deprivation he witnesses at **Lincoln's Inn Fields** in *Angel City* (1994). The homeless community, 'where some of the tent dwellers had been there so long they received Reader's Digest mail shots', emerges in the evening to scavenge for leftovers, oblivious to the bemused stares of tourists looking for The Old Curiosity Shop. 'Angel is an amateur compared to these kids,' says Ripley. 'I wanted to show how hard the city was to these people.' The squatters have since been moved on, returning the Fields to their former graceful, vacant state.

Tucked away behind Lincoln's Inn and **Chancery Lane**, the fourth floor of a building in **Cursitor Street** is the base for **Peter Cheyney**'s (1896–1951) hard-worn, droll private investigator Slim 'Spike' Callaghan, who works London's clubs and ganglands. Former private detective Cheyney also created hardboiled New Yorker Lemmy Caution, and there is more than a touch of the mean streets of America in his Callaghan series. 'We get there somehow – and who the hell cares how?' is the motto that Slim repeats to himself as he wanders the streets of **Holborn**, worrying where the rent for the office is going to come from and what his Fleet Street contacts are up to. In *The Urgent Hangman* (1938), Slim is approached by a woman looking like she could match his hundred-a-day habit, who says she is afraid of being framed for a murder not yet committed. But is she just another 'skirt' trying to pull a fast one? A rich old man's body lying dead against the railings on the south side of Lincoln's Inn Fields seems to answer that question:

> For a few seconds he saw London objectively! Saw it as a place mainly consisting of two parts – a very thin upper crust and a damn thick lower one. The upper crust was the veneer of respectability, 'niceness', cleanliness, which London showed the world; the lower crust – the thick one – all the rottenness, cheap crookery and general lousiness that existed in that jungle in the heart of the metropolis whose boundaries are known to every intelligent police officer. He smiled to himself as he thought how little the majority of Londoners knew about London.

Seated in a quiet corner of the fictional 'ABC Teashop' on 'Norfolk Street' off the **Strand**, rheumy-eyed, birdlike Bill Owen is the old man of **Baroness Orczy**'s* (1865–1947) *The Old Man in the Corner* (1909) (US: *The Man in the Corner*). Listening to one of the very first 'armchair detectives' present the solutions to baffling mysteries from London's dark

Built in 1881 and closed in 1992, **Bow Street Police Station** provided the headquarters for London's first police force, the Bow Street Runners.

and distant corners is Polly Burton – a young reporter with a 'leading halfpenny-worth'. Hungarian-born Orczy was the author of *The Scarlet Pimpernel* (1905), and in the old man created another enigmatic character, who feeds on cheesecake and milk and lays out a range of snapshots to illustrate his cases, all the time knotting and un-knotting bits of string with his strong, bony fingers. In silent awe, Polly is treated to the full works of a robbery in **Kensington**, a murder in **Regent's Park**, a mysterious death on London's oldest underground line (Metropolitan) and the story behind a body found on a disused barge in the **East End**.

The **Bow** district on the fringes of the teeming tourist-magnet of **Covent Garden** is linked to the rise of detection both real and fictional. This was where the Bow Street Runners, the first 'detectives' in the modern sense, were founded by the Fielding brothers. The anonymously published *Richmond, or Scenes from the Life of a Bow Street Runner* (1827) provides one of the earliest fictional accounts of police detection. Another Bow-based novel made a similar impact: *The Big Bow Mystery* (1892) by London-born **Israel Zangwill** (1864–1926) is the first known 'locked room' mystery. In *Blind Justice* (1994), the first of **Bruce Alexander**'s intriguing series, vivid descriptions of Georgian London enfold the mystery of a dead nobleman in a locked room. Thirteen-year-old orphan narrator Jeremy Proctor turns detective with the assistance of the benevolent Bow Street Magistrate Sir John Fielding, the 'Blind Beak', whom Jeremy faces when he is falsely accused of theft and brought before the Bow Street Police Court next door (where the Magistrates Court still operates today). The legendary 'Blind Beak' also features in the Georgian mysteries of **Deryn Lake***.

From Bow Street, a walk down to Waterloo Bridge and the **Victoria Embankment** leads to the famous turreted 'streaky-bacon' red and white brickwork of the former **New Scotland Yard**. From 1890 onwards, detectives were looking out across the busy waters of the Thames, down to **Big Ben** and over the trees of **St James's Park**. In 1967 New Scotland Yard made the short journey to its modern, utilitarian twenty-storey headquarters on **Victoria Street**. The innermost workings of the Yard seldom form part of detective fiction, which focuses more on the legendary prowess of its practitioners of law enforcement. However, using the Yard's fictional storage place for the detritus of unsolved cases – weapons, clothing, toys etc. found near the scene of the crime – **Roy Vickers** (?1888–1965) created the innovative *Department of Dead Ends* (1949). These powerful short stories provide the victims of crime with a belated opportunity for justice, and establish blind chance rather than scientific detection as the means of its delivery.

One of the most prolific writers of the twentieth century, **John Creasey** (pseud. William Vivian Butler, 1908–73) always sympathized with the figure of Claude Eustace Teal, the hapless Scotland Yard Inspector constantly outwitted by **Leslie Charteris**' (1907–93) 'The Saint'. Although he went on to create his own Saintly caricature in 'The

Toff' (the Hon. Richard Rollison), Creasey's reputation lies largely in the resounding authenticity of his police procedurals. Writing under twenty-two pseudonyms, Creasey (whose name attaches to the CWA's annual award for best crime fiction debut) produced some 560 full-length novels in forty years. As **J J Marric** he created Commander George Gideon, whose long and impressive career takes him around the gleaming façades, glossy offices and high-rise warrens of the **Square Mile** and out into the teeming, crime-packed streets of the metropolis. A 'massive, slow-moving, pale man with a quiet voice and unassuming, almost modest manner', Gideon first appears in *Gideon's Day* (1955) (US: *Gideon of Scotland Yard*), where he sets out his attachment to his surroundings:

Baroness Orczy's* *Lady Molly of Scotland Yard* (1910) provides one of the first female (and mildly feminist) detectives, with Lady Molly heading the 'Female Department of the Yard' and assisted by her maid to clear her husband's name.

'I am Inspector Bucket from the Yard, I am' – the former **New Scotland Yard** saw a wealth of illustrious detectives pass through its hallowed doors in the footsteps of **Charles Dickens'*** Victorian detective in *Bleak House* (1852).

'What's on your mind, Chief Inspector?'

'There's always the same thing on my mind,' Roger said. 'A need for facts – a thirst for facts. At Scotland Yard we live by them, can build cases on them, can hang men on them… Like all of us at the Yard, I'm interested in getting justice for the living and the dead…'

John Creasey, *A Beauty for Inspector West* (1954)

It was a crisp morning in April, no rain was about, the look of spring was upon London and the feel of spring was in Londoners. In a vague sort of way, Gideon knew that he loved London and, after a fashion, loved Londoners. It wasn't just sentiment; he belonged to the hard pavements, the smell of petrol and oil, the rumble and the growl of traffic and the unending sound of footsteps, as some men belonged to the country. They could be said to love the soil. The only time that Gideon was really uneasy was when he had a job to handle outside London or one of the big cities. The country hadn't the same feel; he felt that it could cheat him, without him knowing it, whereas here in London the odds were always even... Very few people disliked Gideon, even among those he put inside. That was one of the reassuring things, and it put the seal to his oneness with London.

Also operating out of Scotland Yard, Inspector Roger West is another of Creasey's enduring series characters. A solid, experienced and highly respected detective, West lives happily with his family in **Chelsea**. The adept delivery of an improbable plot in *A Beauty for Inspector West* (1954) is trademark Creasey: as the winners of a soap company's beauty competition are murdered one by one, Chief Inspector West has his hands full with an ambitious subordinate out to make a name for himself. From a dark and dangerous South London common to a shootout on a Chelsea church roof, the tension is palpable, and never more so than between the duelling Scotland Yard detectives. Stoical to the last, West always seems to be one step behind the killer, until the investigation reaches its climax in London's moonlit streets.

That **Dorothy L Sayers*** should have lived and worked in the pleasant squares of **BLOOMSBURY**, home of the British Museum and London literati, seems wholly appropriate. Having lived at **44 Mecklenburgh**

Mecklenburgh Square, WC1 – where Bloomsbury residents can relax in neatly manicured surroundings behind locked gates. The former home of **D L Sayers** can be seen to the rear left, marked by a plaque on the front wall.

Square and later in a flat on the first and second floors at **24 Great James Street**, Sayers adapted her surroundings in *Strong Poison* (1930), as Lord Peter Wimsey tackles a murder investigation in which detective novelist and Bloomsbury resident Harriet Vane stands accused. *Murder Must Advertise* (1933) focuses on Sayers' background in advertising as Wimsey goes undercover as copywriter Mr Death Bredon in 'Pym's Publicity' on **Southampton Row**, where his predecessor has been killed in a fall down an iron staircase. For this undisputed classic, Sayers was able to draw on a decade of copywriting for one of London's largest agencies, **Benson's** on **75 Kingsway**, and even satirizes herself as sardonic copywriter Miss Meteyard. **David Williams*** also remembers treading the infamous staircase during his time in advertising, and places his banker sleuth Mark Treasure here in *Advertise for Treasure* (1984).

Bloomsbury Street held the office of Arthur Crook, **Anthony Gilbert**'s (pseud. Lucie Beatrice Malleson, 1899–1973) cunning, roguish sleuth, whose theory of the 'Invisible Witness' holds that no amateur murderer can exclude a chance witness to the crime. Crook also employs a taciturn ex-crook handicapped by a bullet in the leg – 'set a crook to catch a crook' – and in *Is She Dead Too?* (1955) (US: *A Question of Murder*) sets out to find a housekeeper with dangerous evidence in her possession. In *Murder's a Waiting Game* (1972), Gilbert's stock-in-trade damsel in distress has been cleared of murdering her husband, but now, ten years later, faces blackmail.

'To work in A14 is to see everything that no one ever sees: the violence, misery and despair, the immeasurable distance in the mind of a human being that knows nothing but suffering between its dreams and its death,' wrote **Derek Raymond** (pseud. Robin Cook, 1931–94) in his desperate story of a murdered prostitute, *I was Dora Suarez* (1990). Raymond's 'black' novels focus on an unnamed Detective Sergeant working in the fictional 'Department A14–Unexplained Deaths' of a **SOHO** 'factory' (police station) in **Poland Street**, just off London's busy shopping highway of **Oxford Street**. Born into an upper-class Bloomsbury family, Raymond effected an unusual transition from Eton schoolboy to Soho scoundrel, fronting gambling operations for London gangs and lunching with villains. In his autobiography, *The Hidden Files* (1992), Raymond describes how working the night shift as a London mini-cab driver drew him closer to his destination as a writer:

> Whether I liked it or not I became a minute tooth in a minute cog of the gear train, the way London works, and lives when it isn't working. It took me to parts of the city – with its inhabitants on board – that I previously hardly even knew existed, though I thought I knew the place like the back of my hand… I could never have written the Factory series (the term Factory, by the way, is both the police and villains' word for any police station) if I hadn't done this work…

Close to the **Soho** factory of **Derek Raymond**'s nightmarish vision – the neon-lit streets of London's sex empire.

Crime writer and broadcaster **Simon Brett**'s* hilarious romps featuring actor-detective Charles Paris run the gamut of fictional London theatres, where Paris can often be found observing murderous clashes of egos centre-stage from his corner of the rehearsal room.

London-based actor **Simon Shaw** is the author of a comic crime series featuring vain, arrogant, witty and murderous Philip Fletcher. Working his way around irate directors and bitching troupes, luckless Inspector Higginbottom trails Fletcher around **Theatreland**, only to be foiled by the actor's last-minute skills of disguise.

Trawling the depths of London's dingiest and dirtiest streets, *He Died with his Eyes Open* (1984) establishes the pattern of the detective becoming totally absorbed in the life, and grisly death, of the victim. Highly critical of what he saw as 'middle-class' crime fiction reducing 'the stark horror of unnatural death, and the equally stark social reasons for it, to the level of an industrialized version of hide and seek', Raymond forged his unique series in an urban landscape of real and metaphysical despair and disillusion, playing with literary conventions to forge visceral stories looking for morality in the unlikeliest surroundings of Soho and an amoral London.

Under London's bright lights, most of the violence and drama of the **WEST END** and **Theatreland** thankfully takes place on stage. An experienced theatre producer, **Ngaio Marsh*** (1895–1982) found her second home in the theatres of London thousands of miles away from the dramatic unspoilt beauty of her native New Zealand. England

St Martin's Theatre, West Street, Covent Garden, current home of **Agatha Christie**'s *The Mousetrap* (1952), which has now been running for half a century and is the longest-running play in the world. Christie's own favourite play was *Witness for the Prosecution* (1953).

provides the social milieus and characters of her detective fiction, which demonstrates Marsh's theatrical flair for scene-setting and laying out of clues. Tall, handsome 'Chief Inspector Detection' Roderick Alleyn (named after Elizabethan actor Edward Alleyn) steps into the world of theatre for the first time in Marsh's second mystery, *Enter a Murderer* (1935), in which he witnesses the murder of an actor on the London stage.

Peregrine Jay, the playwright-director of the fictional 'Dolphin' Theatre near the **Thames Barrier** in **Woolwich**, has the misfortune to have his opening night marred by murder in *Death at the Dolphin* (1966) (US: *Killer Dolphin*). Peregrine and Alleyn return to the 'old Victorian Theatre beside the river' for a last night performance in Marsh's final novel, *Light Thickens* (1982). With rehearsals under way for 'the Scottish play' – **Shakespeare**'s (1564–1616) superstition-laden *Macbeth* – the cast has to cope with a series of practical jokes and worsening personality clashes. Inevitably, disaster strikes, and Macbeth loses his head. In a novel brimful of technical and theatrical detail, Alleyn works meticulously through clues, interviews and intuition, but needs the assistance of the youngest member of the cast to solve the mystery.

'You never feel a stranger in London because it's so familiar: you turn a corner and you see something you know, or have read about, or have seen in a film,' says **Marian Babson**. Her ageing thespian detectives – Trixie Dolan, a 'hoofer' (B-Musical dancer), and *grand dame* Evangeline Sinclair, an old film legend – traipse around the bright lights and resplendent interiors of Theatreland in the forlorn hope of once more treading the boards. Trixie and Evangeline first appear in *Reel Murder* (1986), arriving in London for a film retrospective only to discover that people are being killed according to the film scripts. The redoubtable duo are never far away from murder and, deciding to stay on in London, are soon embroiled in further investigations in *Encore Murder* (1989)

'In the direct tradition of Elizabethan, Jacobean and Victorian audiences… the Old Vic, in those days, thrummed with a coarse, racy life that had no equivalent on the West End' – the carefully restored **Old Vic** on the corner of Waterloo Road and The Cut, and former home of the National Theatre, was a particular favourite of **Ngaio Marsh**'s. A student at the School of Speech and Drama from 1920, **Margery Allingham** was also often in the audience.

Marian Babson* outside one of her favourite theatre-bars and London's oldest pub theatre, **The King's Head**, in **Islington**'s **Upper Street**. In *Break a Leg, Darlings* (1995), former movie stars Trixie Dolan and Evangeline Sinclair roam around the pub theatre circuit looking for a willing playwright.

and *Even Yuppies Die* (1993). Babson began her career with *Cover-Up Story* (1971), featuring her early series sleuth Douglas Perkins. A London travel guide and co-owner of a **Villiers Street** PR company with 'some very dodgy clients', Douglas investigates in *Murder on Show* (1972) (US: *Murder at the Cat Show*), only to find himself playing second fiddle to a Siamese cat called Pandora. Many of Babson's detective novels feature cats, and *Nine Lives to Murder* (1994) is a typical blend of theatrical and feline mystery. 'They say that when a cat sees a place she likes, she wants to have kittens in it,' says Marian Babson. 'When I see one, I want to set a book in it.'

Just off **Regent Street**, west of Soho, **Kingly Street** is the location of 'Pryde's' small detective agency where **P D James**'* youthful detective Cordelia Gray cuts her investigative teeth. This is also where, in 1928,

Kingly Street, W1 – **P D James**' Cordelia Gray threads her way 'between the blocked pavement and the shining mass of cars and vans which packed the narrow street' to get to her third-floor office in Kingly Street, reached by negotiating a smelly staircase, dark green damp walls and linoleum-covered stairs in *An Unsuitable Job for a Woman* (1972).

The **London Eye** and **Big Ben** – the wheels of justice keep turning in London's diverse detective fiction.

Camden Tube Station – 'Camden is very vibrant, it's very young', says **Paul Charles**, whose Inspector Christy Kennedy operates in the area where **Ann Granger's** youthful Fran Varady experiences the ups and downs of city life.

the Detection Club first convened, only to be gently satirized in the classic *The Poisoned Chocolate Case* (1929) by its Honorary Secretary **Anthony Berkeley** (pseud. Anthony Berkley Cox, 1893–1971). Chief Inspector Moresby recounts a murder case to the assembled members of the Crimes Circle, who in turn produce alternative solutions, leaving conceited series sleuth Roger Sheringham red-faced.

Running westwards from Piccadilly Circus past Green Park and some of London's most prestigious quarters, **Piccadilly** was the residence of choice for **Dorothy L Sayers**'* Lord Peter Wimsey, whose home at '**110A**' **Piccadilly** is located on the site of today's Park Lane Hotel. A small cul-de-sac with a police station below it, **Vine Street** is the model for 'Bottle Street', where **Margery Allingham**'s* Albert Campion rents a flat at 17A. Originally the St James Parish Watch House, then taken over by the newly-formed Metropolitan Police, Vine Street was once one of the most famous police stations in central London but finally closed in 1997. In *Coroner's Pidgin* (1945) (US: *Pearls before Swine*), Campion returns from war service to witness his grumpy and melancholic manservant Magersfontain Lugg dragging a corpse up the stairs of 17A. The book includes memorable descriptions of the destruction London experienced during the Blitz and describes Campion's feelings towards this 'great city' that has already 'spread its ancient charm about him… he knew from the very smell of it that it was still safe, still firmly respectable, still obdurately matter of fact'.

Agatha Christie's* Hercule Poirot finds perfect symmetry in his second London base at 'Whitehaven Mansions', a newly built block of flats in **Mayfair**. 'But Bertram's Hotel had not changed. It was just as it had always been. Quite miraculously so, in Miss Marple's opinion' – things are just a little too perfect, however, for Miss Marple in the Edwardian surroundings of *At Bertram's Hotel* (1965), inspired by the old-fashioned luxury Christie experienced at Mayfair's **Brown's Hotel** (with entrances in Dover Street and Albemarle Street). Christie is at her quietly intriguing best in this mystery where Miss Marple's suspicions are aroused soon after her arrival in the congeniality of Bertram's Hotel. Beneath its 'dignified, unostentatious, and quietly expensive' charm, something is clearly rotten and while Miss Marple enjoys herself shopping for glass, china and household linen in London's department stores, Chief Inspector Davy follows a trail of clues that lead straight to the hotel doors. Christie also enjoyed **The Ritz** ('Blitz'), **Claridge's** ('Harridge's'), and **The Savoy**.

The rituals and trappings of **WESTMINSTER** and the **Houses of Parliament** are elusive to most, but for those who tread the historic corridors of power, they provide a ready source of material for some ingenious detective stories. Labour MP **Ellen Wilkinson** (1891–1947) – nicknamed 'Red Ellen', and not just for her hair colour – was the author of *The Division Bell Mystery* (1932). The murder in a **House of Commons'** committee room is committed with a revolver fixed up to

Just off Piccadilly, **2 Nassau Street** is home to apothecary and amateur sleuth John Rawlings, of **Deryn Lake's*** (pseud. Dinah Lampitt) atmospheric Georgian London mysteries. Based upon a real-life historical character living at the same address, Rawlings is introduced in *Death in the Dark Walk* (1994) and has his apothecary shop in nearby 'Shug Lane'.

Francis Selwyn (1935–) explores **Westminster** in his Victorian series featuring zealous Sergeant William Verity of Scotland Yard, who probes the seamy underbelly of the city without losing his own morals. From the outset in *Cracksman on Velvet* (1974), Verity's Westminster is seen to be awash with horse dung and soot, the sound of cursing, the rattling of coal wagons and the harsh clash of cartwheels on cobbles, all illuminated by the 'white glare of self-generating gas lamps' and 'the red flare of grease lamps'.

Brown's Hotel, the inspiration behind **Agatha Christie**'s 'Bertram's Hotel' and **Simon Brett**'s 'Greene's Hotel' in *Mrs Pargeter's Point of Honour* (1998).

fire at the sound of the division bell, calling MPs to the vote around 10pm. One-time research librarian at the House of Commons, **Stanley Hyland** (1914–) wrote two irreverent and stylish detective novels set around parliament and the civil service. In *Who Goes Hang?* (1958), a young MP, Hubert Bligh, organizes a committee of MPs to investigate a mummified corpse discovered during repairs to the famous bell chamber of **Big Ben**. In *Top Bloody Secret* (1969), the weighty ceremonial mace is transformed into a lethal weapon when a House of Commons servant is killed.

Former parliamentary reporter **Gillian Linscott** throws her enterprising suffragette sleuth Nell Bray into the thick of early twentieth-century political action at a time when British women still did not have the vote. Over the course of the series, Nell spends time in Holloway

Prison for throwing a half-brick through the window of **10 Downing Street**, rallies support speaking on **Trafalgar Square**, and, at a historic time, stands for Parliament in 1918. Linscott focuses her series around the Movement's offices on **Kingsway**, where, in *Dance On Blood* (1998), Nell is outvoted when she tries to convince her more militant suffragette colleagues that bombing the **Albert Memorial** and running an arson campaign might not be politically opportune. Her visit to 11 Downing Street to help the Chancellor of the Exchequer track down politically explosive letters that have already brought about one 'suicide' marks a new phase in Nell's struggle.

'Evenin' all!' – Labour Life Peer **Ted Willis** (1918–92) created TV's enduring image of the British bobby in (George) Dixon of Dock Green, but if there was a vote for best contemporary British crime writer, then each of the benches of the **House of Lords** would have a likely winner: **P D James** (Conservative) and **Ruth Rendell** (Labour). The Upper House is an ideal example of the 'English Establishmentland' targeted by Irish/British writer and commentator **Ruth Dudley Edwards*** through the jaundiced vision of her series sleuths: the larger-than-life Baroness Ida 'Jack' Troutbeck and the 'drifting observer' Robert Amiss. In *Ten Lords A-Leaping* (1995), Jack takes up her seat in the House of Lords in order to wreak her customary havoc and scupper an anti-hunting bill – until tensions escalate and a number of the noble Lords are found poisoned. Continuing to cast her well-trained satirical eye, Dudley Edwards has used a version of the Spectator building at **56 Doughty Street**, Bloomsbury, for *Publish and be Murdered* (1998), while **Pall Mall** is the focus of *Clubbed to Death* (1992), using 'an amalgam and distortion' of her own Liberal **Reform Club** together with the most famous nineteenth-century club, the beautifully frieze-rimmed **Athenaeum** on **Waterloo Place**.

Further west, amidst the wealth of tourist attractions around the **Regent's Park** area, busy **Baker Street** can boast the most famous address in detective fiction, thanks to **Arthur Conan Doyle*** (1859–1930). However, a little detection is certainly required to arrive at the right residence. Sherlock Holmes lived at '221B Baker Street', but during this period what is now Baker Street was only one third of the length of the present street, with only ninety-two houses in it. The present 221 Baker Street houses a building society that receives post from all over the world – requesting an autograph, or even asking Sherlock Holmes himself for help. Literary tourists can collect a Holmes postcard here, but in the great detective's day this address was in Upper Baker Street, as was the present 239 Baker Street, which now houses **The Sherlock Holmes Museum**. Research suggests that 221B was actually at what is now **31 Baker Street**, although the original Victorian building on that site was demolished many decades ago.

'It is a hobby of mine to have an exact knowledge of London,' says Sherlock Holmes in 'The Red-Headed League' (1891). Conan Doyle's

St Stephen's Tower, housing the bells of **Big Ben**, a striking symbol of London all over the world.

'It was a cold morning of the early spring, and we sat after breakfast on either side of a cheery fire in the old room in Baker Street. A thick fog rolled down between the lines of dun-coloured houses, and the opposing windows loomed like dark, shapeless blurs, through the heavy yellow wreaths.'

Arthur Conan Doyle, 'The Copper Beeches' (1892)

Arthur Conan Doyle – created archetypal London settings in the Sherlock Holmes series.

Baker Street with the ubiquitous hansom cabs of the time.

early descriptions of London do, however, reveal the odd inaccuracy betraying the influence of his native Edinburgh and a reliance on maps rather than a close personal acquaintance with London. Nevertheless, the strong association between London and crime fiction is due in large part to Conan Doyle's skill in creating an atmosphere of capital possibilities: on a cold night, 'the breath of the passers-by blew out into smoke like so many pistol shots' ('The Blue Carbuncle', 1892); the 'opalescent London reek' ('The Abbey Grange', 1904); or the riverside's 'dense drizzly fog' ('The Sign of Four', 1890) In 'The Resident Patient' (1893), Watson makes it clear that the great detective feels most alive in the city:

Not far from Baker Street, a snug little flat in fictional 'Montague Mansions' is home to **Patricia Wentworth**'s (pseud. Dora Amy Elles, 1878–1961) governess turned private eye Miss Maud Silver. Oddly dressed and forever knitting baby clothes when she first appears in *Grey Mask* (1928), Miss Silver is a dogged detector, and every inch of table space in her home is taken up by framed photographs of former clients, from mysteries such as *The Brading Collection* (1950) and *The Fingerprint* (1956).

> A depleted bank account had caused me to postpone my holiday, and as to my companion, neither the country nor the sea presented the slightest attraction to him. He loved to lie in the very centre of five millions of people, with his filaments stretching out and running through them, responsive to every little rumour or suspicion of unsolved crime. Appreciation of Nature found no place among his many gifts, and his only change was when he turned his mind from the evil-doer of the town to track down his brother of the country.

Raffles, a gentleman burglar moving in upper-class London society, appears in *The Amateur Cracksman* (1899) by Conan Doyle's brother-in-law **E W Hornung** (1866–1921) – an enduring character that Conan Doyle referred to as 'a kind of inversion of Sherlock Holmes'.

OUTER LONDON

I felt that London was already too large and loose a thing
to be a city in the sense of a citadel...

G K Chesterton, *Autobiography* (1936)

Despite its continual seizure and assimilation of the suburbs and environs, London remains a collection of villages and communities, many of which still retain their distinctive feel and cultural identity. Just as British fiction as a whole is becoming more regionalized, so writers of today's London detective fiction feel more confident in the far-flung corners of the city – providing a contrast to homogenous London backdrops punctuated by tourist landmarks.

At first glance there does not seem to be much of a connection between **NORTH LONDON** and **Mike Phillips'** (1941–) Central/Eastern European novel *Shadow of Myself* (2000). But the book touches on a defining theme of twentieth-century experience that is as central to London's identity as to Phillips' life and work: migration. In the tightly thronged streets of **Harringay** where he first lived as a child, Phillips sees an 'archaeology of change'. Born in Guyana, Phillips moved into a primarily white, working-class area of London in the 1950s, but returned to Harringay some three decades later to discover the streets had 'mutated into a bazaar of cultures'. After graduating from university, Phillips found himself working next to a young Bernie Grant, later MP for Tottenham, whose often turbulent political career serves as the inspiration for the Silver Dagger-winning *The Late Candidate* (1990). The second novel in the journalist-detective Sam Dean series, this is a

'The wonderful thing about London is that it has the capacity to adapt that emerges from a diverse, multicultural, confident city' – **Mike Phillips** sets his crime fiction in the teeming diversity of **Harringay** and North London, seen here from **Alexandra Palace**.

'…its bulk and shape still possessed the power to impose' – **Alexandra Palace** is a highly symbolic North London landmark for both **Mike Phillips** and his detective Sam Dean.

'I've seen almost everything that I knew in London as a boy change' – **Mike Phillips**.

powerful story about political and social conflict, and survival in this 'beautiful and hard-faced city'. When Sam's childhood friend, local politician Aston Edwards, is found murdered, Sam agrees to write an article about his life. His research takes Sam around old haunts in some of the poorer and more intimidating parts of North London, but it is the murky waters of politics and the hostility of the local police that present the real threat.

A brooding presence of Old England looming over the cynical and manipulative media world setting of *An Image to Die For* (1995), **Alexandra Palace** is a highly symbolic landmark for Phillips: 'When I look at Alexandra Palace, what I see is the past… a past which is so inflexible, and so narrow, that it was slated for destruction, it couldn't survive in modern times.' Reluctantly drawn into the television charade of a supposed miscarriage of justice, Sam Dean unwittingly enters a very real murder case, drawing him into the dangerous and erotic heart of an investigation tinged with despair and touched by madness.

'I have a great affection for Patrick Petrella. My own youth as a writer and his youth as a policeman started together on the northern heights of London.' The career of erudite and enquiring Patrick Petrella, created by Diamond Dagger-recipient **Michael Gilbert*** (1912–), begins as a Detective Constable with the Metropolitan Police's fictional North London 'Q Division'. Incorporating landmarks such as (variations on) **Highgate Cemetery** and **Hampstead Heath**, the 'honeycomb of tight, respectable streets' comprising Petrella's beat hides a varied universe of crime and delinquency described in crisply written, nostalgically elegant novels and short story collections such as *Young Petrella* (1988). Petrella grows in both stature and authority as the series progresses, but remains suspicious of the processes of law so familiar to London solicitor Gilbert.

The 'controlled lunacy' of **Camden High Street** is the perfect patch for **Ann Granger**'s* irrepressible, impecunious young detective Fran Varady. The simple act of offering an old tramp a cup of coffee in *Keeping Bad Company* (1997) leads Fran into a murder inquiry, and to the unwanted attention of her old adversary Sergeant Parry. From the 'resolutely downmarket' pubs in an 'unreconstructed bit of Old London Town' to the shadowy towpath and unhealthy waters of the **Grand Union Canal**, Fran effortlessly immerses herself in deep trouble.

'**Camden** is very vibrant, it's very young… but there's an old world there at the same time,' says **Paul Charles** (1949–), whose Detective Inspector Christy Kennedy series succeeds in capturing both the urban character and community feel of this distinctive part of London. Charles was lured to North London from his native Northern Ireland by the late 1960s music scene, and his beautifully crafted mysteries are infused with the fruits of thirty years spent as agent, manager and promoter in the music business. Quietly philosophical, tea-drinking, music-loving Kennedy lives at **16 Rothwell Street**, immediately next to the panoramic, grassy slopes of **Primrose Hill**, yet still within easy reach of the 'total buzz' of **Camden Town Market**, where he loves shopping for records and books.

'I walk my stories,' says **Paul Charles**. 'There are so many amazing locations around Camden, all within walking distance.'

Primrose Hill – a place for Detective Inspector Christy Kennedy to contemplate his cases and find solace with his lover ann rea [*sic*].

'The shape was illogical, and the entire building looked like it might collapse if hit by a solid gust of wind' – the distinctive blue exterior of the **Design Building** features in **Paul Charles'** *I Love the Sound of Breaking Glass*, with North Bridge House, fictional headquarters of Camden Town CID, visible to the rear.

Once a monastery and now a school, **North Bridge House**, on the busy **Parkway/Gloucester Avenue** interchange, holds the fictional headquarters of Kennedy's Camden Town CID. On the opposite side of the junction stands the distinctive blue **Design Building**, home to the troubled 'Camden Town Records' at the centre of *I Love the Sound of Breaking Glass* (1997). In this warts-and-all history and mystery of the music industry, Charles weaves an ingenious tale of chart-rigging, blackmail and murder, of ruthless ambition and shattered dreams. In part, it is also a touching and funny love story between Kennedy and journalist ann rea [*sic*]. All the Kennedy books have a strong sense of place bounded by unique local landmarks. *Fountain of Sorrow* (1998) has a scene of the crime behind a fountain on the bridge between **Prince Albert Road** and **Gloucester Gate**, and **Dingwall's**, scene of the emergence of punk in the 1970s, features in *The Ballad of Sean and Wilko* (2000). Cases solved, Kennedy returns to his office for a quiet drink: 'Time for tea, I think.'

A short run down the train line from Camden to the 'grumbling and unsettled' air of the **Euston Road**, a surreal note is added to a mystery set amidst the flamboyant Victorian Gothic architecture of **St Pancras Chambers** fronting **St Pancras Station**. In *The Long Dark Tea-Time of the Soul* (1988), **Douglas Adams*** somehow conjures a gateway to Valhalla, home of the ancient Norse gods, from this magnificent building, formerly the Midland Grand Hotel. As far from a conventional detective story as could be expected from the creator of *The Hitchhiker's Guide to the Galaxy* (1979), this is an improbable and allegorical investigative romp laced with sharp social observation, bizarre humour and eye-wateringly funny dialogue. Emerging from the bachelor squalor of his **Islington** flat in search of a fee to break his seemingly permanent state of poverty, Dirk Gently's trademark tardiness results in his only client's head being removed by a 'large, hairy, green-eyed monster armed with a scythe' and left revolving on a record deck. Adams conceived the idea of *Dirk Gently's Holistic Detective Agency* (1987) whilst living in Islington. Where Sherlock Holmes excluded the impossible because what remained had to be the truth, Gently, assessing a world moulded by chaos from his Islington office, heads straight for it. A year after Douglas Adams' untimely death, the draft fragment of *Salmon of Doubt* (2002), a final holistic detective adventure, was published.

The revolutions are equally bizarre in **Peter Lovesey's*** Victorian mystery *Wobble to Death* (1970). Moving 'more like sacrificial victims than gladiators striding into the arena', a motley assortment of contestants enters the vast arena of Islington's **Royal Agricultural Hall** in 1879 to compete in an indoor pedestrian race. Introducing Sergeant Cribb and Constable Thackeray from Scotland Yard, Lovesey's debut novel is based on an actual indoor long-distance race lasting six days, in which contestants covered over 500 miles. In the intimidating atmosphere of the hall, passions are running high, and for some there is more at stake than the prestige of becoming Champion Pedestrian

AGRICULTURAL HALL ISLINGTON

WILL START AT 1 A.M.
MONDAY, JUNE 16th

FINISHING AT 10.30 P.M.
SATURDAY FOLLOWING.

INTERNATIONAL PEDESTRIAN MATCH

COMPETITORS

CHARLES ROWELL
(HOLDER OF THE BELT)
CHAMPION OF THE WORLD

JOHN ENNIS.
(CHALLENGER)
CHAMPION OF AMERICA

BLOWER BROWN
(CHAMPION OF ENGLAND)

DICK HARDING.
(THE JOLLY YOUNG WATERMAN)

E. P. WESTON.
THE EDITOR
OF THE
SPORTING LIFE
HOLDS THE STAKES & WILL
OFFICIATE AS REFEREE.

CONDITIONS

THE ONE WHO
GOES FARTHEST
IN THE
SIX DAYS
WILL WIN
BELT & £500.
BESIDES
HALF THE GATE RECEIPTS

THE BELT:
THE GIFT OF SIR J.L.ASHLEY BART.
WAS FIRST WON BY O'LEARY
AGRICULTURAL HALL LONDON,
MARCH, 1878.
AND ROWELL BEAT O'LEARY
NEW YORK, APRIL, 1879.
& BROUGHT THE BELT BACK TO ENGLAND
IT REMAINS TO BE SEEN WHETHER
ENNIS
CAN BEAT OUR MEN

CHAMPIONSHIP OF THE WORLD.

ADMISSION 1/-   A FAIR FIELD AND NO FAVOUR. THE BEST MAN TO WIN.   FULL MILITARY BAND.

of the World. Quick-witted Sergeant Cribb has to think on his feet to get to the bottom of the real motives for murder in this cleverly plotted, lovingly recreated and well-paced detective mystery. Outside the hall, Lovesey leads us round the wintry, lamplit streets of Islington and **Finsbury**, and through a maze of Victorian morality as Cribb moves slowly but surely towards the apprehension of a less than gentlemanly killer. Taking delight in 'pricking the hypocrisy' of the times, sports enthusiast Lovesey moves on to boxing in *The Detective Wore Silk Drawers* (1971), and in later books tackles distinctive aspects and themes of the Victorian era, when 'many motives [for murder] that are gone now' still possessed a lethal relevance.

Lesley Grant-Adamson* was born in **Finsbury Park**, and bases her Irish private eye Laura Flynn at the Highbury end of Islington. Grant-Adamson returned to live in Islington through the 1980s and 1990s, sharing a flat with her detective at **30 Bewdley Street**, **Barnsbury**. During this time the area around the **Angel** tube where Grant-Adamson had attended school was transformed 'from being rundown tenanted buildings to some of the prettiest and most expensive small houses in London'. Laura herself gets off to a flying start in *Flynn* (1991) (US: *Too Many Questions*) by getting embroiled in a multiple mugging on a tube train and hired for a new job by a Dublin fashion designer who is then pulled dead from the Thames. To complicate matters further, Laura also has to track down her own father. Skilfully weaving together the strands of the story, Grant-Adamson explores different corners of Islington's Irish community and Laura's 'tribe': old Irish families, a priest, an old friend who's 'made it' by the Grand Union Canal, as well as the building trade and the quirky shops that make London N1 so fashionable. Laura returns in *Dead Men's Lies* (2003).

Among Islington's many interesting shops, 'Dido Hoare – Antiquarian Books and Prints', with its smart brown sign and gold

' "There's your field, then," one reporter observed. "Care to wager on the ones that finish the week in coffins?" ' – Victorian endurance racers trying not to *Wobble to Death* in **Peter Lovesey**'s crime debut.

'Until the Big Storm the Big Trees had obscured it, but now I had my own personal version of Big Ben' – looking out of her office window at the **Union Church Tower** clock in Islington's Upper Street, **Lesley Grant-Adamson**'s private eye Laura Flynn can see when it's time for action.

Home to a women's prison, **Holloway** also harbours the run-down warehouse where sexy, stroppy sculptress Sam Jones tries to concentrate on her commissions when her creator, Hampstead-born **Lauren Henderson** (1966–), is not dragging her into murder investigations. In her first sizzling 'tart noir' mystery, *Dead White Female* (1996), Sam investigates the suspicious death of her art tutor. In *Freeze My Margarita* (1998), Sam gets involved in the offstage drama surrounding a production of *A Midsummer Night's Dream* in a **Belsize Park** church hall theatre.

Highbury Crescent, near the 'green lung' of **Highbury Fields** – close to the home of Frances Fyfield's Helen West, and territory of enigmatic free spirit Sarah Fortune, who steers Fyfield's writing in a different, but equally powerful, direction.

lettering and 'shadowy shelves of buckram and leather bindings', is run by **Marianne Macdonald**'s (1934–) amateur sleuth Dido. Located in fictional 'George Street' (just north of **Cross Street**), the shop is within earshot of the bells of **St Mary's** in **Upper Street** and also close to Canadian-born MacDonald's own home in **Muswell Hill**. In *Death's Autograph* (1996), Dido is attacked while on the road in search of book collections to sustain the shop that was a wedding present from her father. When her shady ex-husband Davey reappears on the scene, Dido senses trouble. Then her father receives a threatening letter, her bookshop is burgled and Dido knows she needs help. Ably assisted by the comforting police presence of Detective Inspector Paul Grant, Dido confronts her adversaries in a mystery liberally sprinkled with anecdotes and snippets about the book business. The fourth book in the series, *Road Kill* (2000) finds single mum Dido investigating the death of her nanny's accountant husband – was he cooking the books for someone? When Dido's car is burnt out and her shop is nearly torched, her troubles have only just begun.

One of Britain's foremost writers of literary crime fiction, **Frances Fyfield*** (pseud. Frances Hegarty, 1948–) intertwines the forces of free-thinking, volatile Crown Prosecutor Helen West, whose scarred beauty and soft heart attract criminality like a magnet, with the more rigid and pragmatic Detective Superintendent Geoffrey Bailey. In her London settings Fyfield contrasts 'interiors with exteriors, so that the streets and

the landmarks form a foil to the inside of the houses or institutions, which vary as much as the landscape, from rich, to poor, shambolic to organised, tasteful and old to new and not always hopeful…' Give or take a few topographical liberties, Helen West lives in the basement flat Fyfield herself once occupied in **Highbury**, 'within hearing distance of Arsenal football ground', while 'Islington, as home, is probably the place which inspired most in the beginning. Gloomy Angel Station, as was, the long, long corridors of Highbury Station, the North London line, with its stations which look as if Armageddon is here.' When it is her turn to cook, West heads to Islington to eat out with Bailey, while her clientele is drawn from less salubrious **Hackney**, **Dalston** and **Holloway**. Sex, relationships and gender roles form a fundamental part of Fyfield's fiction, epitomized by *Shadow Play* (1993), a heartrending, chilling story of violence, abuse and sexual possessiveness. *Without Consent* (1996) brings the theme close to home when Bailey's sidekick and serial philanderer DS Ryan is accused of rape. As the investigations move from the Crown Prosecution Service offices out to **Clerkenwell** and **King's Cross**, the urban landscapes reflect the tensions and tragedies of a gripping drama.

'I'm colossally influenced by places, but never tied by the details' – **Frances Fyfield**.

Bailey is comfortable on the London streets he has known since childhood, and covers a broad patch all the way out to **East Ham**. In the Silver Dagger-winning *Deep Sleep* (1991), a disturbing tale of drugs and delusion, Bailey and West are drawn into an East End 'enclave against the world'. Situated on Bailey's route 'between Whitechapel and Bethnal Green through the concrete and redbrick jungle where the remnants of old squares, invisible to traffic, formed the only saving graces of the area in summer', the archetypal East End street of 'Herringbone Parade' turns into the scene of a callous crime:

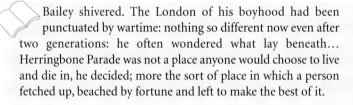

> Bailey shivered. The London of his boyhood had been punctuated by wartime: nothing so different now even after two generations: he often wondered what lay beneath… Herringbone Parade was not a place anyone would choose to live and die in, he decided; more the sort of place in which a person fetched up, beached by fortune and left to make the best of it.

Writing comedy is a serious business and finding settings for detective fiction can be no joke. But when **Mike Ripley*** (1952–) first placed his endearingly laddish detective Fitzroy Maclean Angel in a virtual **Hackney**, one of London's poorest boroughs, the reasoning was simple: 'Hackney, at the time, was a *joke*,' says Ripley. 'Nobody would go and live in the People's Republic of Hackney; it really was *the* naff address.' Apparently, Ripley had never set foot in Hackney until well into the series, when a friend more or less pushed him out of the car and abandoned him there. The rich green fields of the borough were once used as pasture for carriage horses, lending their name to the 'hackney' cabs that – unlike the fields – are still so much a feature of

Divine sign – Angel creator **Mike Ripley** at the tube station.

the capital. Driving a black cab 'as a way of being totally anonymous in London', Ripley's streetwise detective shines his headlights on the 1980s in the Last Laugh Dagger-winning *Angel Touch* (1989). In a London where 'greed was an absolute god' Angel finds insider dealing a lethal business, while the cut-throat world of the free market causes manifest alienation across London. Angel's arsenal of one-liners continues to complement his rules of engagement ('Always park the car at the point of fastest escape') in the manic *Lights, Camera, Angel* (2001). When Angel drives a male film star through a Millennium-crazed capital, the fireworks are just waiting to begin. Angel's new 'baby-sitting' job quickly shunts him from the three-dimensional reality of Hackney to the dangerous and unpredictable fakedom of the movie world.

Combining London street politics with Chandleresque style, **Gillian Slovo** (1952–) swathes her fast-paced detective novels in the drab grey hues of a disaffected Hackney. A far cry from the vast skies, bright light and vivid colours of her native South Africa, Slovo was living in run-down **Dalston** when she created Kate Baeier. Roaming both real and fictional Hackney landscapes, Baeier is a Portuguese freelance journalist turned PI who returns to London to cat-sit for a friend in *Catnap* (1985). What starts with a mugging the minute she sets foot in Dalston soon becomes a full-scale nightmare for Kate, in a landscape devoid of welcome: 'My eyes went down. Dalston, like nature, abhorred a vacuum – every hole and crevice was filled with newspapers, sweet wrappers, and other detritus. A gust of wind disturbed the mixture, and Hackney's version of autumnal leaves swirled round my feet.'

'Kate's both a foreigner and an insider, which in a way is a metaphor for the detective – someone who comes from outside and has to get in close' – **Gillian Slovo**, the creator of the East London-based Kate Baeier series.

The Richton estate was the kind of place most people try and avoid, even during daylight hours. A set of high-rise towers stranded between two busy roads and a once-designated green area that had been turned brown by neglect, it was a no-go area at night for police, social workers, most people on foot and any strangers. What had once been a dream of cheap housing for the general populace had turned into a nightmare for the underclass. A car park made to fill the sixties dream of universal car ownership was now a graveyard for burnt and battered vehicles. Jagged barbed wire cut one area off from the other, combining with the council's other attempt at safety measures – high, bright lights – to make the place look like a maximum-security prison.

Close Call

In *Close Call* (1996), Kate's investigations into the seemingly straightforward case of finding a missing policewoman take her deep amongst 'the jagged tangle of grimy rooftops backlit by the burnished red of a polluted Hackney sunset'. Kate wryly contrasts the line of battered **Homerton** shopfronts with the lush allure of 'bright and clean and optimistic' **Richmond**, which, however, hides a much older guilt.

EAST LONDON crime is touched by the sordid, high profile past of gangsters such as the Krays, and darkened by the long shadow of Jack the Ripper, legendary Victorian murderer of **East End** prostitutes, whose identity is hotly disputed to this day. Areas such as **Whitechapel** and **Spitalfields** might have been synonymous with poverty and immigration for centuries, but today live side by side with trendy quarters such as **Hoxton**.

A working-class writer with a strong social conscience, **Arthur Morrison** (1863–1945) rejected the Victorian ideal of a Holmesian 'Superman' detective in favour of solicitor's clerk-cum-sleuth Martin Hewitt. Gifted with a cheerful, round countenance, common sense and good eyesight, Hewitt is introduced in the short story collection *Martin Hewitt, Investigator* (1894) as the 'detective as ordinary man… embodied'. Firmly set in believable and characteristic London locales, and employing ingenious plots, the lyrical and moving Hewitt stories mark the beginning of an age of New Realism in detective fiction. Defining a social landscape of London slum life and death, Hewitt's exploration of **Bethnal Green** and **Stepney** in *Tales of Mean Streets* (1894) is disorientating: 'Where in the East End lies this street? Everywhere. The hundred-and-fifty yards is only a link in a long and a mightily tangled chain – is only a turn in a tortuous maze.'

'I wanted to try and convey in words what Gustave Doré does in engravings' – says **Anne Perry**. 'Dudley Street, Seven Dials' by Gustave Doré captures the appalling realities of life for the Victorian poor that are so much a feature of Perry's writing.

'The background to a story should be so vivid that you think you're there, but not so intrusive you're conscious of the author's voice saying: look how much research I've done' – **Anne Perry**, faithful chronicler of the inequalities and injustices of Victorian London.

Steeped in the soot and fog of late 1880s Victorian London, the best-selling mysteries of **Anne Perry*** (1938–) originate in the dark myth of Jack the Ripper. Born in the south-east of London, Perry used to listen to tales of the infamous murderer and frequently returns to the East End in her writing. Using an 1888 *London A to Z* to enable readers to trace her street geography, Perry also draws a well-defined moral landscape, exposing the flaws and hypocrisy of the times. Her detectives, Charlotte and Thomas Pitt, both possess a strong sense of social justice and are introduced in *The Cater Street Hangman* (1979), where Charlotte's access to upper-class drawing rooms proves invaluable to Thomas' inquiries. When the two are wed, it is not without reminders that Thomas has married above himself, and while his investigations often lead from **Bow Street Police Station** in **Covent Garden** out to the damp and dreary East End, Charlotte continues to prod gently but insistently into the dark recesses of Victorian high society.

Whitechapel, the City's poor relation on the main Essex road, was a notorious area of slums, crime and prostitution. In *The Whitechapel Conspiracy* (2001), Thomas makes enemies in high places after testifying in court against a high-ranking soldier and scholar who is subsequently hanged. Seconded to an undercover mission in Spitalfields to investigate revolutionary tension in the area, Thomas takes up a job at a silk factory. Meanwhile, Charlotte and her loyal Cockney maid Gracie put their own feelers out, and find clues to the hanged man's motives: a political conspiracy which could have far-reaching consequences.

> This was Whitechapel. Charlotte thought about what the name meant literally, and how ludicrous it was for this grimy, industrial area with its narrow streets, dust-grey, broken windows, dog-leg alleys, chimneys belching smoke, the smell of drains and middens. Its history of horror lay so close beneath the surface it was sharp and painful in the heart.

Perry's second Victorian London mystery series is set in the mid-1850s, after the end of the Crimean War, and features Inspector William Monk and nurse Hester Latterly, who first meet in *The Face of a Stranger* (1990). When ambitious, abrasive Monk awakens in hospital, he has no idea where – or who – he is. Hester, who has nursed alongside Florence Nightingale, possesses both the courage and the integrity to help Monk in his search for the truth. The search for a missing businessman in *Cain His Brother* (1995) leads Monk, now turned private investigator, towards the man's twin brother, a shadowy, dangerous figure living in the **Limehouse** slums bordering the Thames.

Operating further along the river at **Bermondsey** and **Canning Town**, one-legged PI Jimmy Jenner is the creation of TV screenwriter and ex-policeman **John Milne*** (1952–). An East Ender by birth, Jenner loses his leg in the line of duty with the Metropolitan Police but emerges in *Dead Birds* (1986), limping, but very much alive, and versed in the Sam

Bermondsey – a **Shad Thames** warehouse conversion symbolizing a landscape of nostalgia and disaffection in **John Milne**'s Jimmy Jenner series.

'We were deep in Shad Thames by now. The spice warehouses still had that dank, eastern pungency, though they'd stopped carrying spices thirty years ago. It's in the walls. In the mortar. Between the cobbles. I turned away… I breathed deep. I love that smell. My youth savoured of Courage breweries, fresh bread, bonded sherry under railway arches, malt vinegar in the vats on the Tower Bridge Road, spice on the docks in Shad Thames.'

John Milne, *Alive and Kicking*

Spade school of detection. The succession of betrayals, beatings, beautiful girls and cynical cops continues in *The Moody Man* (1988), as Jenner tries to keep track of an elusive colleague and ends up the prime suspect in a murder investigation. Milne's beautifully cadenced, caustic prose and stark stills of London life lead Jenner from the relative safety of his **Stoke Newington** home to the nostalgic but nightmarish *noir* of Spitalfields, where drunks reel in the frozen darkness and 'sudden flames of light' flare from market traders setting up for work.

'I usually avoid Bermondsey. It turns me maudlin. Sometimes I feel as if everything in my life started and ended in Bermondsey. I know it started there' – the complex, stylish and poignant *Alive and Kicking* (1998) takes Jenner back to childhood days playing on the Thames-side mud at Bermondsey, and to his dead brother's links with a South London gangster. From the opening scene of an attempted shooting outside a pub in **Mile End**, it is clear that Jenner's divorce case surveillance is going to land him in deep trouble. And when the going gets really tough, who better to lend a helping hand than his ex-wife, a serving police officer? With ghosts from the past lining the route through the **Blackwall Tunnel** towards the old warehouses and working

'Fed by a clear, sweet spring rising in Hoxton, just one of the many to be found in the marshes of Finsbury and Moor Fields, it had originally been known as the Perilous Pond because of its reputation for dangerous swimming conditions' – apothecary John Rawlings investigates an eighteenth-century leisure complex in **Deryn Lake**'s* *Death in the Peerless Pool* (1999). The real-life resort, with its clients from the 'counting houses and shops in the City', lay close to where **Peerless Street**, north of Old Street tube station, stands today.

docks on the south bank, there is a genuine yearning for lost London in Milne's romantic but unsentimental vision:

> I rode shivering across Tower Bridge in the hour before dawn. Below me the tarted-up southern bank glittered across the water, Bermondsey by moonlight. My Dad unloaded barges where there are restaurants now. My feet had trodden those pavements so much when I was a boy I felt as if there should be ruts, Jenner-ruts worn into the surface of the flags… Passing the darkened windows I wondered about the people behind them. God knows who lives in Bermondsey now. Everyone I knew has left or is dead. Everyone I knew is obliterated. In nineteen-seventy the docks closed and in nineteen-seventy-one Bermondsey closed.

When a cask is unloaded onto the busy **St Katharine's Docks** in **Freeman Wills Crofts**'* debut masterpiece *The Cask* (1920), a grisly find leads Inspector Burnley into investigations on both sides of the Channel, a favourite pattern for Crofts' novels. From the early 1970s St Katharine's became the first dock to be redeveloped.

'Any place that has seen so much social, cultural and economic change and conflict is fertile ground for generating stories.' Entering the landscape of 'tough people and criminal possibilities' described in **Michael Gilbert's*** *Rollercoaster* (1993), **Deborah Crombie*** (1952–) pays homage to the neighbourliness and independent spirit of the **Isle of Dogs** in *Kissed a Sad Goodbye* (1999). Immersed in the wharves and quays of 'the Island' and overshadowed by the towering presence of the **Canary Wharf** tower, the highest landmark in London (and the UK), this is a haunting tale linking modern murder with the wartime evacuation of Dockland

Dockland landscapes past and present – the tea clipper Cutty Sark at **Greenwich**, with **Canary Wharf** and the **Isle of Dogs** in the background.

An overview of north-east **London** – 'I felt that London was already too large and loose a thing to be a city in the sense of a citadel' **G K Chesterton**, *Autobiography* (1936).

'Brilliantly the Temple Fountain sparkled in the sun and laughingly its liquid music played' – **Charles Dickens'** *Martin Chuzzlewit* (1843) describes a scene that remains largely unchanged today, with the **Inns of Court** providing an oasis of tranquillity amidst the hustle and bustle of Legal London.

Westminster Abbey – where Hugh Corbett gains the ear of the king in **P C Doherty's** medieval mysteries.

children. Weaving in testimonies of oral history, Crombie recreates that 'special feeling of isolation' of this very distinctive part of East London and indulges her fascination with the tea trade, as Superintendent Duncan Kincaid and Detective Sergeant Gemma James investigate the murder of the manager of a long-established tea company. 'Once most of these places are tarted up, none of us who grew up here on the Island can afford to live in them,' says a local police officer, pointing to the motivation of the property developers who view the island as their territory.

Few crime writers can match the vivid imagination and prolific pen of soldier, journalist and scriptwriter **Edgar Wallace*** (1875–1932). Born in **Greenwich** and adopted by a **Billingsgate** fish market porter, both banks of the Thames played a major role in Wallace's formative years. In the shadow of Billingsgate's fish-shaped weather vanes, Wallace absorbed the vocabulary and sea-faring flavour of the riverside and docks, and before entering journalism also worked as a merchant seaman. From his first novel, *The Four Just Men* (1905), it was clear that Wallace enjoyed experimentation and taking risks – the offer of £500 for anyone able to solve the mystery rebounding badly when he and his publishers discovered that their readers were cleverer than anticipated! Many of Wallace's novels are thrillers, but his most famous detective is surely the 'lugubrious and unhappy' J G Reeder, a deceptively meek individual with a razor-sharp intellect and an encyclopaedic knowledge of poultry. 'I have a criminal mind,' says Wallace's inimitable detective, whose mixture of cunning and ruthlessness enables him to tackle the most fearsome of criminals despite his apparent physical frailty. Introduced in *The Mind of Mr J G Reeder* (1925) (US: *The Murder Book of Mr J G Reeder*) working for the Public Prosecutor's Department, Mr Reeder covers cases all over London. Home is south of the river in **Brockley Road** near the **Lewisham High Road**, but in 'The Case of Joe Attymar' from *Red Aces* (1929), Mr Reeder moves along the murky waters of the River Thames and around Greenwich and Rotherhithe docks on the trail of a master criminal.

Edgar Wallace – 'London is a large place full of strange, mad people,' says Mr Reeder in 'The Investors' (*The Mind of Mr J G Reeder*). Reading Edgar Wallace's extravagant, hugely entertaining novels it would be hard to disagree.

The concept of a 'Second City of London' was originally floated by the politician Lord Owen in the late 1980s. When **Gwendoline Butler*** was looking for a new challenge for her CID detective John Coffin, the re-emergence of historic parts of East London and the unprecedented transformation of the docklands provided the necessary inspiration. With Coffin installed as Chief Commander of the Second City, Butler has been able to involve him in investigations into high-level conspiracy and murder whilst still allowing for a degree of hands-on detection. Coffin first appears back in the 1950s, operating alongside Inspector Winter in the fashionable area of **Blackheath**, a bijou example of village London where Butler was born.

Gwendoline Butler – a pioneer of the women's police procedural.

Evoking dockland history, *A Coffin from the Past* (1970) has a strong political theme as Coffin investigates the death of a controversial MP in a mystery 'based on a tombstone found in an old city church by my husband in Clerkenwell,' says Butler. Married to famous actress Stella

'The twin, white domes of the Royal Naval College irresistibly drew the eye' – the view over **Greenwich** and the **Docklands** feature in **Deborah Crombie**'s *Kissed a Sad Goodbye* and forms part of **Gwendoline Butler**'s 'Second City of London' controlled by Commander John Coffin.

In **Mo Hayder**'s (1962–) tense, crisp detective shocker *Birdman* (2000), five bodies are unearthed in an industrial yard close to the **Greenwich Millennium Dome** and Detective Inspector Jack Caffery tracks a sadistic serial killer through the streets of south-east London. In *The Treatment* (2001), Caffery is drawn into investigations in the **Brixton** and **Herne Hill** area.

Pinero, Coffin is inextricably linked to the theatre, and the pair live in the tower of a converted church, with 'St Luke's Theatre' in the main church below. A visit to the plush riverside home of a former British prime minister in *A Double Coffin* (1996) leads to Coffin hearing a bizarre confession and opens an intriguing and macabre mystery that maintains its suspense until the very last. History is never far beneath the surface in Butler's work, and when the buried past and a simmering resentment rise into the present, Coffin and his team need to be at their sharpest to solve the case.

Sandwiched between Brixton and Peckham, **Camberwell** is a good base for **Stella Duffy**'s (1963–) fearsomely energetic private eye Saz Martin, despite the 'rubbish and broken tyres doing their best to hold back the greenery which threatened to cheer the place up'. Living on the floor of a 1960s Camberwell council flat and trawling the designer bars and clubs of south-east London, Saz experiences the highs and lows of city life – and probably the most graphic lesbian sex in crime fiction. After an early morning run, the dynamic PI spends her days investigating drug dealing, gambling and high-class prostitution. In *Wavewalker* (1996), Duffy's personal favourite, Saz is hired by a mystery employer to investigate an internationally acclaimed healer leaving a trail of suicides. In *Fresh Flesh* (1999), an original exploration of parenthood, Saz is living in her newly pregnant partner Molly's

Hampstead flat, but also revisits her old Brixton haunts in the line of duty. And at 4.30am, the soft morning light is 'prettifying Camberwell Green into something slightly closer to Camberwick Green…'

Clearly influenced by American *noir*, and perhaps as a reaction to the housing boom that has seized much of **SOUTH LONDON** in its relentless grip, detective fiction here tends to occupy the territory of sink estates, gangsterdom and the shapeless sprawl of no-go areas. **Brixton** is much-changed now from the burning streets and massed police presence during the riots of the 1980s and mid-1990s. In place of social deprivation, heavy-handed policing and strained community relations, today's CCTV, double-glazing and chic bars signal an upwardly mobile area. Reminders of the past are never far away in **Ken Bruen**'s *noir* nightmare world, where police patrol streets flooded with drugs and violence and HM Brixton Prison readies itself for a fresh intake. A tale of bloodlust and revenge, *The Hackman Blues* (1997) is not for the faint-hearted. When volatile, gay ex-con Tony Brady is hired to find a local villain's missing daughter, the only possible outcome is bedlam. Deciding that 'the modern version of hell might be Railton Road on a wet Wednesday night', Brady traces the missing girl to a club 'halfway down Electric Avenue' – which is when his troubles really start.

Stella Duffy – her Saz Martin series hits the streets of south-east London running.

Dishing out rough justice in Bruen's 'White Trilogy' are DS Brant ('Brant looked like a thug and he was real proud of that') and Chief

'This place was not about getting away from it all for a quiet half, it was about getting into it all, any of it' – the streets of **Brixton** keep **Stella Duffy**'s Saz Martin buzzing in *Fresh Flesh*, but are awash with violence in **Ken Bruen**'s *noir* novels.

Home to private eye Nick Sharman, thriving **Tulse Hill** was a run-down area when **Mark Timlin** lived here and began writing his series.

'My favourite film of all time is *The Wild Bunch*' – **Mark Timlin** sprays South London with more bullets than the Wild West in his Nick Sharman series.

Inspector Roberts, breaking all the rules in a trio of brutal novellas. In *A White Arrest* (1998), Bruen's bleak, bruised prose depicts a lawless South London: from **Stockwell** ('where the pitbulls travelled in twos') to **Walworth Road** and **Elephant and Castle**, justice depends upon the speed of the draw. The compelling carnage continues in *Taming the Alien* (1999), where Brant and Roberts have to deal with arson, rape and a baseball bat-wielding villain nicknamed the 'Alien', and comes to a close in an orgy of murder, beatings and grim humour in *The McDead* (2000).

'Brixton now is like Notting Hill: no-smoking, carrot-cake, cappuccino,' says **Mark Timlin** (1944–), who was raised in nearby **Tulse Hill**, where his private eye Nick Sharman lives and operates. Setting out to write a 'British Philip Marlowe', Timlin has created a series with more corpses than a London cemetery, bent coppers, fast motors and non-stop action. A former colleague turns up in pieces all over London in *Find My Way Home* (1996) and Sharman tours around Dalston and **Denmark Hill** in search of answers. A big bad Jonah with an unhealthy appetite for trouble and an animal magnetism that women find just irresistible, Sharman's habit of losing friends and lovers to violent death is less appealing.

South London provides a filmic backdrop for Timlin's torn, despairing prose barbed by wickedly dark humour. In *A Street that*

Rhymed at 3am (1997), bodies are again littering the streets after Sharman takes a seemingly straightforward job 'babysitting' a big-time American drug dealer turned informer. Sharman's involvement with some highly dangerous Yardie gangsters leads him from the 'independent state of Brixton' into darkest **Deptford** and its 'notorious Lion Estate', and on to a quiet street just off the **Old Kent Road**:

Neate Street, London, SE, three o'clock in the morning on Christmas Day. A street that rhymed at 3 a.m. Could be the title for a song. No one lived on Neate Street. There wasn't a house or block of flats along its half-mile length. It was just a road that led nowhere, and it reminded me of my life. The main line from Kent to Waterloo ran along one side, high on an embankment over railway arches made from brick that had long ago blackened in the acid south London air. On the other side was a scrubby park that disappeared into the night. There were four street lamps dotted along that side of the road, and one sputtered and fizzed like it would give up the ghost any moment. That was the only sound I heard, apart from my own footsteps and heartbeat as I walked round the corner carrying the case of dope.

'A street that rhymed at 3am' – **Neate Street, Walworth**, provides a candidate for best crime title and a setting for more High Noon drama for Nick Sharman.

Clapham Common Bandstand – a favourite landmark for **Natasha Cooper***, who has lived in **Clapham** for more than twenty-five years, and for her swish detective Willow King. When she first appears in *Festering Lilies* (1990) (US: *A Common Death*), Willow is living in a dank apartment at the wrong end of Clapham, working as a civil servant by day on **Clapham High Street** and writing as romantic novelist Cressida Woodruffe by night.

A world away from street riots and shootouts, the wealth and splendour of **WEST LONDON** breeds a different kind of detective fiction – but no less deadly. Forming a gateway to the west, **Paddington Station** and nearby **Praed Street** feature in two of **John Rhode's*** (pseud. Cecil Street, 1884–1965) best mysteries. Dr Lancelot Priestley is a mathematician and scientific detective introduced in *The Paddington Mystery* (1925), an ingenious tale that still retains much of its inventiveness. Priestley has to clear the name of his future son-in-law, who returns from a late-night drinking session to find a sodden body in his bed. The cathedral-like iron girder roof of Paddington Station still lords it over **Praed Street**, which 'beneath its squalor possesses a vein of native shrewdness' in *The Murders in Praed Street* (1928). On a foggy night a Praed Street herbalist is summoned to hospital on a hoax call and stabbed to death. Another murder in the street follows, and then another, despite the heavy police presence – can Priestley stop the killing?

> The fog was like a saffron blanket soaked in ice-water. It had hung over London all day and at last was beginning to descend. The sky was yellow as a duster and the rest was granular black, overprinted in grey and lightened by occasional slivers of bright fish colour as a policeman turned in his wet cape. Already the traffic was at an irritable crawl. By dusk it would be stationary. To the west the Park dripped wretchedly and to the north the great railway terminus slammed and banged and exploded hollowly about its affairs.
>
> Margery Allingham, *Tiger in the Smoke*

'It almost seems as though Praed Street regarded Paddington Station as an intrusion, and those who throng to and from it as unwelcome strangers' – two of **John Rhode**'s best mysteries revolve around the **Paddington** area.

The fog continues to envelop London in one of **Margery Allingham**'s* finest novels, *Tiger in the Smoke* (1952). Playing on the capital's historic nicknames ('The Big Smoke' or 'The Smoke'), this chilling psychological mystery is set largely in the **Bayswater** area, where a young Margery used to walk with her father and invent stories of what went on behind the lighted windows. Shrouded in secrecy and menace, London assumes a character and role of its own as a knife-wielding psychopath breaks out of jail. Detective Chief Inspector Charles Luke has his intuition and resolve tested to the full as he and Albert Campion track a ragbag gang of ex-soldiers in the hope of finding the elusive

Margery Allingham revisits the streets of her childhood in two of her most chilling mysteries: *Tiger in the Smoke* and *Hide My Eyes*.

'London to me is like a character,' says Anna Lee creator **Liza Cody**.

killer. The mood of violence and danger is enhanced by the heavily militarized atmosphere of post-war London.

'The autumn morning air was soft and smelled of rain and the London street scene was done in pastel shades under a sky of smoked pearl' – Allingham's love of London (she was born in **Ealing**) shines through in another classic: *Hide My Eyes* (1958) (US: *Tether's End*). In this ingeniously plotted, nail-biting detective thriller, Charlie Luke places his credibility on the line as he tries to track down a callous and extremely dangerous robber and conman who thinks nothing of killing to hide his tracks. Campion, by now 'a friend, an expert witness, and, at times, a very valuable guide into little-known territory', backs Luke's hunch as the search closes in on the 'labyrinth of Victorian middle-class stucco' where the killer has his lair.

'The world is still a jungle, though the settlements are larger and the linking paths, though they vary, are mostly well made and seem deceptively safe,' wrote **John Bingham** (pseud. **Michael Ward**, the seventh Lord of Clanmorris, 1908–88) in his Kafka-esque *A Fragment of Fear* (1965). **Kensington** and **Notting Hill** are transformed into a menacing urban jungle of hunter and hunted as crime writer James Compton finds himself up against forces he cannot comprehend. The psychological insights first displayed in *My Name is Michael Sibley* (1952) are again evident in Bingham's stylish exploration of the seamy side of society, as Compton's flat in Kensington's narrow **Stratford Road** becomes the epicentre of a nightmare. The murder of an elderly lady Compton briefly met on holiday sparks a relentless cascade of threats, intimidating letters, phone calls, break-ins at his flat, and then the murder of a messenger in a lane off **Notting Hill Gate**. With the police growing increasingly hostile to his anxieties, the dogged if intimidated Compton has to do his own detecting.

'My mission in life is to blow holes in things a little bit,' says native Londoner **Liza Cody** (pseud, 1944–) whose private eye Anna Lee works for 'Brierly Security… sat incongruously above the loud and popular boutique like a bowler hat on a disco dancer' in fashionable **Kensington High Street**. Introduced in *Dupe* (1980), gutsy ex-policewoman Anna takes the subtle approach to detection: gaining the trust of her clients and suspects, confident enough of her own moral judgement not to abuse it. Anna lives in a friend's Kensington house, 'on the cusp between Shepherd's Bush and Notting Hill, two of London's most populous villages, but in the back garden, sheltered by walls and the city's secret greenery, it could have been in the deep country'.

Cody's gently thoughtful, humorous series is set against a no-frills West London landscape, where a tide of property speculation is about to sweep into the lives of ordinary, middle-income families. Unpretentious, independent Anna is at her best when dealing with London's vulnerable youth. In *Bad Company* (1982), Anna works alongside the 'comforting bulk' of friend and colleague Bernie Schiller on a surveillance operation for a custody battle between their

Hammersmith client and his schoolteacher wife. Their daughter seems a pleasant, if precocious, fourteen-year-old schoolgirl to Anna, who is unaware that she will soon be sharing a cold, damp basement with the girl's schoolfriend when a witness intimidation scheme goes wrong. An intriguing and tender detective story, *Head Case* (1986) initially appears to be a straightforward missing person case but turns into a full-blown murder mystery focused on a child prodigy. Anna has to be at her most resilient and tenacious to protect the child, uncover the truth, and resist the unreasonable demands of her employer and the girl's distant and formal father.

When, in his 1901 essay 'A Defence of Detective Stories', G(ilbert) K(eith) Chesterton* (1874–1936) called the urban setting for crime fiction 'more poetic than the countryside… because it is not only lonely but beautiful', he was using his favourite literary device, the paradox. The London settings of Chesterton's detective stories about a deceptively meek and dumpy Catholic priest from Essex, Father Brown, have an atmosphere all of their own, resonating with an urban poetry rooted in the author's **Kensington** childhood. Born at **32 Sheffield Terrace**, at the foot of **Campden Hill**, Chesterton's enjoyment of walking and his training in art translate into powerful physical descriptions – light and shade, colour and tone – of landscapes with a strong moral dimension underpinned by an undogmatic if determined Catholic conviction.

G K Chesterton's childhood growing up on the south-facing slopes of **Campden Hill** sparked an interest in landscape evident in his classic Father Brown stories.

'As an artist I had always attempted to provide crimes suitable to the special season or landscapes in which I found myself,' says Chesterton's arch-criminal Flambeau, who in 'The Blue Cross' is pursued by Inspector Aristide Valentin across London to end up on a hill in **Hampstead Heath**: 'A perfect dome of peacock-green sank into gold amid the blackening trees and the dark violet distances'. A **Belgravia** hotel features in 'The Queer Feet', where Father Brown's priestly habit, frayed umbrella and clumsy

Notting Hill provides the setting for one of the earliest detective novels, **Charles Felix**'s strikingly modern *The Notting Hill Mystery* (1865). Narrated through a series of reports and letters from life assurance investigator Ralph Henderson to his employers, the mystery focuses on the sinister Baron R, holder of not one but five separate life policies on his wife – who is now dead. Using scraps of documentary 'evidence', Henderson finds himself caught in a literally mesmerizing mystery.

naïvety are again shown to conceal a shrewdly analytic and versatile mind. A man with ample experience of human shortcomings, honed in the confessional during his religious ministering, Father Brown is at his best in 'The Invisible Man', where the villain leaving menacing letters turns out to be a man whose presence is so commonplace as to go unnoticed – just like Father Brown, in fact.

Fashionable movie backdrop and site of Europe's biggest street carnival, **Notting Hill** is the territory of determined TV researcher and amateur sleuth Alex Tanner, created by **Anabel Donald**. Always on the lookout for commissions and contacts, Alex grew up on the 'pinched' streets near a local council estate and is wary of the trappings of success. From her flat in the 'marginally smart' surroundings of **Ladbroke Grove**, Alex has to contend with toxic fumes from the nearby **Westway** flyover that make 'carpets and curtains go from new to grubby before the cheque that you bought them with clears'. Still dreaming of following her childhood heroes Philip Marlowe and Lew Archer down the mean streets of America, Alex is hired by an anonymous Ms X in *The Glass Ceiling* (1994) to stop the murder of famous feminists. She also has to trace a missing father using TV footage of the Notting Hill Carnival and the savvy of a well-educated street kid assistant:

> I'm not usually up at dawn unless I've worked all night, but it is a time of day I'm fond of in London. I left the motorway as the sun rose and drove through the almost-deserted streets, thinking that now, for an hour or so, the city would belong to me and the few thousands of real Londoners going to work or delivering milk or driving the buses, beginning the first steps on the tread mill that keeps the city going. Wordsworth was wrong. It isn't an animal or a person, with a mighty heart: it's a gigantic machine that needs to be driven by me and people like me.

Going downhill? – 'marginally smart' **Ladbroke Grove** heading away from **Notting Hill** towards the **Westway** flyover.

In *An Uncommon Murder* (1999), Alex turns off her usual route home from Notting Hill tube – 'Westbourne Park Road (smart, expensive, residential) into one of those big, wide garden squares (very smart, ridiculously expensive, stucco-fronted, residential)' – and assists the victim of an attempted mugging. However, the old lady turns out to be an invaluable source for Alex's research into a 1950s' society murder.

Diamond Dagger-recipient **H R F Keating** (1926–) lives in a quiet street between Bayswater and Notting Hill not far from the banks of the **Grand Union Canal** – dug in the late eighteenth century to connect London with the Midlands. Best-known as the creator of Bombay CID Inspector Ganesh Ghote, Keating's more recent police procedurals are conjugations of detectives' weaknesses and dilemmas. His characters operate within the fictional city of 'Greater Birchester' – notionally a cross between Manchester and Birmingham, but inspired by Keating's favourite urban London landscapes.

'I'm interested in the dilemmas facing detectives' – **H R F Keating**.

In *The Hard Detective* (2000), the author of influential studies of crime fiction introduces intelligent and determined Superintendent Harriet Martens. As the righteous instigator of the zero-tolerance 'Stop the Rot' campaign, Harriet meets her match in the figure of a deranged killer targeting police officers. A slightly smelly Canal is seen to bisect the community, especially in terms of football allegiance, and the disused warehouses, muddy waters, blind alleys and dark bridges reflect the uncertainties and complexities of life that Harriet usually refuses to entertain:

> Under the louring rain clouds, seeping now only an off-and-on drizzle, Harriet went pacing the canal's black towpath, her feet squelching slightly on the gritty surface at every step. The walls of the long-deserted warehouses at her side glistened with so much damp that they seemed to be made as much of water as of brick. The sluggish green canal itself, its filmed-over surface lightly pocked with the descending droplets, was giving off a yet sharper odour, metallic and clinging.

London is blown by icy winds and sleet in *A Detective In Love* (2001), as Harriet investigates corruption at 'Persimmon House', the fictitious headquarters of the capital's 'Maximum Crime Squad', which Keating situates close to his home.

The 'glutinous' waters of the **Grand Union Canal** also run through the patch of Detective Constable 'Dangerous' Davies, aka the 'Last Detective', created by **Leslie Thomas** (1931–). Dangerous occupies the lowest rank in the Metropolitan Police, and having 'been thrown down more flights of stairs than any man in London', is only called upon if there is absolutely no one else to do the job. Born in **Kensal Rise**, Dangerous's patch encompasses the area around **Willesden** and **Kensal Green**, described by Thomas with lyrical imagery in *Dangerous by Moonlight* (1993):

'Its greened unmoving water divided the whole region, its modest but still ornate bridges pinned the banks together' – the **Grand Union Canal**, where *Dangerous Davies. The Last Detective* enjoys feeding the ducks, but also takes an involuntary dip.

Winter suited Willesden. Its trees were created to drip, its canal to wear a muffler of mist, its pavements and roofs to reflect the lights of winter streets and the cloudy winter moon; few daytime things decorated the north-west London sky more poetically than the steam clouds from the power station cooling towers flying like the hair of God.

'The many colours, creeds and cultures wedged into that north-western corner of London' do not mean much to Dangerous, a parochial man who rarely strays far from the landmarks of the canal and power station, and who spends his free time at the local Bingo hall. Home is a seedy B&B 'near the Jubilee Clock in Willesden' under a choked industrial sky, where the cooling towers of the power stations loom 'like monstrous chessman' over the low terraces with roofs hanging 'like parched tongues'. After spending the night between the tombs in the beautiful expanse of **Kensal Green Cemetery** (on **Harrow Road**) to ward off a bomb threat in *Dangerous Davies. The Last Detective* (1976), Dangerous at last grabs himself a murder case: the unsolved killing of a young girl on the canal towpath a quarter of a century previously.

'A second before he had been in one of the drabbest regions he had ever set eyes on, and now, as if a scene had been rapidly shifted on a stage, he saw a green triangle, plane trees, a scattering of Georgian houses. Such, he supposed, was London, ever variable, constantly surprising.'

Ruth Rendell, *Murder Being Once Done* (1972)

A short distance geographically to the east, but a world away culturally, well-heeled residential **Maida Vale**, where **Baroness Orczy's*** female detective in *Lady Molly of Scotland Yard* lived, is the London home of **Ruth Rendell***. Close examination of societal norms and the many individuals whose lives, for various reasons, do not conform with the expectations and pressures of mainstream society, have long been a hallmark of Rendell's work. Many of her acclaimed psychological thrillers are set in London, but it is unusual to see her long-running series detective, Inspector Reg Wexford, in town.

'Wexford had seen many a dawn in Kingsmarkham, but never till now a London dawn' – in *Murder Being Once Done* (1972), Wexford arrives in the **Chelsea/Fulham** borders to stay with his nephew, who works at Scotland Yard. Investigations are underway into the death of a young woman found in a family vault in the cemetery of 'Kenbourne Vale' ('bigger than Kensal Green and more bizarre than Brompton'), located between **North Kensington** and **Kilburn**. A tad homesick for Sussex's green meadows and pine forests, and definitely peeved at being excluded from his nephew's murder inquiry, Wexford embarks on his own course of action. Ambling into a wasp's nest of property development, parenthood and possessiveness might not be the best thing for Wexford's blood pressure, but the man from the provinces has a thing or two to teach the city police.

One of the London villages to have retained its distinct community feel, **Shepherd's Bush** is 'an ordinary, busy, unglamorous, tightly-packed hive of people all just trying to get along,' says **Cynthia Harrod-Eagles**. Her Detective Inspector Bill Slider was born on the huge **White City Estate** at a time when it was 'a poor but respectable working class area, where everyone kept their net curtains white and their doorsteps Mansioned… and where family ties were very strong'. With **Wormwood Scrubs** prison a stone's throw away and 10 Rillington Place, home to the infamous murderer John Christie, nearby, Harrod-Eagles had an early interest in crime and criminals.

Her psychologically astute police procedurals have a conversational, humorous and lyrical style, with musical themes and solid, real-life locales. *Orchestrated Death* (1992) introduces Slider, dodging promotion despite his wife's pressure, investigating a murder on the White City Estate involving a Stradivarius and a giant can of olive oil. Even Slider finds the topography of his home ground disorientating:

Born in 'the Bush' – **Cynthia Harrod-Eagles** steers Detective Inspector Bill Slider around her home territory of **Shepherd's Bush**.

> Slider had had business on the estate on many an occasion; usually just the daily grind of car theft and house-breaking, though sometimes an escaped inmate of the nearby Wormwood Scrubs prison would brighten up everyone's day by going to earth in the rabbit warren of flats. It was a good place to hide: Slider always got lost… Slider was of the opinion that either you were born there, or you never learnt your way about.

A country man at heart, Slider instinctively appreciates the old-fashioned, unpretentious community feel of the area. His disillusionment with the 'Catatonia' of suburban home life sometimes erupts, but ultimately Slider accepts that 'he had to prefer vacuity to vice'.

Slider enters the world of television in *Blood Lines* (1995), when a music critic and guest celebrity on a show at the **White City** TV Centre has his throat slit. There are plenty of suspects, as no one in this media warren appears to have an alibi. The setting of *Shallow Grave* (1998) is loosely based on the **Bedford Park** estate just outside the Bush. Slider,

Sliding into West London – a typical **Shepherd's Bush** terrace.

an architectural enthusiast, and enervated by 'bungaloid' imitation architecture, has his eyes on the Old Rectory – only to find a dead body in a hole on the terrace.

'Some people find the whole place depressing – not me. It's real – not pretty, but alive,' says Sara Kingsley of the **Acton** area where she lives. The creation of sociologist **Anne Wilson**, Kingsley is an engaging detective, a young Jewish community counsellor and single mother of two living in the middle of Acton, off **Churchfield Road**. Acton might be 'full of dark, dingy pubs with about as much charm as a wrestler's armpit', but Kingsley likes its 'miniature woodland gardens' and its groundedness. When one of her clients dies shortly after coming to see her in *Truth or Dare* (1996), Kingsley is drawn into her complex first case, upsetting more than one London applecart.

'I have always been fascinated by the difference between appearance and reality,' says **Jean Stubbs** (1926–), who uses **Wimbledon Common** as the central location for *Dear Laura* (1973), the first in her Inspector Lintott trilogy of Victorian mysteries. Having been 'steeped since childhood in Charles Dickens' London', Stubbs based her detective upon the real-life Victorian Inspector Field – using a South London setting where the author herself lived for many years. Focusing on Laura Crozier, mistress of a wealthy household, *Dear Laura* explores the double-standards of late nineteenth-century London: 'beneath the cosiness and tea cups lay an underworld in which eighty thousand prostitutes and four thousand brothels existed in London alone'. While Lintott struggles with the emerging feminism of his own daughter, the villa on Wimbledon Common conceals the dark secrets of the Crozier family:

The villa, built in 1808, stood apart and slightly back from its neighbours on Wimbledon Common. In that dim February evening towards the end of the nineteenth century, it gleamed dully and then more radiantly as the lamplighter touched gas to flame and walked on. From his vantage point at the far side of the Common, Dr Padgett saw the whole establishment as a citadel in state of siege; or a doll's house in the distance; so minute were its appointments, so perfect its evolvement.

'The Common became one vast golden space under the evening sky, and she hesitated to draw the curtains against such splendour' – **Wimbledon Common** plays host to Victorian intrigue in *Dear Laura*.

In today's flight path of aircraft from nearby **Heathrow**, the western suburb of **Littleton** becomes the commuter suburb of 'Roth' in **Andrew Taylor**'s* powerful and ambitious Roth Trilogy – a literary dig through the layers of two families' pasts against a Church of England background. Set in 1970, *The Judgement of Strangers* (1998) unfolds a claustrophobic suburban state of mind through the jaded eyes of a newly-remarried vicar. Sexual frustration, jealousy and brutal murder accompany Roth's trajectory from village isolation to busy suburb. The new tenants of the country house of 'Roth Park' (**Littleton House**, now home to the Shepperton film studios) seem suspicious as bossy churchwarden Audrey Oliphant sets out to catch the killer of her cat, Lord Peter. 'But Miss Oliphant isn't really Miss Marple,' says Andrew Taylor, 'and Roth isn't a village any longer…'

CHAPTER TEN

The South-East & Home Counties

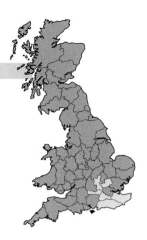

> All down the hedges here grows the wayfarer's tree with its flat creamy bracts of blossom, and beneath, edging the meadows like a fringe of lace, the whiter, finer, more delicate cow parsley... It is like downland up here, the trees ceasing until the forest of conifers begins over there to the east, chalk showing in outcroppings and heather on the chalk...

Ruth Rendell, *An Unkindness of Ravens* (1995)

The **SOUTH-EAST** and **HOME COUNTIES** (the counties surrounding London) represent Britain's wealthiest corner and, beyond the symbolic white cliffs of **Dover**, provide many visitors with their first impressions of England's green and pleasant land. Although vast amounts of greenery have long-since surrendered to commuter sprawl and the Stockbroker Belt, the counties of **Berkshire**, **Surrey**, **Sussex** and **Kent** still retain many areas of natural beauty – encompassing the wooded chalk ridges of the **Downs**, world-famous gardens and a wealth of historic houses. If there was ever an ideal setting for **Agatha Christie**'s* 'St Mary Mead', this would be it, and with a literary heritage including

'In the golden sunlight of late afternoon the grey stones were warmed and tranquil looking. Not a castle that had ever stood siege, or had tragic memories of the slaughter of attackers and defenders imposed upon it' – **Windsor Castle** is a familiar sight for **Jennie Melville**'s police detective Charmian Daniels, who spends the beginning of *Windsor Red* at the Garter Ceremony.

Christopher Marlowe (1564–93), **Charles Dickens** (1812–70) and **Rudyard Kipling** (1865–1936), the region certainly lends itself to traditional detective fiction. A welcome satirical edge to the home comforts is provided by the South-East's clutch of comedy writers.

'It's a township inside a castle that I am looking at. I had not realised so many people lived here in their own community. Not just the Court with its special routines and life, but people like the Military Knights and the soldiers under the Constable of the Castle and the police and all the people who keep the whole place running… a world within a world.'

Jennie Melville, *Windsor Red*

Symbolizing the Home Counties' wealth, prestige and heritage to perfection, the picturesque royal town of **Windsor** lies in **BERKSHIRE**, just beyond the M25 west of London and a short distance from the **Runnymede** home of **Jennie Melville** (pseud. Gwendoline Butler*). In *Windsor Red* (1988), Melville's Inspector Charmian Daniels arrives in Windsor after a transfer from nearby 'Deerham Hills', the setting for earlier mysteries in the series. Charmian is officially on sabbatical, but soon finds her research into female crime and criminals disrupted. First, a friend's baby disappears, then limbs are discovered in a rubbish sack outside Charmian's home in (fictional) bohemian 'Wellington Yard', and soon headless torsos are turning up around the town. Deceptively quirky and light in its descriptions of Windsor's elegance and style, there is a disturbing edge to the novel, a disquieting sense of another Windsor somewhere in a parallel universe very much at odds with its outer appearance. As the series develops, Charmian rises through the ranks to become Chief Superintendent Daniels but remains based in her home town of Windsor. Today Britain's longest continuously inhabited royal residence, **Windsor Castle** also takes centre stage in **Gwendoline Butler**'s* Georgian-era historical crime series featuring Major Mearns and Sergeant Denny.

In *The Affair at Little Wokeham* (1943) (US: *Double Tragedy*), former railway engineer **Freeman Wills Crofts*** (1879–1957) describes the tiny **SURREY** village of **Blackheath** ('Little Wokeham'), near **Guildford**, that

'For nearly a mile in two other directions the heath ran on, open and wild and primitive, with its miniature hills and valleys and plains covered with heather and bracken, gorse and birch, pine and an occasional clump of oak' – the magnificent expanse of **Blackheath** provides an atmospheric backdrop to **Freeman Wills Crofts**' *The Affair at Little Wokeham.*

Surrey boasts many of the gardens designed by the influential Gertrude Jeckyll, who as a girl lived at Bramley House, near **Guildford**, and her fifteen-acre gardens at **Munstead Wood** (south of **Godalming** – pictured) are amongst the most famous in England. In *The Mantrap Garden* (1986), **John Sherwood**'s sleuth Celia Grant is called in to sort out a fictitious Jeckyll garden run to seed, only to find herself involved with the dark secrets of an eccentric family.

was his home for many years. Investigating in this quiet backwater, precise and determined Inspector Joseph French enters a maze of deception much in the spirit of **Francis Iles**'* classic *Malice Aforethought* (1931). Crofts' tightly plotted novels invariably find French unpicking closely woven tissues of lies and alibis, often by systematically checking travel times and arrangements. In *The Hog's Back Mystery* (1933) (US: *The Strange Case of Dr. Earle*), French investigates the disappearance of three locals on a Surrey ridge – seemingly a murder case without bodies. *Crime at Guildford* (1935) (US: *The Crime at Nornes*) again concerns a murder committed near the historic town of Guildford, together with a major jewellery theft from a firm of London diamond brokers.

A keen gardener, **John Sherwood** (1913–) lives in the 'Garden of England' (Kent), but his green-fingered sleuth Celia Grant weeds out the clues in a series of complex mysteries set mainly in the Surrey area. A practical, hard-working horticulturalist with a deceptively mild exterior, Celia runs a rare-plant nursery in a narrow lane one mile outside 'Melbury' village (close to **Guildford** and **Reigate**) with her young and determinedly working-class assistant Bill. Celia first appears in *Green Trigger Fingers* (1984), working on a garden that becomes the scene of the crime in a 'gilt-edged beauty-spot village' close to Melbury, where gossip is the chief industry. In the face of spite and snobbery – the very *idea* that the murderer could be 'One of Us' – Celia tries to uphold the honour of her friend, the village storekeeper, whose absent son stands accused of chopping two 'weekenders' to death.

Celia is active in the village life of Melbury and proud of its well-kept gardens and showpiece main street, 'a jumble of red-roofed houses and cottages built over a spread of five centuries on no particular plan… mellowed into a coherent master-piece'. This is not a timeless landscape, however: Melbury has lost its local shop and has to make do with one

Josephine Bell* (pseud. Dr Doris Bell Ball, 1897–1987) practised medicine at **Guildford** hospital for many years. Institutional landscapes peopled by overworked, idealistic medics are a feature of her mystery series in which amateur sleuth Dr David Wintringham assists the detectives of Scotland Yard.

bus a week, while a large garden centre down the road presents a major threat to Celia's small business. Sherwood's mysteries come complete with footnotes on species and seedlings, and *Creeping Jenny* (1993) focuses on the highlight of the gardening calendar: the Chelsea Flower Show. With the event looming, Celia and the police uncover plans by a radical group to terrorize the festival; plans that link Celia's timid new employee and *Lysimachia numularia*: Creeping Jenny.

Julian Symons (1912–94), whose *Bloody Murder: From the Detective Story to the Crime Novel* (1972) is still a definitive guide to the genre, specialized in exploring the nature of violence behind faces of respectability. *Colour of Murder* (1957) is a suburban Jeckyll and Hyde tale, portraying an unhappy marriage and an archetypal domineering mother-in-law. When John Wilkins meets an attractive woman in his local library, he begins to suffer a series of 'blackouts' and his humdrum existence descends into murderous obsession. *The End of Solomon Grundy* (1964) is a modern classic set in the claustrophobic comfort of 'The Dell' – a fictional semi-suburban Surrey housing scheme simmering with barely repressed violence, class snobbery and racism. The novel's eponymous anti-hero first appears to be the sympathetic defender of individuality and equality in The Dell's 'gracious, civilised living' (cosy, white, middle-class strait-jacket), but becomes increasingly unpredictable and volatile. 'I don't belong here,' says Grundy early in the book: 'too much bloody *order*'. Sacked from his job as a cartoonist, trapped in a soulless landscape and stale marriage, Grundy's frustration is manifest. When a girl is found murdered in a Mayfair mews, Detective Superintendent Jeffrey Manners is sure he has the guilty man – but the elusive, enigmatic Grundy cannot be pinned down so easily. With trial scenes at the Old Bailey interwoven with investigations in the pulsing urban heart of London, this unsettling mystery clearly targets the 'new élite' living in 'dozens of other Dells built in England during the past few years'.

Ruth Rendell, who has broadened the horizons of detective fiction and made the fictional Sussex town of 'Kingsmarkham' world famous.

Ruth Rendell* (1930–) began her long and illustrious career in crime writing with *From Doon With Death* (1964), introducing redoubtable Chief Inspector Reginald Wexford in the 'Mid-Sussex' town of 'Kingsmarkham' – a location initially influenced by the **WEST SUSSEX** town of **Midhurst**, but entirely fictitious and ending up situated nearer to **Lewes** and **Brighton**. In a striking debut, Rendell quickly establishes her trademark style of literary allusion interwoven with strands of Golden Age puzzle, police procedural and psychological thriller. Reg Wexford is seen to be a solid, middle-aged family man and a brusque but caring investigator with a strong sense of justice and a steely determination to uphold the law. As his puritanical sidekick Mike Burden is well aware, the fine weather of Wexford's keen and literary mind is accompanied by sudden storms of thundery ill-temper, and never more so than when confronted by the smug, self-satisfied complacency of Middle England. Rendell's first mystery fairly bristles

Calm before the storm? –
Midhurst, Ruth Rendell's
initial inspiration for
'Kingsmarkham'.

with indignation at the apathy and arrogance reigning in this corner of suburban commutersville as Wexford and Burden tackle the mysterious and grisly death of a respectable, ordinary housewife. 'It all goes on,' says the dead woman's husband disbelievingly, 'as if nothing had happened.'

While the Kingsmarkham area undergoes considerable change and urbanization as the series develops, the social landscape remains uppermost in Rendell's work as she handles controversial and highly emotive subjects with considerable dexterity. In *An Unkindness of Ravens* (1985), a neighbourly good deed uncovers a complex and tragic plot involving militant feminism, concealed identity, assault, bigamy and murder. *Simisola* (1994) tackles small-town racism against a background of rising unemployment and social change. Wexford's investigations into the disappearance of one of Kingsmarkham's few black inhabitants lead him to look within himself and challenge his own prejudices.

'When I retire, he had told his wife, I want to live in London so I can't see the countryside destroyed.' At the beginning of *Road Rage* (1997), a despairing Wexford walks in 'Framhurst Great Wood', which is threatened by a new road scheme. This is a place Wexford has enjoyed for many long years and there is a lyrical, nostalgic tone to the descriptions of the endangered forest and riverscape – the only British habitat of the map butterfly, *Araschnia levana* ('Almost every one of my novels has a butterfly or moth in it,' says Rendell). As Wexford's family becomes the direct target of environmental activists trying to block the new bypass, Rendell uses her detective for a caustic comment on Britain's car-dominated society – 'Would he be prepared to give up his car for the sake of England? What a question!'

Although still able to enjoy the Sussex woodlands he considers 'the most beautiful in England', Wexford has plenty on his mind in *Harm Done* (1999), as Rendell continues to render uncomfortable home truths

Simon Brett outside his home
in the 'Agatha Christie-style
village' of **Burpham**.

'The sea goes out a long way at
Fethering, revealing a vast, flat
expanse of sludge-coloured
sand. When the tide is high,
only pebbles show, piled high
against the footpath and the
wooden breakwaters that
stretch out from it like the
teeth of a comb' – **Climping**
beach close to Simon Brett's
'Fethering' in *The Body on the
Beach.*

through his unflinching standpoint. Investigating a series of bizarre
abductions, Wexford and Burden find their hands full when mob rule
descends upon a Kingsmarkham housing estate. From the public
hysteria at the release of a convicted paedophile to the private agony of
a wife battered and abused in her own home, Rendell challenges our
whole concept of morality and justice. Rendell's acknowledged 'fondness
for gardens, plants and flowers' and Sussex's natural wooded landscapes
juxtapose neatly with the complex, disturbing profile of human dilemma
and 'natural' justice.

Nestling in the woodlands of the **South Downs**, the picturesque
Agatha Christie-style village of **Burpham** has been home for some
twenty years to versatile comic writer **Simon Brett*** (1945–). With its
population of exactly 200 unchanged since 1800, this secluded corner
of Sussex provides the perfect ingredients for mystery and social
comedy. The first of Brett's 'Fethering Mysteries' featuring retired civil
servant Carole Seddon starts on a November day on the South Coast
five miles to the south of Burpham. Carole's hopes for 'benign
anonymity' in the inward-looking community of 'Fethering' (a pun on
nearby **Tarring**) are frustrated in *The Body on the Beach* (2000), when
she finds a body only for it to disappear before the police arrive.
Fortunately, Carole's neighbour Jude believes her. Unfortunately, the
two women decide to embark on an investigation behind the village
façade of 'double-glazed windows and double-glazed minds'. The beach
at the mouth of the river 'Fether', where the body is first found, was
inspired by the stretch of sandy beach broken by wooden sea defence

The hideaway village of **Burpham** – home to Simon Brett and 'not a million miles' away from the hamlet of 'Weldisham' in *Death on the Downs.*

barriers near **Littlehampton**. Here, the tide transforms the 'lethargic trickle' of the outlet of the river Arun twice daily into 'a torrent of surprising malevolence' that threatens to engulf Carole as the mystery moves towards its climax.

There is further intrigue in *Death on the Downs* (2000), when Carole stumbles across a skeleton while sheltering from the rain in a dilapidated barn on the West Sussex Downs. 'A lot of the plot hinges on converting barns into houses, getting planning permission, that kind of thing, which is quite a big local issue,' says Brett, whose blend of old-fashioned English whodunnit and light comedy brings him close to home with the hamlet of 'Weldisham'. The action of *Torso in the Town* (2001) takes place in and around the ancient and strategically placed 'Fedborough' (**Arundel**), a town 'notoriously distrustful of outsiders'. In real life, **Arundel Castle** looms large over the town, but Brett's imagination presents 'Fedborough Castle' as the ruins Cromwell's soldiers left behind rather than its current impressive, rebuilt state.

The laughs continue in **EAST SUSSEX** with Nick Madrid creator **Peter Guttridge** (1951–), who explores the region's pagan past in *A Ghost of a Chance* (1998). Commissioned to spend Walpurgis Night (30th April) near a haunted prehistoric burial chamber on the Downs, society journalist Madrid gets more than he bargained for. This is a time when witches traditionally revel with the devil, but the sight of a dead man hanging upside down from an ancient oak in the churchyard is not quite what Madrid had expected. And then there is the small matter of a tall stranger with a dog's head roaming the ancient landscape illuminated by a full moon 'silvering the flint paths and giving a spectral look to the slice of sea at **Birling Gap**'. On the trail of the killer, Madrid hobnobs with opera connoisseurs at **Glyndebourne** and investigates in a **Brighton** caught up in Millennium madness, attending seances, getting in the way on film sets and skirting the antique shops of **The Lanes**.

Peter Guttridge outside the **Half Moon** pub, **Plumpton**, where a good part of *A Ghost of a Chance* was written. The 1979 painting on the wall here provides a vital clue.

The Regency terraces of Brighton's genteel neighbour **Hove** provide the settings for prolific **Laurence W Meynell**'s (1899–1989) Hooky Hefferman series. Journalist and private investigator Hooky is a connoisseur of South Coast bars but is often to be found in the wholly respectable surroundings of his formidable aunt's Hove flat.

Guttridge blends satire with mystery and fantasy in his series, but over the years has seen real-life crime draw closer to the tucked-away Sussex hamlet where he lives: 'I'd drive over the Downs to Brighton and see the odd burnt-out car... then suddenly they started appearing on that two-mile stretch across the Downs... Last year, the first burnt-out car appeared at the bottom of my lane.' Madrid is a seasoned traveller, but the contrast between busy Brighton, 'the California of Europe when it comes to loopy trends', and the sleepy Downs provides some of the most evocative sense of place, as Guttridge explains:

'The Downs is a quite remote area, and at night, as it goes dark, you see this curious light across the top of the Downs, which is the pollution from Brighton. So you're in the middle of one atmosphere – very quiet, very still, the birds are singing, and the bats are going by – but at the same time there's this throbbing, thriving atmosphere just over the Downs. Coming out of buzzing Brighton, you move into another kind of mode, and I like the idea of using that change of mood in my fiction.'

Plumpton Place (private), the impressive moated Elizabethan manor redesigned in the 1920s by Edwin Lutyens is visible from **Peter Guttridge**'s study window and inspired haunted 'Ashcombe Manor', a 'big, gloomy pile set among woods' turned into a New Age conference centre in *A Ghost of a Chance* (1998).

'I took a stroll in the curious old-world garden which flanked the house. Rows of very ancient yew trees, cut into strange designs, girded it round. Inside was a beautiful stretch of lawn… the effect so soothing and restful' – the 'deeply peaceful' atmosphere of **Groombridge Place** is disturbed by a 'fantastic nightmare' in **Arthur Conan Doyle**'s *The Valley of Fear.*

In the Holmes pastiche *The Beekeeper's Apprentice* (1994), by US author **Laurie R King** (1952–), fifteen-year-old Mary Russell meets the great detective on the Downs in 1915 and Holmes acquires an apprentice who is more than a match for his wits.

In 1907 **Arthur Conan Doyle*** moved to the East Sussex town of **Crowborough** on the edge of **Ashdown Forest**. From his study in the large Jacobean brick house (Windlesham – private) by the golf course, Conan Doyle had a dramatic view of the **Weald**, the low-lying stretch of land separating the chalky ridges of the North and South Downs. In *The Valley of Fear* (1915), nearby **Groombridge Place** provides the inspiration for 'Birlestone Manor', accessed by a drawbridge across a 'beautiful broad moat, as still and luminous as quicksilver in the cold winter sunshine'. The garden where Watson walks has recently been re-established, and a small museum was opened in 1995. With war rumbling ominously in the background, 'His Last Bow' (1917) finds sixty-year-old Holmes enjoying retirement in the South Downs, keeping bees, playing the violin and smoking his pipe – until tempted back into action for one last case.

'To me, there has always been something faintly creepy about an off-season English seaside resort,' says **Martin Russell** (1934–), who was living not far from **Hastings** when he created his journalist detective Jim Larkin. Russell's fast-moving novels are all direct in style and wryly lyrical in tone, but *Deadline* (1971), 'perhaps the one book in which the setting came first', has a convincing air of abandonment and foreboding. Russell cloaks his fictional composite of South Coast

Martin Russell, whose *Deadline* captures the atmosphere of an out-of-season South Coast resort.

Hastings seafront – an inspiration for **Martin Russell**'s South Coast resort where investigative journalist detective Jim Larkin has his first taste of murder.

Writing as **Staynes and Storey** (US: **Susannah Stacey**), Jill Staynes and Kent-based Margaret Storey have created wise and subtle Inspector Robert Bone, who investigates around **Tunbridge Wells**. Their debut, *Goodbye, Nanny Gray* (1987), centres on the murder of a nanny in a village, and *Grave Responsibility* (1990) is a bleak and macabre tale of multiple murder in a peculiar family.

Rochester's most famous son, **Charles Dickens***, immortalized the town at the mouth of the **Medway** river where he grew up as 'Mudfog' and 'Dullborough', and set much of his unfinished *Mystery of Edwin Drood* (1870) here in 'Cloisterham'.

resorts in an atmosphere of bracing winds, frilly chintz, missed opportunity and repressed passion, as Larkin arrives in town to work on a local newspaper. 'Other towns have silly seasons; ours is half-witted all year round,' jokes one of Larkin's colleagues, but the witticisms stop when a girl's body is found – in two parts – on the shingle beach half a mile from the pier. Soon after, Larkin has to thwart an attack on a female colleague as they walk along the seafront, 'past rows of identical bow-windowed façades, where... at the moment it seemed as though lighted rooms and a friendly welcome were things undreamt of. Their footsteps rattled in the gloom. He had a sense of isolation, as if the townsfolk had retired with united secret tread to some distant territory to watch the pair of them challenge an unspecified threat.' As the grisly murders continue, the 'secret tread' of the town's apparent apathy explodes into the loud steps of vigilante action – and Larkin is their first catch.

The mild climate and fertile soil of **KENT** have gained the county a reputation as the 'Garden of England', where the landscape is dotted with orchards and the angled cowls of oast houses stand as distinctive symbols of the hops industry. Kent points the heel of England towards the Channel and the Continent – making the area particularly vulnerable during World War II, as described in **Christianna Brand**'s (pseud. Mary Christianna Lewis, 1907–88) classic *Green For Danger* (1944). One of the last writers in the Golden Age tradition, Brand wrote this atmospheric medical whodunnit as a monument to the Voluntary

Aid Detachment teams of first-aiders whose tireless work she had witnessed during the Blitz. Shabbily dressed but dogged Detective Inspector Cockrill of Kent Police arrives late at the fictional 'Heron's Park' military hospital, where a patient has been killed on the operating table and the only suspects are doctors and nurses. Superbly schemed, the novel paints a powerful background of war: shells bursting in the sky, sirens breaking 'into their unearthly howl', the booming of distant guns and the 'bomb-scarred landscape' littered with fragments of bomb-casing and shattered lives. The stark horror of the wartime scenes stands in utter contrast to the surroundings of a Kentish pub where the survivors are finally able to reflect upon their new-found peace:

> The apples were young and green upon the boughs and all the air was sweet with the scent of a dying summer day. They walked in silence through the country lane, and in the rich fields the rabbits sat up to watch them, rubbing black noses on little, furry paws. The last soft rays of the sun gleamed on the whitened stems of the trees, and foxglove and ragged robin caught at them as they passed, as though to hold them for a moment longer in the magic of the Kentish twilight.

North-west of **Maidstone**, the unspoilt village of **Birling** was well known to **Ngaio Marsh***, as the place where her close friends, the Rhodes family, had their country mansion. The Rhodes provided the inspiration for the upper-class 'Lampreys' in Marsh's *A Surfeit of Lampreys* (1941) (US: *Death of a Peer*), where **Birling Place** (private) inspired 'Deepacres Park', the Lampreys' family seat. Devoted to each other, the Lampreys are eccentric, fond of jokes – and desperately short

Josephine Tey* enjoyed many walks in the Kentish countryside and often stayed at **Wadhurst** on the Kent-Sussex border. For the lush landscape of *Brat Farrar* (1949), Tey uses scenery between **Dover** and **Folkestone**: 'Over that far ridge the land sloped in chequered miles to the sea and the clustered roofs of Westover. But here, in the high valley, shut off from the Channel gales and open to the sun, the trees stood up in the bright air with a midland serenity: with an air, almost, of enchantment.'

'I prefer writing about the stage to any other topic, but one must have variety of settings' – **Ngaio Marsh**, *Black Beech and Honeydew* (autobiography, 1966).

'That classic, that almost archaic picture – a country blacksmith's shop in the evening' – standing opposite All Saints Church, **Birling Forge** provides the model for 'Copse Smithy's' working forge in **Ngaio Marsh**'s *Off With His Head*.

The massive Sarsen stone circle guarding a 5,000-year-old burial chamber at **Coldrum Longbarrow** provides the scene of the crime in **Ngaio Marsh**'s *Off with his Head*.

Opposite: A walk through the 'Garden of England' – 'Perhaps, in a hundred years' time this landscape, which probably looked very similar now to the way it had a century ago, would have changed beyond recognition' – **Dorothy Simpson**'s Inspector Thanet ponders the future of his beloved Kentish landscape in *Dead and Gone*.

Dorothy Simpson interweaves murder mystery with an intimate knowledge of the Kentish countryside in her Inspector Thanet series.

of money. When a wealthy uncle is invited in the hope of a loan, he ends up murdered, and Chief Inspector Roderick Alleyn has to pick a route through the Lampreys' charades, deceptions and red herrings to solve the mystery.

'Over that part of England the Winter Solstice came down with a bitter antiphony of snow and frost. Trees, minutely articulate, shuddered in the north wind.' After being snowed in at Birling Place in the winter of 1954/5, Marsh carried the experience into one of her strongest novels, *Off With His Head* (1957) (US: *Death of a Fool*). Ancient traditions are very much alive in the feudal Kent surroundings of 'Mardian', unlike the village smithy who loses his head outside 'Mardian Castle', inspired by the (private) castle in neighbouring **Leybourne**. The group of standing stones glinting with frost in the novel can be seen today nestling in a quiet hollow beneath the chalk escarpment near **Trottiscliffe**, north of Birling.

Travelling to the scene of the crime, Alleyn sees an analogy in the wintry Kent countryside:

'Has it ever occurred to you,' Alleyn said, 'that the progress of a case is rather like a sort of thaw? Look at that landscape.' He wiped the mist from their carriage window. Sergeants Bailey and Thompson... stared out with the air of men to whom all landscapes are alike. Mr Fox, with slightly raised brows, also contemplated the weakly illuminated and dripping prospect. 'Like icing,' he said, 'running off a wedding cake. Not that I suppose it ever does.' 'Such are the pitfalls of analogy. All the same, there is an analogy. When you go out on our sort of job everything's covered with a layer of cagey blamelessness. No sharp outlines anywhere. The job itself sticks up like that phony ruin on the skyline over there but even the job tends to look different under snow. Blurred.'

Having lived near **Maidstone** for many years, **Dorothy Simpson** (1933–) uses attractive Kentish settings for her neatly crafted Inspector Luke Thanet mysteries set in a fictional 'Sturrenden' (with both name and surroundings similar to the southern Kent town of **Tenterden**). Simpson's background in marriage guidance informs Thanet's supportive relationship with his wife (who works in the Probation Service) – a stark contrast to the complex family tangles Thanet encounters professionally amidst the grand houses of the Kentish monied classes. Introduced in *The Night She Died* (1981), Thanet lives deep in a maze of country lanes and has strong ties with the countryside of his native Kent, 'the irregular patchwork of fields bordered by hedges and punctuated by specimen trees which is the essence of the English countryside.'

The wintry **Weald** is a land of furrowed fields and bare trees witnessing the fatal return of a prodigal brother in *Dead By Morning* (1989). By

Catherine Aird, whose crime debut, *The Religious Body*, features a newel post with a removable knob as murder weapon.

contrast, it is sweltering summer when Thanet and his trusty sidekick Sergeant Mike Lineham delve into undercurrents of hatred, sexual envy, addiction and family friction in *Dead and Gone* (1999). Simpson's interest in wild flowers shines through in her characters, while away from the scene of the crime Thanet demonstrates his knowledge of natural history by counting the number of native species in a hedge to establish its age ('one per century'). The hedge Thanet chooses offers hawthorn, '…the most common one; dogwood – that's the one with the reddish stems; elder; hornbeam – that goes a wonderful golden apricot colour in the autumn, hazel… just think. Five hundred years old.'

In 1946, when **Catherine Aird** (pseud. Kinn Hamilton McIntosh, 1930–) came to live in **Sturry**, a village a few miles outside **Canterbury**, she experienced a winter never to forget: 'We moved in here in October, and it was pretty nearly the end of March before we got to see the end of the garden.' Although the 'Calleshire' setting of her police procedurals shares elements with Kent, it is a wholly imagined county. In this way, Aird aims to distill the essence of a timeless, archetypically English setting, society and atmosphere. Her landscapes are steeped in stoicism, understatement, fair play and justice – and underpinned by a satisfying streak of humour.

'I really think of him as common man, oppressed by his superiors and disappointed by his underlings,' says Aird of her Detective Inspector C D Sloan, who is often found unravelling mysteries in institutional environments such as the secret scientific establishment in *His Burial Too* (1973), a prison in *A Dead Liberty* (1986) and a hospital in *After Effects* (1999). Sloan first appears in *The Religious Body* (1966), where the ordered tranquillity of 'St Anselm's' Convent (neatly juxtaposed with the more rumbustious environment of the nearby 'Cullingoak Agricultural College') is shattered when the body of Sister Anne is found at the foot of the cellar steps. When it turns out that Sister Anne had actually been a wealthy woman, the motive seems clear. But Sloan has his doubts, and slowly, methodically, uncovers the evidence that will trap the killer.

'My father,' says **Liz Evans**, recalling childhood holidays, 'had been abroad once and he figured that was once too often, so whilst others enjoyed sun and sangria, we got to shiver behind windbreaks and splash around in all those freezing grey rollers rushing onto the northern coast of the **Isle of Thanet**.' The hardships of holidays spent on the sandy beaches in the shade of low chalk cliffs fringing the Isle of Thanet bred a resilient sense of humour that underlies Evans' detective series and has thickened the skin of her bold and brash PI Grace Smith. Capering her way around a rather dispirited Kentish coast struggling to find a new identity after the downturn in tourism and agriculture, Grace squats in a basement flat in 'Seatoun' – a down-at-heel English seaside town on the south coast. Seatown was inspired by **Margate** and **Cliftonville**, at the easterly tip of Kent, but also by the faded elegance of nearby **Ramsgate** and the more upmarket **Broadstairs**. A former

A young **Liz Evans** on the beach, possibly pondering the plot of *Who Killed Marilyn Monroe?*

Margate – the energy and industry of Kent's coastal resorts is captured in **Liz Evans'** 'Seatoun'.

police officer, Grace is hired to investigate the murder of a beach donkey in *Who Killed Marilyn Monroe?* (1997), taking her around Seatoun's police station, donkey stables and retirement homes.

When not in the office or at her squat in one of Seatoun's 'ubiquitous four-storey Edwardian boarding houses', Grace enjoys greasy fry-ups and the garish lights of the promenade as much as the changing colours of the sea. When, in *Don't Mess with Mrs In-Between* (2000), a client asks Grace to track down three complete strangers because she wants them to inherit her not inconsiderable fortune, Grace can't believe her ears. She soon succeeds in tracking down the lucky recipients, but has not bargained for local passions, illegal immigrants, violence and murder. More recently, *Barking!* (2001) 'harks back to the time when Kent was the centre of the hopping industry,' says Evans, 'and the East Enders descended every autumn for their annual "Opping Oliday" '.

The seaside town of **Broadstairs** was a favourite holiday spot for **Charles Dickens***. The resort also provides the setting for *Murder in Pug's Parlour* (1986), introducing **Amy Myers'** Victorian master chef and amateur detective Auguste Didier, who investigates the death of a Dickens club chairman. Kent-born Myers lives on 'the far side of the Medway' in a village by the North Downs, with her sleuth's English-French background reflecting the region's proximity to mainland Europe.

CHAPTER ELEVEN

Oxford & The Cotswolds

It is true that the ancient and noble city of Oxford is, of all the towns of England, the likeliest progenitor of unlikely events and persons.

Edmund Crispin, *The Moving Toyshop* (1946)

Many detective writers have been educated under the 'dreaming spires' of **OXFORD**, where the aura of dignified purpose and timeless seclusion of nearly forty colleges continues to inspire mysteries today. Scholarship and detection share methods and aims, and the cloisters, quads and neat lawns of academia provide ample grounds for murderous hide-and-seek. Away from the personality clashes, devious dons and scholarly scatterbrains of tightly closed college communities, detective fiction has increasingly explored Oxford's less salubrious quarters, factories and council estates. Whether the Thames (called **Isis** here), **Cherwell**, or the Oxford Canal, the city's waterways are never far away.

The 'dreaming spires' of **Oxford**.

Dial M for Murder – the **Bath** phone box at the centre of **Christopher Lee**'s *The Killing of Sally Keemer* (1997).

Between a rock and a hard place – away from mainland murder investigations, **St Mawes** in Cornwall is a favourite location and prospective retirement home of **W J Burley**'s Inspector Wycliffe.

Burford – the Cotswold town provides an example of the archetypal English landscape so influential for the writing of **Ann Granger** and **Betty Rowlands**.

Oxford has been the seat of a university since the early thirteenth-century. Although, technically, not the oldest of the Oxford colleges, Merton was the first to adopt the college model where tutors and students share the same roof, and can trace its roots back to 1264. This date coincides with the historical setting of *Falconer's Crusade* (1994), the first of **Ian Morson**'s (1947–) atmospheric medieval detective series featuring Regent Master William Falconer. Morson was educated at **University College** (just to the north of Merton), which forms a focus for Falconer's investigations into a series of murders against a backdrop of shifting academic allegiances. Operating at a time when Oxford was in the grip of the 'clash of church and religiosity with the burgeoning ideas of science and empirical thought', Falconer is based at the historical **Aristotle's Hall** (formerly at the corner of **Logic Lane** and **Merton Street**, but no longer standing), and Aristotelian logic is the yardstick of his detection.

'Falconer's feet squelched through the mud on the spot where the girl had been killed. He thought again about the truths he had collected about the death, so terribly few to date.' The exposed platform of **St Mary the Virgin** (the forerunner of today's fourteenth-century church on **High Street**) 'cocooned in poles and ropes, and surrounded by apparently haphazard piles of stone', becomes the scene of a life and death struggle in *Falconer's Crusade*. Today, the views from the official University Church are amongst the best in Oxford. Morson's vivid descriptions of the unruly, smelly and noisy landscape of medieval Oxford draw on its 'sense of layers of time all existing in

For his tour de force *An Instance of the Fingerpost* (1997), **New College** Fellow **Iain Pears** (1955–) swaps the Italian art world for his workplace. Set around the cobbled alleys and colleges of 1660s Oxford, the novel tells the story of a young woman standing accused of murder through the testimonies of four academic witnesses.

Christ Church – Oxford's largest and most prestigious college and one-time employer of Oxford detective fiction pioneers J C **Masterman** and **Michael Innes**.

the present'. In his career, Falconer solves the murders of a foreign ambassador and an actor in a Christmas play with a mixture of science, Aristotelian logic and intuition. Much of Falconer's time is spent traipsing through muddy backstreets, avoiding the jostling crowds and away from the line of fire between town and gown. All that remains today of **St Martin's**, whose bells rally the townsfolk, is **Carfax Tower**.

Scribbling away in his study in the gabled **Old Palace** at the corner of **Rose Place** and **St Aldate's** (across the road from **Christ Church College**) was **Ronald Knox** (1888–1957), one of the first Sherlockian scholars and an extraordinary character on the academic circuit. Knox was also the author of the 'Ten Commandments' of detective fiction forbidding the use of supernatural agencies, Chinamen, identical twins, poisons unknown to science, and other popular escape routes for hard-pressed writers. During his time as Catholic University Chaplain, Monsignore Knox took a break from theology and Theocritan hexameters to raise money for the Chaplaincy by writing a fairly pedestrian detective series focused on Miles Bredon, a researcher with the 'Indescribable' insurance company. *The Footsteps at the Lock* (1928) features an empty canoe on the upper reaches of the Thames, which *should* contain a highly-insured young man.

John C Masterman (1891–1977) was teaching Modern History at **Christ Church** when he wrote the seminal *An Oxford Tragedy* (1933), set in an imaginary 'St Thomas' College' with a sympathetically drawn cast of dons, staff and students. A classic study of human behaviour, this was one of the first detective novels to depict the tranquillity of Oxford colleges being shattered by violent death. When an unpopular

Fellow in Classics is found dead in the Dean's rooms, many of the victim's faculty colleagues are under suspicion, and it is left to Ernst Brendel, a Viennese lawyer with a passion for crime and detection, to establish 'the drama behind the murder'. Over twenty years later, in *The Case of the Four Friends* (1956), a neat 'diversion in pre-detection', Brendel returns to St Thomas' Senior Common Room to tell his fellow bridge players how he had known that a crime was going to be committed, and how he went on to prevent it.

Born in Oxford, **Dorothy L(eigh) Sayers*** (1893–1957) later discovered here the environment of 'intellectual integrity' that allowed her to place Harriet Vane on an equal footing with Lord Peter Wimsey, as well as to achieve her aims as a writer. Sayers returned to Oxford in 1912 to study French at **Somerville College** (on **Woodstock Road**), where she was one of the first occupants of the Maitland Building, nurturing a precocious mind and advanced linguistic ability in the congenial environment of a women's college.

The idea for her first crime novel, *Whose Body?* (1923), came to Sayers while playing a story-telling game with her Somerville friends. Later, memories of the ghost of a nun that was supposedly haunting Somerville in her undergraduate days, together with proposing the toast at Somerville's annual convocation – 'Gaudy' – dinner, inspired *Gaudy Night* (1935). Independent-minded, intelligent and sensitive detective novelist Harriet Vane returns to 'Shrewsbury College', a fictionalized Somerville (placed on **Balliol Cricket Ground** over to the east of the city) for the Gaudy. Soon Harriet is investigating an outbreak of poison pen letters and mischievous vandalism that arouses strong emotions in the close-knit college community. This classic high-brow mystery

Oxford was not only **Dorothy L Sayers'** birthplace, but also the author's spiritual home.

In **Edmund Crispin**'s *Swan Song* (1947) (US: *Dead and Dumb*), ex-Somerville girl and crime writer Elizabeth is getting a bit bored in out-of-term Oxford, but life becomes a bit more dangerous when she finds that someone is lacing her tea with aconite.

The Darbishire (originally 'East') Quadrangle at **Somerville College**, the original for the quadrangle described in the opening paragraph of *Gaudy Night*.

The **Warden's Window**, a tiny opening in the **New College** 'bridge' above New College/ Queens Lane, under which Lord Peter Wimsey and Harriet Vane finally embrace. At the beginning of *Busman's Honeymoon* (1937), they marry in **St Cross Church**, opposite Balliol Cricket Ground, the site of 'Shrewsbury College'.

'For a crime writer, Oxford was a good place to go,' says **Val McDermid***, who read English at **St Hilda's** and gives her Manchester PI Kate Brannigan a background in working-class East Oxford. 'Oxford dons have always had an affinity with the crime novel – and not just Michael Innes writing it. It wasn't unusual to go for a tutorial and see your tutor's reading material on the table and a green Penguin among it…'

harnesses a mystery plot to a serious debate about the choices facing women between the life of the mind or 'real' life (in the 1920s, years after finishing her course, Sayers was amongst the first women to be awarded a degree). Looking down from the roof of the circular **Radcliffe Camera**, Harriet sees 'all Oxford springing underfoot in living leaf and enduring stone, ringed far off by her bulwark of blue hills…' Later, all of Oxford holds its breath as Harriet and **Balliol** man Lord Peter take a walk together down **New College Lane**.

To the foremost representative of the 'donnish school' of detection, **Michael Innes** (pseud. John Innes Mackintosh Stewart, 1936–94), the world of Oxford colleges provided 'a capital frame for the quiddities and wilie-beguilies of the craft'. Introducing Shakespeare-quoting Oxford graduate Inspector John Appleby, Innes' intricately plotted *Death at the President's Lodging* (1936) (US: *Seven Suspects*) is essentially a 'locked-college' mystery. The President of 'St Anthony's College', Dr Umpleby, is found shot dead in his room, bringing all the Fellows under suspicion as Appleby takes stock of the timeless Oxford surroundings:

> Dusk was falling and the trim college orchard seemed to hold all the mystery of a forest. Only close to him on the right, breaking the illusion, was the grey line of hall and library, stone upon buttressed stone, fading, far above, into the darkness of stained-glass windows. Directly in front, in uncertain silhouette against a lustreless Eastern sky, loomed the boldly arabesqued gables of the Caroline chapel. An exhalation neither wholly mist nor wholly fog was beginning to glide over the immemorial turf, to curl round the trees, to dissolve in insubstantial pageantry the fading lines of archway and wall. And echoing over the college and the city, muted as if in requiem for what lay within, was the age-old melody of vesper bells.

With great diplomacy, Innes locates his version of Oxford in the environs of 'Bletchley', half-way between Oxford and Cambridge, where Appleby displays the intuition, humour and empathy much needed amongst a clutch of Machiavellian dons plotting behind the 'long row of grey-mullioned, flat-arched Tudor windows'. Innes' detective novels are a don's delight: elegant and spirited, though not always adhering to the law of probability. Peopled by eccentric characters, Innes' Bletchley is a world where privilege and farce go hand in hand.

If books have always been the lifeblood of Oxford, they have certainly played a substantial role in Oxford death, too. The **Bodleian Library** receives a copy of every title published in the UK and now holds some seven million books. In *Operation Pax* (1951) (US: *The Paper Thunderbolt*), the air of the 'Bodley' carries the reassuring aromas of ancient learning: 'old leather and vellum and wood… if this smell evaporated it would be a sign that the soul of Oxford had departed its tenement of grey, eroded stone, and that only its shell, only its tangible and visible surfaces, remained'. When a petty criminal escapes kidnapping and experimentation as a human guinea pig at a quiet private clinic in Oxfordshire, he hides in the enormous vault of the Bodleian under **Radcliffe Square**. Jane Appleby, John's undergraduate sister, witnesses the plight of the fugitive: 'All around her was a massive apparatus of learning: cliffs of books in the Camera, in the Codrington, in the Bodleian – and even beneath her feet, she knew, more and more learning, profound, unfathomable, in subterranean chambers deep down below the cobbles on which had been flung by some horrible and surreptitious violence the wretched little man. It was like being very thirsty on a broad, broad ocean.'

The **Bodleian Library** –
'There are many silences in the
Bodleian Library, from the
impure quiet of the Camera,
where crêpe soles squeak and
lawyers breathe heavily, to the
analeptic calm of Duke
Humphrey. But no silence
compares with the silence of
the Stack.'

Robert Robinson, *Landscape
with Dead Dons* (1956)

Literary allusion was the stock
in trade of **Wadham**-educated
Cecil Day-Lewis (1904–72),
Poet Laureate from 1968, who
wrote a series of inspiring
detective novels as **Nicholas
Blake**, featuring urbane
Oxford graduate Nigel
Strangeways and a cast of
fascinating characters.

Michael Innes remained the inspiration for **Edmund Crispin**
(pseud. Robert Bruce Montgomery, 1921–78) whose detective novels
are filmic and farcical in style, often ending with chases or mad
scrambles. Donnish detective fiction might revel in the intricacies and
arcane rituals of closed-shop academia, but Crispin was one of the first
to step out of the quadrangle. Inspired by Crispin's tutor at **St John's**,
eccentric Professor Gervase Fen of 'St Christopher's' is introduced in
The Case of the Gilded Fly (1944) (US: *Obsequies at Oxford*). With his
wild hair spiking off in all directions, Fen has a genuine dislike for Jane
Austen and other icons of English literature and loves playing literary
games of the 'unreadable books' or 'hateful characters in literature'
variety. His students adore him, though he has been known to lie and
to use them as bait to trap a killer.

Fen steers his back-firing red convertible roadster 'Lily Christine III' unsteadily through Oxford in *The Moving Toyshop* (1946), Crispin's best-known novel. At the beginning of the novel, Fen's friend, the poet Richard Cadogan, hitch-hikes towards a holiday in Oxford he will not forget in a hurry:

> Oxford is the one place in Europe where a man can do anything, however eccentric, and arouse no interest or emotion at all. In what other city, Cadogan asked himself, remembering his undergraduate days, could one address to a policeman a discourse on epistemology in the witching hours of the night, and be received with neither indignation nor suspicion? ... Through a rift in the trees he caught his first real glimpse of Oxford – in that ineffectual moonlight an underwater city, its towers and spires standing ghostly, like the memorials of lost Atlantis, fathoms deep.

The imposing neo-Gothic **Randolph Hotel** at 1 Beaumont Street is an Oxford institution and a meeting place for crime writers and characters alike. Opposite its mellow stone frontage, stands **Edmund Crispin**'s – and Inspector Morse's – old college, **St John's**.

Wandering into town down **Iffley Road** in the middle of the night, Cadogan spies the open door of a toyshop and enters – only to find a dead body and receive a blow to the head for his trouble. When Cadogan returns the following morning, the 'toyshop' turns out to be a grocer's, and there is no sign of the body...

Robert Robinson (1927–) was educated at fourteenth-century **Exeter College** (renowned for the most elaborate neo-Gothic chapel in Oxford). His *Landscape with Dead Dons* (1956) is a spoof of eclectic college architecture that might well have been inspired by the **Tower of the Five Orders of Architecture** on the eastern side of Exeter's beautifully proportioned, seventeenth-century **Old Schools Quad**. Inspector Autumn is called in from London to stop the destruction of priceless books at the **Bodleian**. But the very evening of his arrival, the Vice-Chancellor of 'Warlock' College, where Autumn is staying, is found lifeless among the statues on the chapel roof. *Landscape with Dead Dons* features a hilarious finale of naked dons chasing the villain through the streets of Oxford towards the **Randolph Hotel**.

Sometimes, in a reflective mood on a golden Oxford afternoon, when the sun illuminates 'the pale-cinnamon stone of the colleges', Chief Inspector Morse would feel 'deeply grateful that he had been privileged to spend so much of his lifetime' here. His creator, **Colin Dexter** (1930–), has done more than any other writer to make Oxford known to the world – balancing its tourist landmarks, mellow stonework and spires with less visited parts of the city such as **Jericho** or **Cowley**. Morse is fond of a drink, especially when it's free, and is pedantic, vulnerable and even romantic beneath a gruff exterior. Morse's crossword-honed intelligence, erudition and love of classical music (especially Wagner) is a match for any don's, although his academic career at **St John's** was cut short by an entanglement with an undergraduate from **St Hilda's**. Morse's relationship with workaday Sergeant Lewis is more solid. Lewis, whose idea of paradise is a plate of eggs and chips in his **Headington**

'Oxford has almost become an extra, a character,' says **Colin Dexter**, whose Inspector Morse novels offer an inimitable combination of psychology, cerebral challenge and Oxford landscape. In his Morse novels, Dexter reputedly uses over 11,500 different words – more than Shakespeare, Dickens or Austen.

Room with a view – Room 310 of the **Randolph Hotel** features in *The Jewel that Was Ours* (1991).

'A short passage through to the River Thames dug by the fourth Duke of Marlborough in 1796...' – the triangular **Duke's Cut** on the Oxford Canal is scene of a Victorian crime in *The Wench is Dead.*

home, is the perfect foil for Morse's far from infallible intuition and does much to keep the melancholia of Inspector 'Morose' at bay – and his feet on the ground.

Dexter spun his Byzantine plots from his home in **North Oxford**, a part of town long famed for the erudition and eccentricity of its inhabitants. Morse's ground-floor bachelor flat was close enough for Dexter to imagine him wandering up and down the **Banbury Road** to the nearest off-licence. Attached to Thames Valley police at **Kidlington**, to the north of the city, Morse first investigates in *Last Bus to Woodstock* (1975), where the prime suspect for the murder of a young hitchhiker is a don at 'Lonsdale' College.

The superbly crafted, Gold Dagger-winning *The Wench is Dead* (1989) opens with Morse in lecherous form as he recovers from a perforated ulcer in the **Radcliffe Infirmary** on Woodstock Road. Morse soon finds himself intrigued by the Victorian tale, left by his bedside, of a young woman whose body was found at **Duke's Cut** on the **Oxford Canal** (built in the late eighteenth century, now the haunt of fishing enthusiasts and pleasure boats). As Morse enters the pages of an intriguing mystery of death and deception, he begins to zero in on possible motivations for murder, but realizes that any evidence must surely be long gone. And then in walks Lewis with a box from the City Police HQ in **St Aldate's**, containing the dead woman's shoes.

'Many Oxonians know "Wytham" as the village on the way to the wood. But Morse knew the spot as the village, situated on the edge of the wood, which housed the White Hart Inn…' Dexter's second Gold Dagger was received for *The Way Through The Woods* (1992), in which interest in the unsolved case of a missing Swedish tourist is revived via a series of lively and mysterious letters in *The Times*. With Morse apparently heading into a complex romance with a woman of equal intellect, a body is found in the eastern part of **Wytham Woods**. As the trail leads towards the stone-faced Italianate crescents of **Park Town**, it seems that Morse is unable to see the wood for the trees, but before long he is back and scrutinizing both.

Picking up Colin Dexter's brushes and palette, but painting contemporary Oxford very much in her own style, is **Veronica Stallwood**, whose series features historical romance novelist and outspoken sleuth Kate Ivory. 'Stately figures still dress up in colourful academic gowns and betassled headgear and drift across velvet lawns drinking champagne and eating strawberries,' says Stallwood, 'but I like to show my readers a glimpse of the mismatched socks and grubby trainers they're wearing underneath.' Stallwood portrays a new generation of Oxford academics who worry about funding and no longer speak generic, affected English. In *Oxford Exit* (1994), Kate investigates in the **Bodleian**, which Stallwood knows well, having worked here in 1988 when the cataloguing system was being dragged into the computer age. Working undercover, Kate has to find out who is stealing books and erasing computer records in the online catalogue – and to discover the connection with the death of a library trainee the previous year.

In *Oxford Fall* (1996), Kate is about to start temping as a fundraiser for 'Bartlemas' College (located close to the site of Merton College), when its handsome development officer is killed. Apparently drunk, the man falls from the college's 'Tower of Grace', a soft golden stone fifteenth-century tower, 'tall and square, surmounted by crocheted pinnacles' with panoramic views over Oxford. With her reputation preceding her, and having met the victim shortly before his downfall, Kate starts to receive warning notes. Close to the **High Street**, the beautiful Fellows' Garden seems an oasis of aromatic leaves and flowers, stone nymphs and birdsong, but there is also a whiff of something more sinister in the air.

Kate Ivory may encounter some discrimination, but seldom the elements of Oxford academia who would have preferred to see women remain firmly outside the quad. The links between misogyny and murder are tackled in **Joan Smith**'s (1953–) contemporary detective series featuring Loretta Lawson, a lecturer in English literature and feminist theory who has moved to Oxford from London. In *Don't Leave Me This Way* (1990), Laura's investigations in a former men-only college highlight the continuing marginalization of women in Oxford academic life. In *What Men Say* (1993), Loretta's colleague Bridget is under suspicion of murder.

The model for 'Lonsdale College' featured in Colin Dexter's Morse novels is **Brasenose College** on the High Street. In *The Riddle of the First Mile* (1983), the headless body of the master of Lonsdale is fished out of the Oxford Canal.

A former librarian at **St Hilda**'s and **Christ Church**, **Margaret Yorke** (pseud. Margaret Beda Nicholson, 1924–) penned traditional detective stories featuring Oxford don Patrick Grant before turning to her trademark psychological thrillers.

Another female English scholar and accidental sleuth, Terry Williams is the creation of **Tony Strong**, and solves her first case in *The Poison Tree* (1997), an ingenious and erotically charged debut full of Oxford locale. During his research, Strong stayed at one of the newer colleges, **St Peter's**. 'St Mary's' College is where Terry undertakes her doctorate thesis in detective fiction, and she needs all her literary training to find the author of letters discovered behind wallpaper in her house in **Osney Island**, the scene of a savage sexual murder in the past. But in this intriguing quadrangle of streets enclosed by streams and ditches to the west of the city, Terry might be saying too much to the wrong people.

The Poison Tree references the 'crumbling clock tower and ugly squares of Fifties buildings almost like a grotesque parody of one of Oxford's ancient colleges' at **Cowley** to the east of the city. Not long before Britain's first mass-produced car was launched at the Rover car works here in the 1920s, the old Oxfordshire village of Cowley was the birthplace of **Gladys Mitchell***. Her amateur sleuth and psychiatric consultant to the Home Office, Mrs (later Dame) Beatrice Adela Lestrange Bradley, can match any don detective for eccentricity. In the dedication to *Dead Men's Morris* (1936), Mitchell recalls 'with delight' the holidays spent cycling around the countryside east of Oxford, while *Late, Late in the Evening* (1976), set in a small Oxfordshire village, won her the Silver Dagger.

The **Botanic Gardens**, opened in 1621 as Britain's first, beside **Magdalen College**. In *Oxford Fall*, **Veronica Stallwood** develops the theme of a Garden of Eden defiled by corruption and rivalry, while Lord Peter Wimsey and Harriet Vane go punting on the Cherwell near Magdalen Bridge in **D L Sayers'** *Gaudy Night*.

To the west of Oxford, the **COTSWOLDS** form a fifty-mile range of gently undulating limestone hills (largely in **Gloucestershire**) that were once at the centre of the medieval wool trade. With its rolling green pastures, dry-stone walls, ancient woodlands, winding rivers, secluded towns, picture-postcard villages, majestic churches and merchants' houses in rare harmony, this is quintessential rural England.

Rainbow's End – **Chipping Norton** and **Bliss Mill** at the heart of the Cotswolds.

Deep in the unspoilt isolation and pearly, light-grey stone of the southern Cotswolds, **Betty Rowlands** finds inspiration for her amateur sleuth and best-selling crime writer Melissa Craig. At home in the 'unruffled tranquillity' of a stone-roofed cottage in the beautiful Gloucestershire village of 'Upper Benbury', a composite location 'somewhere between **Cirencester** and **Cheltenham**', Melissa has the unfortunate knack of falling headfirst into murder investigations. Originally a 'townie', Melissa has come to appreciate the gentle charms of the landscape by the time she investigates in *The Man at the Window* (2000), having been 'irresistibly drawn to the… stunning view across the secluded valley with its quietly flowing brook, cattle grazing on the sloping pasture and the patch of woodland rising to the skyline'.

Rowlands mainly uses composites of real places, and the very first Melissa Craig mystery, *A Little Gentle Sleuthing* (1990), found its inspiration in a disused shepherd's hut encountered on an afternoon ramble. One of Rowlands' favourite books is *Malice Poetic* (1995), in which a week-long writer's retreat at the peaceful hamlet of 'Uphanger' promises to be just the tonic for Melissa to complete her latest novel and contemplate her deepening relationship with Detective Chief

Betty Rowlands has lived for over thirty years in a Cotswold village having much in common with the one where her series sleuth, Melissa Craig, has made her home. Both enjoy quite spectacular views of the countryside from their gardens.

Ann Granger – 'I was very conscious of not wanting to write about an olde worlde, folksy, non-existent type of English village'.

Another resident of the Cotswolds, **M C Beaton*** is the creator of bullying, retired PR executive Agatha Raisin, who finds life in the Cotswolds village of 'Carsley' far from dull. Agatha livens up the local baking competition in *Agatha Raisin and the Quiche of Death* (1993) by submitting a Harrods' quiche but ends up investigating the poisoning of one of the judges.

Inspector Ken Harris. The owner of the 'Uphanger Manor Learning Centre', close to the Wiltshire border, claims to have developed a new method of tuition but needs Melissa's help with the threatening, anonymous verse messages he is receiving.

The stone is a shade softer in the north-east corner of the Cotswolds where **Ann Granger** (1939–) sets her series featuring Foreign Office civil servant Meredith Mitchell and her long-term lover Superintendent Alan Markby. Granger's 'Bamford' is a composite of the market towns in the area: notably the picturesque Georgian wool town of **Burford**, and the larger, more industrialized **Chipping Norton**. Granger sees this semi-urbanized corner of the Cotswolds as characteristically English: 'It is a beautiful landscape, but it's also typically English in that it has always absorbed different influences and turned them into its own.'

Whilst Meredith commutes into London from her terraced cottage in 'Station Road', Markby feels unrepentantly 'proprietorial' about Bamford, reflected in his green-fingered approach to policing: 'It was his patch and just as he kept his garden carefully tended and free of weeds, he felt it was his duty to keep Bamford free of contamination, to dig out any evil that took root there.' In *Murder Among Us* (1992), the conversion of a rambling mid-Victorian Gothic hall into a restaurant and hotel complex threatens the untidy, smelly and impoverished horse and donkey sanctuary run from its grounds. Meanwhile, the campaign to protect 'historic' Bamford turns sour when one of the committee members is found dead in the wine cellar at the hotel's opening gala.

Ann Granger often uses large country mansions to illustrate issues of changing rural identity and the different perspectives of 'the countryside'. *Shades of Murder* (2000) weaves together the cyclical nature of history with issues of inheritance and rural property prices, through four generations of a rambling, rather forbidding Victorian Gothic family home:

> ...the old place slumbered in a dark mustard-coloured sleep against the background of trees and rolling countryside. Puffs of white cloud hung motionless above it, testimony to the lack of breeze. The impression was of an oil painting. It was there but somehow not real.

The owners of the house, two elderly sisters, are struggling with the upkeep of the dilapidated property and are considering selling up, when a young Polish man turns up out of the blue, claiming to be a long-lost relative.

CHAPTER TWELVE

The South

We don't have murders in Bath. It's bad for the image.

Christopher Lee, *The Killing of Sally Keemer* (1997)

There is a definite air of refinement about the South's detective fiction, immersed in history and classic architecture, but exploring the sharply defined contours of the social landscape beneath. Sliding inexorably towards the edge of this sceptred isle, the geographical features of the South are also more perceptibly English, as if in defiance of the turbulent waters of the Channel and the Continent beyond.

It seems almost impossible to conceive the genteel Georgian terraces, antique shops and Roman heritage sites of **BATH** as places of deadly deeds and murder most foul. But in the same way that the solid stone terraces of Edinburgh have attracted a new generation of crime writers, so the warm Bath stone of this ancient spa city in the Avon Valley has

Bath – the city that **Daniel Defoe** (1660–1731) called a resort 'of the sound as well as the sick and a place that helps the indolent and the gay to commit that worst of murders – to kill time' – has seen more than its fair share of fictional murder and mayhem.

The West Front of **Bath Abbey**, a favourite view for **Peter Lovesey**'s Peter Diamond as he sits and ponders in the **Abbey Churchyard**.

'Mr Pinkerton felt suddenly very strange and alone, and rather frightened. He had not thought of Bath as being an enormous and unfriendly place. He stood staring up through the drizzling rain at the city, rising like some gigantic amphitheatre in tier after tier of beige-coloured stone, studded with spires and domes and towers. He had not got the faintest idea where to go.'

David Frome, *Mr Pinkerton has the Clue*

proved irresistible to writers of detective fiction determined to slip behind its façade of refinement and respectability. Although the crime writers here are not generally native Bathonians, they share a delight in tackling the myth that certain things just do not happen in this showpiece of elegance and prosperity.

When Mr Pinkerton, the curiously nondescript little detective created by US writer **David Frome** (pseud. Zenith Brown, 1898–1983) arrives in the city in *Mr Pinkerton has the Clue* (1936), he feels lost and lonely. But there's nothing like a murder enquiry to brighten a detective's day, and soon Mr Pinkerton is nosing around the corridors of the 'Blandford

House' hotel in search of clues. The imposing grandeur of **Great Pulteney Street** is the ideal setting for Frome's unashamedly frivolous but ingenious mystery, which explores the city's main tourist sights and freely pokes fun at class-conscious 1930s Britain and its bumbling, deferential police.

Peter Lovesey* (1936–) was living south of Bath in **Westwood** village when he began his first Peter Diamond mystery, *The Last Detective* (1991). Head of the Bath murder squad at **Manvers Street**, Peter Diamond is a big man in every sense: certain in his actions, uncertain in his moods, often tactless, but usually big-hearted enough to apologize after. Unlike most fictional detectives, Diamond is happily married and lives in a comfortable semi in **Weston**, a north-western Bath suburb. As his wife jokes, Diamond's should be a quiet life: 'This is Bath, the Floral City. Nobody can spare the time to commit murder.' Sadly, she is mistaken, and Diamond sets out to investigate the death of the wife of a university professor organizing a major **Jane Austen** (1775–1817) exhibition.

In the contemplative surroundings of the **Abbey Churchyard**, Diamond often finds himself staring upwards at the figures of angels climbing, and falling from, the ladder to heaven on the Abbey's West Front. Any thoughts of Diamond climbing the career ladder are dashed in this first novel, as he resigns on principle after clashing with his superiors, but returns in time to investigate in *Upon a Dark Night* (1997). A young woman is dumped, unconscious, in the car park of a private hospital, another falls to her death from the roof of a house at the west end of **Royal Crescent**, arguably the most majestic terrace in Britain. But what links these two incidents to the suicide of an old farmer in a nearby village? Diamond, with a little prompting from the intimidating bulk of 'Rose', a homeless shoplifter, needs to be at his sharpest to solve a case of mistaken identity, greed, missing treasure and murder.

In *The Vault* (1999), a concrete-encased hand found in the vaults under the **Roman Baths** and delivered to Diamond at Manvers Street, sparks off an investigation taking in the Bath art, antiques and second-hand books circuit. With its colourful shopfronts, bohemian atmosphere and the **River Avon** running nearby, **Walcot Street** is one of Peter Diamond's favourite areas. It also provides the setting for **Michael Z Lewin's** (1942–) *Family Business* (1995), where the Lunghi family investigate fraud and murder amongst the antiquities and artefacts.

A deceptively inconspicuous man, the 'Bath Detective' – Inspector James Leonard of Bath City Police – is the creation of former BBC correspondent **Christopher Lee** (1941–). First appearing in *The Bath Detective* (1995), Leonard is a Campionesque character, much given to polishing the steel-rimmed glasses that shield his blinking but penetrating eyes. With a royal visit planned for Bath, the last thing the city fathers need is the body of a vagrant dumped in the Roman Baths, and every effort is made to suppress the murder inquiry. Cycling around the city in his tweed suit, munching gingerbread men from a **Broad Street** bakery, Leonard presents an unlikely foe for master manipulator

'Diamond had never read a book by Jane Austen. He found it difficult to identify with the detectives in TV whodunnits who quoted Shakespeare and wrote poetry in their spare time' – **Peter Lovesey** introduces his own 'rough diamond' to the streets of Bath in *The Last Detective*.

Christopher Lee, like his Inspector Leonard, sought refuge in Bath 'even though we both had doubts about what went on behind very proper and well-painted Georgian front doors'.

Royal Crescent, John Wood the Younger's graceful terrace of thirty houses and over a hundred columns, is scene of the crime in **Peter Lovesey's** *Upon a Dark Night*, and the focus of some murderous manipulating in **Christopher Lee**'s *The Bath Detective*.

'People are people... and passions and tensions will drive people to murder, wherever they are. But in a place like Bath, of course, it all has to look rather unruffled on the surface' – **Morag Joss**.

Montague James, manoeuvring his 'merry-go-round' from the multi-hued stone curve of the **Royal Crescent**.

Leonard contemplates his cases in the (real-life) relaxed ambience of **Woods** restaurant and bar 'just across' from 'Albert Street' (**Alfred Street**) under the amiable gaze of its streetwise owner, Selsey. Just a few yards down the road, the lamplit phone box at the end of the cul-de-sac behind the **Assembly Rooms** provides the scene of the crime for *The Killing of Sally Keemer* (1997). Lee's terse humour, clipped prose and unsuppressed vitriol for the city's snobbish elite come close to touching the enigma of Bath. In the final act of the trilogy, *The Killing of Cinderella* (1998), the city's **Theatre Royal** on Saw Close is a suitable setting for a complex murder drama. But by the time the pantomime comes to town, Leonard is growing increasingly disillusioned:

> Bath had been fashionable for two hundred years and more. It thrived on not changing on the surface. The sameness in the fabric disguised little. It had been built by incomers for incomers and it continued that way. It was a friendly city but only for friends... You could eat as well as anywhere, drink as finely and get mugged, knifed or raped as well and as randomly as in any celebrated European metropolis of historical and architectural interest. Leonard was tired of it all.

Striking a chord with music lovers, **Morag Joss** (1955–) introduces international cellist and sleuth Sara Selkirk to Bath in *Funeral Music* (1998). Engaged to play at the **Pump Room**, the centre of the city's

Hay Tor, Dartmoor – constantly in **Agatha Christie**'s vision whilst working on her first murder mystery, *The Mysterious Affair at Styles* (1920).

Tintagel Castle, Cornwall – touched by Arthurian myth, the rugged splendour of this historic site inspired the overblown castle in **Jessica Mann**'s *Faith, Hope and Homicide* (1991).

The **River Teign**, in **Dartmoor National Park** – illustrating the 'ancient, unaltered feel to Dartmoor' that **Michael Jecks** finds so inspirational for his fourteenth-century West Country mysteries.

society circuit in Georgian times, Sara discovers a body in the **Sacred Spring** overflow of the Roman Baths. As she investigates, Sara blends effortlessly into the city, but retains a 'kind of Glasgow nosiness, directness' and an outsider's eye for its pretensions.

Classically trained Joss, who lists the actual musical works used in her novels, uses music to create atmosphere and enhance mood, noticeably in *Fearful Symmetry* (1999). This case of suspected plagiarism between two composers opens with a murder on **Camden Crescent**, another of Bath's stunning Georgian sweeps, overlooking the city and the Avon Valley towards **Bathwick Hill**. The trail eventually leads to a house in **The Circus**, where the claustrophobic symmetry symbolizes the novel's themes of isolation, obsession and secrecy.

Bath's outlying countryside is equally impressive, and considerably less tourist-choked. Tucked away in a beautiful hidden valley, just three miles from the centre of Bath, **St Catherine's** is the location of Sara's 'Medlar Cottage', modelled largely on Joss' first house in the area. In *Fruitful Bodies* (2001), Sara takes pity on her destitute, alcoholic former teacher, and allows her to stay at the cottage, creating discord between Sara and her lover, Detective Chief Inspector Andrew Poole. When the healing environment of the 'Sulis Clinic' is shattered by illness and death, Andrew tackles the official police investigation in his usual headstrong manner. Sara meanwhile slips behind the scenes, where music draws her towards the truth, but also into danger.

For **Margaret Duffy** (1942–), the 'City of Flowers' is a city of contrasts, and she explores many of them in her Detective Chief Inspector James Carrick and Joanna MacKenzie series. Duffy's landscapes are attuned to

Sara Selkirk's favourite haunt, the **Pump Room**, has been at the hub of Bath social life for centuries. The refined air of its Corinthian columns and chandeliers provides a clue to the mystery in *Fruitful Bodies*.

Bath's dominance leaves its near-neighbour **Bristol** with little detective fiction of its own. Writing as **Ruth Carrington**, thriller novelist Michael Hartland (1941–) introduces Bristol-based barrister and sleuth Alison Hope in *Dead Fish* (1998). Taking on the defence of a doctor accused of murdering his wife, Alison is soon enmeshed in a complex case of violence and witness intimidation. The landscape of Old Bristol is much admired by Alison, who reflects on 'how like a village this city could feel'.

Pierrepont Street and its quilting shop provide the inspiration for US patchwork enthusiast **Lizbie Brown**'s (pseud. Mary Marriott) detective and expert quilter Elizabeth Blair, whose own shop is in 'Pierrepont Mews'. Together with her partner and private investigator Max Shepard, who has his office above the quilting shop, Elizabeth investigates in mysteries such as *Double Wedding Ring* (1999), all bearing the name of beautiful quilts.

day-to-day living in Bath, where traffic congestion can cause tempers to fray and shoppers search in vain for functional rather than aesthetic goods. With an office above a herbalists' shop in **Milsom Street**, former CID officer MacKenzie still rues the fact that her relationship with Carrick cost her a police career. A Scot with vague aristocratic connections, Carrick is an educated and cultured man but often aligns himself with the underclass he pursues. In *Dressed to Kill* (1994), a boorish, small-minded woman is found battered to death. At the same time, a priceless reliquary disappears. The climax to Duffy's atmospheric detective thriller takes place in the ultimate Bath setting: the ancient Roman **Great Bath**, dating from the first century AD, where 'water at the rate of a quarter of a million gallons a day wells up from the ground, water that started off as rain on the Mendip Hills ten thousand or more years ago'.

The **Great Bath** – where Sara Selkirk hangs 'over the stone balustrade, marvelling at the steamy green pool' in **Morag Joss**' *Funeral Music*, and where **Margaret Duffy**'s *Dressed to Kill* draws to a conclusion in an 'ethereal, almost timeless scene'.

'A flight of broad, shallow steps in an elegant inverted horseshoe tapered at the ends' – **Pulteney Weir** is scene of the crime in **Peter Lovesey**'s *The Vault*. The weir is also the scene of a gruesome discovery in **Margaret Duffy**'s *Prospect of Death*.

Out celebrating Burns Night in *Prospect of Death* (1995), Carrick wakes up in hospital unable to remember a thing, with his car written-off and facing accusations of drink-driving. In this gripping mystery it is left to MacKenzie – aided by Duffy's thriller series character Patrick Gillard – to help prove his innocence, while Carrick tackles the case of a local film producer's body fished from the river. Carrick's investigations lead from the antique shops and crowded bedsits of the city centre to the picture-postcard villages a few miles south-east of Bath. From here it is a short journey into the 'maze of narrow lanes, mostly unnamed and unsignposted' that disappear into deepest Somerset and Wiltshire.

The fictional county of 'Broadshire', familiar to readers of **Anthea Fraser*** (1930–), is located in the northern half of **WILTSHIRE**, a landscape of 'sweeping hills, farms, woodlands, and honey-coloured stone buildings', that is one of Fraser's favourite parts of the country. Far from being the 'village mysteries' they are often referred to, the settings of Fraser's Broadshire novels often involve urban and suburban areas peopled by characters 'leading normal, uneventful lives, who are suddenly catapulted into danger'. In Fraser's favourite novel, *Three, Three, The Rivals* (1992), enigmatic Detective Chief Inspector David Webb and his solid sidekick DS Ken Jackson leave their base in the fictional town of 'Shillingham' to head for the elegant Georgian market town of Webb's native 'Erlesborough'. Modelled on **Marlborough**, with its wide High Street, arcades, park and ruins a few miles south of **Swindon**, Erlesborough brings Webb face to face with a traumatic incident from his past. The **Kennet and Avon Canal**, masquerading as the 'Broadshire and Avon', was one of his favourite childhood haunts, and it is from these murky waters where Webb once fished and paddled that the body of an old man is retrieved.

Dubbed 'Spiderman' by his colleagues, Webb is also an enthusiastic artist given to setting up his easel in the quiet fields close to home in the picturesque Broadshire countryside. Whilst his watercolours are for

'My passion for knowing exactly where everything is situated probably stemmed from reading the Nero Wolfe books by **Rex Stout**. Each detail of that old brownstone was consistent in every book, and picking up a new one felt like visiting home. I hoped my readers would feel the same about Broadshire' – **Anthea Fraser**.

Texas-born **Deborah Crombie**, whose Kincaid and James series explores English landscapes and history.

'The Tor seemed to hang above the treetops, a massive presence that dwarfed all other elements in the landscape' – **Glastonbury Tor** is at the centre of **Deborah Crombie**'s highly charged mystery *A Finer End.*

relaxation, says Fraser, 'towards the end of an investigation, he roughly sketches the scene of the crime and draws caricatures of the suspects in the locations in which they claimed to be when the murder was committed'. In *The Twelve Apostles* (2000), Webb travels north to an area of remote woodland on the borders of Gloucestershire where a skeleton has been unearthed in an unforgiving landscape carved by the last Ice Age. But it is in Shillingham that Webb must discover the link between a set of valuable silver spoons and the dying words of a clergyman.

Overlooking the wide expanse of the **SOMERSET Levels** from atop its grassy knoll, **Glastonbury Tor** is one of the most famous symbols of mystical England, a spiritually charged site rich in Arthurian legend. The town of Glastonbury is still defined by the transience of passing pilgrims: New Age followers, history lovers, curious tourists and revellers bound for the annual rock festival. The sparse, haunting ruins of **Glastonbury Abbey**, some of the earliest foundations of English Christendom, are particularly atmospheric.

'The sense of time transcended in the grounds of Glastonbury Abbey made an indelible impression on me,' says **Deborah Crombie***, whose enticing novel *A Finer End* (2001) crosses 800 years of history as the past pressures the present to atone for an ancient wrong. At the centre of the novel is the real-life account of architect Frederick Bligh Bond's excavations at the abbey, seemingly 'guided' by long-deceased monks through a process of automatic writing. As Superintendent Duncan Kincaid enters a complex investigation that challenges his preconceptions and beliefs, his relationship with newly promoted Inspector Gemma James enters a new phase as well.

Inspired by a great affection for the **West Somerset** coast where she owned a cottage for many years, **Lesley Grant-Adamson** (1942–) explores the distinctive character of the area in *Undertow* (1999). 'The novel is actually about place,' says Grant-Adamson, 'how such an unnerving place might affect the attitudes of people who live there, setting them apart from those in conventional villages. *Undertow* is all sky and sea, a story of the elements and their influence on human nature.' This riveting tale of isolation and exclusion focuses on the judgement of a community and the catalytic impact of a writer's arrival in the village. As she enters a 'world governed by water', Alice is drawn into a murder mystery from the past that asks as many questions of herself as of the people who live on the peninsula: 'The sea sang, a long way out, but on the turn. Things went away and they came back. Situations, people, tides. You had to deal with things, because they always came back.'

'The history of this coast was told in storms. They had redefined the bay, shaped villages and people's lives' – exposed **Steart Point** in West Somerset becomes 'Stark Point' in **Lesley Grant-Adamson**'s *Undertow*.

Some five miles inland of Steart, the tidy, workaday village of **Stogursey** where Grant-Adamson owned her High Street cottage provides the inspiration for 'Nether Hampton' and 'Withy Cottage' in *Patterns in the Dust* (1985). Series sleuth and gossip columnist Rain Morgan makes her first appearance holidaying in this 'typical sleepy little English village', where the discovery of a body in the grounds of nearby Nether Hampton castle, inspired by Stogursey Castle (private) arouses her more than ample curiosity. In this well-balanced, traditional murder mystery, Grant-Adamson fits her geographical and social landscapes together seamlessly; from the cornfields and rolling **Quantock Hills** beyond, to the village pub and Bridge evenings, and into the heart of the mystery at Nether Hampton Hall.

Lesley Grant-Adamson – her connections with the Somerset coast are influential in her detective fiction.

The wintry **DORSET** 'Vale of Pen Cuckoo' is the scene of an ingenious crime in *Overture to Death* (1939), as **Ngaio Marsh*** combines her passion for theatre with an eye for rural landscape. When Chief Detective-Inspector Roderick Alleyn of Scotland Yard starts looking for motives amongst the stone cottages and narrow streets of 'Winston St Giles', it becomes clear that this 'is no tame landscape'. The social landscape proves to be no less tame, as the traditional position of the village squire ('here I stand... and here my forebears have stood, generation after generation, and looked out over their own tilth and tillage') is challenged by the new generation ('I'm never quite sure,' says his son, 'what tilth and tillage are'). Alleyn, who arrives in the Vale thinking 'this looks like hidden treasure', steers his way neatly through the trials and tribulations of English rural life and is formidable in his pursuit of an audacious murderer.

Opposite: **Corfe Castle** – shrouded in mystery and a familiar landmark for **Gladys Mitchell**.

Always inspired by antiquities and ancient ruins, former schoolteacher **Gladys Mitchell*** (1901–83) retired to **Corfe Mullen** in the early 1960s. Mitchell's mysteries, if occasionally over-complex, are underpinned by her interest in witchcraft and psychoanalysis, and have a strong originality, as well as vividly drawn settings. Dorset provides the evocative backdrop to *Adders on the Heath* (1963), *Dance to Your Daddy* (1969)

Gladys Mitchell, creator of eccentric detective Mrs Bradley.

Rural **Shaftesbury** – traditional Dorset villages are visited by surreal mysteries in the novels of **Gladys Mitchell** and by a suspicious 'suicide' in **Minette Walters'** *The Scold's Bridle*.

'Isolation, claustrophobia, secrecy, introversion, prejudice, seeing 'foreigners' as enemies are themes in my stories' – **Minette Walters** introduces great variety of form and landscape into her mysteries.

Minette Walters attended Salisbury's famous **Goldolphin School**. With **D L Sayers***, **Josephine Bell*** and **Antonia Fraser** amongst its former pupils, the school has a proud crime-writing tradition.

'It stood on the edge of the sea, almost as if it had risen from the waves' – **P D James** uses the National Trust-owned nature reserve and castle of **Brownsea Island** in **Poole Harbour** as the setting for 'Courcy Island' in the second Cordelia Gray mystery, *The Skull Beneath the Skin* (1982). In classic Golden Age style, James washes the eccentric millionaire's castle in Gothic hues, as Cordelia is drawn into a murderous drama in the island's private theatre.

and *Lovers, Make Moan* (1982). Appearing in over fifty novels, Dame Beatrice, described as a sinister pterodactyl with a Cheshire Cat smile, solves dark, bizarre and ghostly crimes, with a unique mixture of psychology and hocus-pocus. Mitchell takes Adela Bradley all over the country, showing a convincing command of dialect and a fascination with British rituals and relics. Gladys Mitchell's second detective, Timothy Herring, a young architect with a brief to preserve historic buildings, appears in six novels written under the pseudonym **Malcolm Torrie**, including *Heavy as Lead* (1966) and *Churchyard Salad* (1969).

From high on the Dorset hills of Ngaio Marsh's Pen Cuckoo, it is just possible to discern the spire of **Salisbury Cathedral** on the far horizon. This is a familiar landmark for **Minette Walters** (1949–), who places the protagonist of her enthralling mystery *The Dark Room* (1995) in Salisbury's exclusive 'Nightingale Clinic'. A young woman is convalescing after a serious car accident and her dysfunctional family and brutal millionaire father are on the prowl. From their base in nearby **Winchester**, the police are chasing shadows and looking for easy answers – but the real answers are locked away with violent nightmares in the dark room of the patient's subconscious.

Based within easy reach of Dorset's coastal paths and stunning clifftop views, Walters combines psychological insight with explorations of the south-west landscapes she so enjoys. She is a great lover of country walks, and the **Dorset Ridgeway** is a particular favourite, offering views of sea on one side and rolling English hills on the other. Occupying the land of **Thomas Hardy**'s (1840–1928) 'Wessex', the closed communities of rural Dorset feature in the Gold Dagger-winning *The Scold's Bridle* (1994), but the strongest landscape is found within the more conventional detection of *The Breaker* (1998). Part of the south-west area that became Britain's first UNESCO World Natural Heritage Site, the **Isle of Purbeck** is a beautiful peninsula lying south across the massive harbour of the ancient seaport of **Poole**. When a woman's body washes up in **Chapman's Pool**, within sight of **St Alban's Head** and the South West Coast Path, there are a number of immediate suspects. Using her experience of sailing, Walters includes plenty of vital maritime detail and forensic evidence in a thrilling 'whydunnit' focused firmly on Dorset's limpid coastal waters.

Moving to very different landscapes, Walters trades the Dorset coast for a fictional sink estate between the major Hampshire ports of **Southampton** and **Portsmouth** (where real-life vigilante riots erupted in August 2000), as she tackles the subject of paedophiles and vigilante justice in *Acid Row* (2001).

Portsmouth is also the setting for a first-rate police thriller introducing DI Joe Faraday, as **Graham Hurley** (1946–) explores the seedier side of his home city in *Turnstone* (2000). Faraday's first-floor flat overlooking the fishing boats, wading birds and glistening mudflats of **Langstone Harbour** (east of the city) seems a long way from the council estates and trouble-torn streets of a 'Pompey' rife with drugs

and violence. But when Faraday is drawn into the search for a girl's missing father, any thoughts of peace are out of the window as this disturbing and demanding case pushes him to the brink:

> More and more Faraday found himself asking what it was about the place that made it so particular, so infuriatingly special… He'd lived here for over twenty years and he'd grown to love the seafront, with its busy views, and the quiet, shadowed cobblestones of Old Portsmouth, still haunted by the tramp of the press gang, but this was the tourist's Pompey, flagship Portsmouth… What it didn't capture, or explain, were the subtler glimpses of a very different city. Even at a distance of two generations, poverty and war still seemed to shape the people he dealt with.

Hurley genuinely tries to prise Portsmouth's identity out from behind its tourist façades and presents much more than a mere backdrop of a naval giant. In *The Take* (2001), Faraday has his hands full with both private and public tragedy. Grief-stricken DS Winter is looking for someone to blame, while Faraday again feels the pressure of an impossible caseload on some of Britain's toughest streets.

'The first time we sailed into it, I recognized how isolated it was and how difficult it would be to retrieve a body from any of the beaches nearby' – **Chapman's Pool** on the **Isle of Purbeck** provides **Minette Walters** with the scene of the crime in *The Breaker*.

Back in 1886, **Arthur Conan Doyle*** was a less than successful doctor residing in Portsmouth's **Southsea** area. It was here that he began to draft a detective story called 'A Study in Scarlet' (1887) involving Ormond Sacker and a certain Sherrinford Holmes. Ormond went on to become Dr John H Watson, while Sherrinford emerged as the most famous detective in history.

St Peter Port, capital of Guernsey, provides the setting for Eileen Dewhurst's Anna Weston and Tim Le Page novels.

Seemingly far-removed from crime and violence, the attractive Channel Island of **GUERNSEY** provides a truly authentic setting for **Eileen Dewhurst**'s* (1929–) Anna Weston and Tim Le Page series. Located some sixty miles south-west of the English coast where Dewhurst notionally places her Phyllida Moon novels in 'Seaminster', sun-drenched Guernsey is renowned as a popular and safe tourist resort. *Death in Candie Gardens* (1992) finds veterinarian Anna Weston forsaking a failed marriage and the cosmopolitan mass of London for the island's tranquillity, where she meets Detective Inspector Tim Le Page of **St Peter Port** police. A short walk from Le Page's villa, Anna discovers the body of a man sprawled across the railings of **Candie Gardens**, and suddenly Guernsey seems less like an island paradise.

'I am indicating the precise spot where the body is found, close to the stout tree from which another victim hanged himself later in the book' – **Eileen Dewhurst** points to the scene of the crime in Guernsey's **Candie Gardens**.

Dewhurst depicts Guernsey in a favourable light, especially for its lack of crime, but also explores the problems of closed communities and exposes the narrow-mindedness of some incomers for whom murder is a personal affront rather than a tragic loss of human life: 'It's too bad, Inspector, really it is. We retire to Guernsey at enormous expense, and this is what happens!' Enjoying a new-found security in *Alias the Enemy* (1997), Anna is bewildered and threatened by a series of bizarre attacks. Travelling widely around the island, this sequel is strewn with red herrings that divert an anxious Le Page from the trail of a deranged killer.

CHAPTER THIRTEEN

Devon & Cornwall

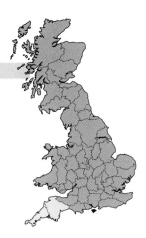

> Over the green squares of the fields and the low curve of the
> wood there rose in the distance a grey, melancholy hill, with a
> strange jagged summit, dim and vague in the distance, like
> some fantastic landscape in a dream.
>
> Arthur Conan Doyle, *The Hound of the Baskervilles* (1901)

Devon and **Cornwall** share the presence of the sea – wild and restless in places, placid in others – and a friendly, unhurried pace of life. Concealing and revealing, history and archaeology are the major influences on the detective fiction that has emerged from these two beautiful counties.

DEVON is distinguishable from its more rugged neighbour to the west of the **River Tamar** by its rolling lush green pastures, a coastline indented by rivers, creeks and bays, a rich maritime history and pronounced Mediterranean atmosphere. For many, Devon's thatched cottages have come to symbolize the lost landscapes and values of Old England, but this is also a modern, thriving county.

Built high on a plateau above the **River Exe**, Devon's capital city **EXETER** is full of architectural delights and reminders of the city's long trading history. Despite severe bombing during World War II, some of the ancient centre has survived, and the city's underground water conduits, cobbled streets and narrow alleys have remained largely unchanged since medieval times. The two Norman towers of **St Peter's Cathedral** rise massively above the horizon, looming over an ornately carved West Front and sheltering the world's longest continuous stretch of Gothic vaulting. The adjacent **Cathedral Close** and **Green** offer timeless tranquillity against a backdrop of cafés and timber-framed shops.

The crowded streets, crammed, haphazard housing and hazy smoke of medieval Exeter provide an atmospheric setting for former Home Office pathologist **Bernard Knight**'s (1931–) thirteenth-century Crowner John series. Justice and law enforcement in medieval times were erratic and often arbitrary, with summary executions and many serious crimes remaining unsolved. Under King Richard the Lionheart, coroners were appointed to uphold the law, but, as Knight observes,

'The soaring church with its two great towers' – **Exeter Cathedral** is an inspirational sight for detectives ancient and modern.

also to collect 'every penny for the royal treasury, impoverished by Richard's costly wars'. A certain amount of discretion is therefore required from Crowner John, Sir John de Wolfe, an upright, brusque and forceful man, with the stubborn streak essential for effective detection in any era. Although Crowner John lives in **Martin's Lane** (connecting the Cathedral and **High Street**), most of his inquests are held in the 'bare stone box' of the **Shire Hall** courthouse and often as not lead to executions, hangings and mutilations at the busy gallows of **Magdalen Street**. Remnants of the Roman and medieval wall surrounding Exeter at the time of Crowner John are still visible today, as are the ruins of the red stone bridge over the broad, shallow waters of the Exe, a crucial lifeline for medieval trade.

The Awful Secret (2000) finds Crowner John stalked by a mysterious figure as he nurses a recently mended broken leg. Despite these handicaps, the valiant civil servant is soon on the trail of pirates based on the island of **Lundy** off the north coast of Devon, and the landscapes of the book switch between the busy, smelly streets of Exeter and the spectacular coast in sight of the 'great cliffs, where **Exmoor** abruptly tumbled into the sea opposite distant Wales'. Meanwhile, a Knight of the Temple of Solomon, known to Crowner John from his crusading days, claims to be in possession of an 'awful secret' that threatens the very foundations of the Church.

Michael Jecks* revels in the seasonal festivity of bustling Exeter when his Dartmoor detectives Sir Baldwin Furnshill and Simon Puttock are summoned to the cathedral for Christmas 1321 in *The Boy-Bishop's Glovemaker* (2000). Here to receive the prestigious gloves of honour from the annually elected Boy-Bishop, Furnshill and Puttock are soon caught up in intrigue and murder within the massive walls of the cathedral itself, as the season of goodwill looks like turning into an increasingly bleak midwinter.

'From the ruddy colour of its local sandstone, it was always known as Rougemont, built by the Conqueror in the northern corner of the old Roman walls' – the remains of **Rougemont Castle**, where **Bernard Knight**'s Crowner John has a cramped chamber in the tall gatehouse.

'From here… the moors did look inviting in the sunshine – a deceptive series of softly moulded green hillocks in the distance, rolling and merging one into the other, touched with bright yellow and gold where the sunlight caught the gorse, with occasional licks of purple and mauve where the heather lay. The scene looked as rich in colour as the robes of an emperor, the flanks of the hills spattered here and there with white where sheep grazed' – **Dartmoor** appears to have changed little from the fourteenth-century scene described by **Michael Jecks** in *A Moorland Hanging* (1996).

'It was the first time Kate had been inside the Minster and its sheer size overpowered her. The soaring arches, the richness of the stained glass, the cold, rounded marble effigies filled her with a sense of awe, bearing witness as they did to a daily round of worship stretching back seven hundred years.' Exeter Cathedral also serves as an inspiration for **Anthea Fraser***. Her 'Broadminster' is loosely based upon Exeter, and the cathedral area features prominently in the opening novel of the series, *A Shroud for Delilah* (1984), and later in *The Nine Bright Shiners* (1987). The 'roofs and chimneys clustered skywards in a glorious lack of uniformity' form the enclosed historic heart of the Broadminster landscape.

'It was not until several weeks after he had decided to murder his wife that Dr Bickleigh took any active steps in the matter.' The riveting mind games of the classic inverted tale *Malice Aforethought* (1931) by **Francis Iles** (pseud. Anthony Berkeley*, 1893–1971) are played out in the small Devonshire hamlet of 'Wyvern's Cross'. An outsider in an area where 'birth counted for everything and achievement nothing', Dr Bickleigh is unable to impress the local worthies and much put-upon by his bossy wife. The tension is palpable as the good doctor's inevitable mental deterioration swells a tide of disaster which Chief Inspector Russell from 'Merchester' police can only stem after a series of spellbinding twists.

Home to hardy ponies, sheep and cattle, the expanse of moor and rocky outcrops (tors) of **DARTMOOR** begins a few miles west of Exeter, forming a timeless and mysterious landscape of heather-clad hills and exposed boggy plains, of stone rows and tiny winding brooks. Much of Dartmoor is bleak and exposed , but the north is surprisingly green and leafy and juxtaposes perfectly with the scorched umbers and hennas of the tor-topped open moors. The whole is criss-crossed by ancient trails waymarked by great stone crosses, and water cuts defining areas of ancient tin mining and peat-cutting.

Michael Jecks at the foot of the medieval village cross in **South Zeal**. Visiting the village on the northern edge of the National Park, with its old stone cottages, atmospheric inns, ancient chapel and stone cross, is like stepping back in time.

Infamous for its harsh justice, **Lydford Castle** is home to **Michael Jecks'** medieval bailiff Simon Puttock.

'Without a doubt, Dartmoor is somewhere in my mind whenever I write,' says **Michael Jecks** (1960–), whose fascination with history, and especially the turbulent early fourteenth century, led him to create a historical detective series:

> '...' 'To me Dartmoor seems to sum up the whole atmosphere of medieval Devon. Bleak, barren, damp, grey and unforgiving, its atmosphere casts a shadow over all my stories, even those set in towns and cities. There really is something timeless and unchanging about the moors, to the extent that readers can visit the place and instantly imagine themselves transported back in time to the fourteenth century.'

Focusing on the demise of the once powerful Knights Templar, *The Last Templar* (1995) introduces Simon Puttock as the newly appointed bailiff of **Lydford Castle**, and Sir Baldwin Furnshill as his friend and master of 'Furnshill Manor' (inspired by **Fursdon Manor**) at **Cadbury**. A former Knight Templar himself, Furnshill's experience and pragmatism are a necessary foil to Puttock's dogged detection and firm convictions in a murder investigation raw with jealousy and vengeance.

On more than one occasion, Furnshill has cause to regret his appointment as Keeper of the King's Peace in bustling **Crediton**, some six miles north-west of Exeter. In *The Crediton Killings* (1997) he has to tackle a dangerous band of mercenaries and a series of brutal murders.

Fox Tor Mires, the inspiration for the great 'Grimpen Mire' in Conan Doyle's classic *The Hound of the Baskervilles.*

The precise geographical centre of modern-day Devon, Crediton was once a most prosperous wool town, but today the only reminder of its former glory is the impressive red-stone **Church of the Holy Cross**, Devon's first cathedral. Jecks blends humour and adventure as medieval Crediton comes to life with the jugs of ale, raucous laughter and murderous plotting in the town's inn, the competing cries of market traders, and clatter of horses' hooves on the cobbled streets outside. The clamour of the town and its stench of sewage and butchery are in total contrast to the densely canopied forest tracks and desolate, dangerous moorlands.

'…we will take the London fog out of your throat by giving you a breath of the pure night air of Dartmoor. Never been there? Ah, well, I don't suppose you will forget your first visit.' One of the greatest detective stories of all time, *The Hound of the Baskervilles* (1901) by **Arthur Conan Doyle*** has immortalized the Dartmoor landscape. The legendary 'enormous coal-black hound', the sheer sight of which induces the most terrible heart-stopping fright, roams the wilds of Dartmoor and has already killed Sir Charles Baskerville. By the time he arrives at Baskerville Hall to protect Sir Henry Baskerville, Sherlock Holmes has already dismissed the notion of the supernatural, suspecting that human motivations lie behind the scenes. In a story rich in atmosphere and Gothic play of shadow and light, the enduring image is that of the dark, quivering 'foul slime' of the great 'Grimpen Mire', where Holmes and Watson first encounter the Hound in the flesh – almost certainly inspired by **Fox Tor Mires**, to the south of **Princetown**.

The wilds of Dartmoor also exerted their ancient magic on the world's most famous author of detective fiction, **Agatha Christie*** (1890–1976). With their ingenious plots, compelling narrative and uncomplicated prose, Christie's mysteries are models of Golden Age detection. Surprisingly, given that mystery writers at the time focused more on the elements of puzzle and deduction than setting and sense

Agatha Christie, whose detective novels are outsold only by the Bible and Shakespeare, always remained attached to her home county.

Still used as a prison today, **Princetown Prison** is the scene of escapes in both **Arthur Conan Doyle**'s *Hound of the Baskervilles* and **Agatha Christie**'s *The Sittaford Mystery*: 'D'you hear the bell? There's a convict loose.'

of place, the landscapes of over a dozen of Christie's novels can be traced to her native Devon. In the summer of 1917 Christie used a two-week holiday to work on the manuscript of her first crime novel, *The Mysterious Affair at Styles* (1920), at the **Moorland Hotel**, beneath **Hay Tor**. 'I think I learned to love the moor in those days. I loved the tors and the heather, and all the wild part of it away from the roads,' she wrote in her *Autobiography* (1975).

   The Sittaford Mystery (1931) (US: *The Murder at Hazelmoor*) offers a glimpse of the remoteness of Dartmoor communities in the depths of winter. With snowdrifts isolating 'Sittaford' village, 'perched right on the shoulder of the moor under the shadow of Sittaford Beacon', a seance is under way at 'Sittaford House'. An eerie rapping on the table conveys to the sitters that Captain Trevelyan, who lives six miles away in 'Exhampton', is dead. When her fiancé is arrested, intrepid Emily Trefusis soon discovers that Sittaford is a place of many secrets. From the top of the Tor, a 'pile of rock of fantastic shape', Emily looks down 'over an expanse of moorland, unbroken as far as she could see, without any habitation or any road' and to the 'grey masses of granite boulders and rocks' lying below as she searches for a solution.

Agatha Christie was born Agatha Mary Clarissa Miller in the more amenable environment of **Torquay**, its palm-planted seafront, hidden coves and sweeping expanse of **Tor Bay** making it the standard-bearer of the 'English Riviera'. Home was the large Italian-style stucco villa of Ashfield, which was always to remain dear to her heart, in **Barton Road** (pulled down in the early 1960s) on one of Torquay's seven hills. Today, a 'Christie Mile' stands as testimony to the enduring charm and remarkable success of her work – leading to locations such as the **Grand Hotel**, where Agatha and her first husband Archibald Christie honeymooned in 1914, and Torquay **Town Hall**, where she worked as a nurse during World War I, gaining the knowledge of poisons that served her well in dreaming up over eighty deaths by poison. In 1938

Agatha Christie made her dapper detective Hercule Poirot a Belgian in honour of the Belgian refugees who came to settle in **Torquay** (Tor parish) in 1914.

Agatha Christie and her second husband, archaeologist Max Mallowan, bought the stately Georgian **Greenway House** (private) on the Dart estuary a few miles south of Torquay, in woodland sweeping down to the river. Christie was to spend most summers here, and uses Greenway (amongst others) as the model for 'Nasse House' on the river 'Helm' in *Dead Man's Folly* (1956). The gardens of Greenway House are open to the public during the summer (National Trust).

Reached by sea-tractor at low tide, rocky **Burgh Island** lies across a short sandy stretch off **Bigbury-on-Sea** near Kingsbridge. Dominated by its intriguing Art Deco hotel, the island's sea cliffs and detached air feature in two novels: *Ten Little Niggers* (1939) (US: *And Then There Were None/Ten Little Indians*) is one of Christie's most baffling mysteries, while *Evil Under the Sun* (1941) finds Poirot relaxing at the 'Jolly Roger Hotel' on 'Smuggler's Island', only to become embroiled in an emotional triangle.

With its imposing hilltop **Royal Naval College** symbolizing a proud maritime history, the deep-water port of **Dartmouth** is an unspoilt haven rising steeply above the River Dart a mile inland from the coast. The town provides the inspiration for the 'Tradmouth' novels of **Kate Ellis** (1953–) featuring Detective Sergeant Wesley Peterson and his boss, Detective Chief Inspector Gerry Heffernan. Archaeology and history underpin the series as Ellis interweaves evidence unearthed from the past with contemporary murder. When a woman is found hanging in the churchyard of the ancient village of 'Stokeworthy' in *An Unhallowed Grave* (1999), Wesley has to uncover the dead woman's past to apprehend her killer. His old friend Neil Watson is busy with a dig at

The **Imperial**, which quickly became Torquay's most fashionable hotel, features as the 'Majestic' in *Peril at End House* (1932), where Hercule Poirot and Captain Hastings are staying on holiday in 'St Loo' – ostensibly located in Cornwall (a favourite Christie device) but recognizably Torquay.

Kate Ellis interweaves crimes past and present in her Devon mysteries.

Slapton Sands feature in *The Armada Boy* (1999) in which an American veteran makes a fatal return to his wartime haunts around the village of **Slapton** ('Bereton') and 'its vast beach, which was the scene of the real-life D-Day landing practices in 1944' (today commemorated by an obelisk).

medieval 'Stokeworthy Manor' (inspired by the beautiful medieval **Bradley Manor** near Newton Abbott) and as the two men swap notes, past and present are destined to collide.

> '...' 'I arrived in Devon by chance sixteen years ago. The last minute offer of a holiday at a friend's apartment in Torquay led to a journey on the Paignton to Kingswear railway to the ancient port of Dartmouth. We approached the town by boat and it was love at first sight... When I set about writing my first novel... I wanted an area with an interesting and varied history and landscape: sea, countryside and towns. The South Hams of Devon, the area around Dartmouth, Totnes and Torquay, with its seafaring connections, historic towns and beautiful countryside populated by locals, newcomers and holiday-makers alike, seemed to be the obvious choice.'

Born in **Staverton**, north-west of Dartmouth on the River Dart, **John Ross** (pseud. Jonathan Rossiter, 1916–) weaves thirty years of experience in the police force into his procedurals featuring sardonic, flirtatious Detective Superintendent George Rogers, operating out of the 'extremely ancient town of Abbotsburn'.

From his home on the historic eighteenth-century waterfront of 'Baynard's Quay' (**Bayard's Cove**), former merchant navy officer Gerry Heffernan is quick to take to the water in his boat. 'St Margaret's', where Heffernan sings in the choir, is modelled on **St Saviour's Church**, which incorporates timbers from the captured flagship of the Spanish Armada. Wesley Peterson adapts more gradually to his new surroundings, but enjoys wandering Tradmouth's cobbled streets and taking the ferry across to picturesque 'Queenswear' (**Kingswear**).

In *The Bone Garden* (2001), the lost gardens of 'Earlsacre Hall' are being 'stripped of the weeds and briars that had choked them and hidden their form', and excavated. When an ancient skeleton is found in the walled garden, Wesley Peterson suspects a link with recent murders in the area, sensing 'an air of expectation, of preparation' about the hall. A series of seventeenth-century letters suggest that Peterson is even closer to the heart of this case than he suspects.

Dartmouth provides the inspiration for the 'Tradmouth' of **Kate Ellis'** Wesley Peterson and Gerry Heffernan series.

The rugged beauty, extraordinary quality of light and independent spirit of **CORNWALL** make it a much-loved destination for tourists and artists alike. Dipping a tough, rocky toe into surprisingly warm waters at the south-westerly tip of the country, the economic tide here has yet to turn and Cornwall has stayed one of the poorest counties in Britain. This remains largely an elemental landscape, with storms pounding the coastline and abandoned tin mines, while persistent winds rasp at the edges of ancient tombs, castles and monuments. The same elements that shaped the sculpture of Barbara Hepworth also inspired the romantic thrillers of **Daphne du Maurier** (1907–89), for whom spirit of place was paramount.

Native Cornishman **W J Burley** (1914–) observes the landscapes of his home county through the detached gaze of Yorkshireman Charles Wycliffe, a superintendent with West Country CID. A resolute, ruminative and compassionate 'English Maigret', Wycliffe travels around Cornish towns and into the countryside, mostly investigating within the closed communities so dear to detective fiction: villages, country houses, homes and businesses. Burley retains a great affection and keen eye for the rhythms of nature throughout the series, as seen in *Wycliffe and the Last Rites* (1992): 'In the valley it was already evening, the light had a golden hue and the birds were silent. The tide was running out and there were banks of mud being worked over by the gulls. A tidal creek or inlet is not a single landscape, but a cycle of landscapes following the changing patterns of time and tide.'

'My interest was to work out how his view of Cornwall would develop, and how it would differ from my own' – **W J Burley** explains his vision for detective Charles Wycliffe.

Born in **Falmouth**, which features in *Wycliffe and the Redhead* (1997) and other Wycliffe mysteries, Burley has been resident for almost forty years in **Holywell** near **Newquay**. In *Wycliffe and the Dunes Mystery* (1993), Cornwall's notorious scouring winds uncover the partially

'Great mounds of sand, crowned with spiky marram grass' – the sand dunes at **Holywell** create a strange and alien landscape in *Wycliffe and the Dunes Mystery*.

mummified corpse of a young man in the sand dunes near **St Ives**. Under pressure from all sides, Wycliffe faces a fifteen-year-old murder mystery and a carefully woven web of deceit from his suspects. Although set close to **Phillack**, on the easterly edge of St Ives Bay, the dunes visible from the upstairs windows of Burley's Holywell home provide the main inspiration for the mystery. Symbolizing Cornwall new and old, *Wycliffe and the Guild of Nine* (2000) features an artists' colony based on the site of a disued mine on **Zennor Head**, west of St Ives.

For almost thirty years, Wycliffe and his wife Helen have lived in the Watch House, a secluded former coastguard station on the western banks of the Tamar, a river 'with at least as much significance for the Cornish as the Channel once had for the English,' says Burley, who plans to retire his detective to the picturesque village of **St Mawes** on the **Roseland Peninsula**, a twenty-minute ferry trip away from Falmouth.

> She was strongly aware of driving towards a terminus. To the south and west she could see the sea. Land's End was ahead. This was Europe's limit, nothing else before America except the dots of the Scilly archipelago and open sea. It was indefinably exciting. Tess felt at once liberated by the emptiness ahead, and secure in the comforting landscape whose high, overgrown hedges enclosed and directed her onwards, westwards.
>
> Jessica Mann, *Hanging Fire*

'You collect up material evidence and you make deductions from it' – **Jessica Mann** often parallels the processes of archaeology and detective fiction.

Elizabeth George* places 'Howenslow', the ancestral seat of her aristocratic Scotland Yard detective Thomas Lynley, on the exposed south-westerly tip of Cornwall, reached by private plane via the airstrip at **Land's End**. A holiday with his fiancée in *A Suitable Vengeance* (1991) turns into a nightmare for Lynley, with murder and betrayal tearing at family ties.

The small village of **St Clement**, overlooking the river near **Truro**, has provided **Jessica Mann** (1937–) with a home for over thirty years. In her wryly observed mysteries, Mann uses the Cornish landscape to arouse strong emotions in her characters, and frequently weaves in 'the effect of the distant past on the present' through her interest in archaeology. Mann's resourceful series sleuth, archaeologist Tamara Hoyland, appears in six novels, but it is Tamara's university mentor, Thea Crawford, who arrives in Cornwall in *The Only Security* (1973) to take up her position as Professor of Archaeology at the 'University of Buriton' (an old name for **Penzance**). Faced with resentment and bitterness from her weak-willed academic colleague and his domineering wife, things turn from bad to worse when Thea finds herself involved in a murder investigation that seems connected to an archaeological dig. Skeletal remains found in the sand dunes of 'Pentowan', very close to **Godrevy** lighthouse, reveal a small, exceptionally valuable crucifix...

Whether the bleak moorland hills on the coast around **Zennor** (*Telling Only Lies*, 1992) or 'the small fields and gorse patches of the furthermost corner of Britain' at **Land's End** (*Hanging Fire*, 1997), landscape is often a prime motivator for human passions and weaknesses. This is perhaps strongest in *Faith, Hope and Homicide* (1991), a detective thriller set in a huge Victorian castle clearly influenced by **Tintagel**, an ancient site and Norman castle shrouded in improbable

The remains of tin workings
on a lonely hill near **Zennor**.

Arthurian legend. The bombastic 'Arthur's Castle' of Mann's mystery
is the headquarters of the Grail Foundation, a venture funding scientific
quests, and a seat of power in more ways than one.

With a heritage including the St Ives and Newlyn schools of painting,
it is Cornwall's way of life as much as its landscape that continues to
lure artists. **Falmouth**-born **Janie Bolitho*** (1950–) bases her painter
detective Rose Trevelyan, an attractive widow in her late forties, in the
fishing community of **Newlyn**, 'which still has the largest fleet in Britain'.
Rose's appreciation of the landscape, together with a ready adaptability,
means that she fits well into the community in this 'part of mainland
England that was like no other… The climate, the people and the way
of life were more reminiscent of southern Europe.' Rose has the trained
eye of the artist and is a woman whom people trust instinctively – useful
attributes for any investigator.

Rose first appears in *Snapped in Cornwall* (1997), where her
investigations lead to the attention of the victim's husband, a growing
friendship with local art dealer Barry Rowe, and the more than casual
interest of local DI Jack Pearce:

Janie Bolitho taps into
Cornwall's artistic heritage.

'Inspiration comes from the magnificent view of the bay and its sweeping coastline I can see from my window,' says **Janie Bolitho** of her vista over **Newlyn**. 'The colours are always unbelievable.'

> Jack whistled as he walked down the hill towards the sea.
> Lights from the salvage tug anchored in the bay rippled over the water, and, to the west, a fishing boat chugged out of the harbour. It was a calm evening; the faint slap of water against pebbles was the only sound apart from an occasional passing car. Above the harbour the tiered lights of the houses of Newlyn twinkled. He paused and breathed in the air with its hint of kelp. An oyster-catcher called as it flew from the shore.

Embroiled in a tale of greed and deception, the view from Rose's window out across the rooftops of Newlyn to **St Michael's Mount** in the distance provides the balance she badly needs. *Buried in Cornwall* (1999) opens with Rose setting out to paint an old tin mine, with unforeseen consequences.

'There was a distant sound of waves flicking against rocks and far off to the east the Lizard lighthouse blinked a pinprick of yellow in grey gloom.' **Robert Richardson** (1940–) explores the tensions within an artistic community at 'Porthennis' (derived from 'Porthenis', which is the ancient name for the bijou cliff-hanging fishing village of **Mousehole**) in *The Dying of the Light* (1990). Series detective Augustus Maltravers arrives to watch his lover take the role of Desdemona in an open-air performance of Othello at a theatre reminiscent of **Porthcurno**'s **Minack Theatre**, but is soon on the trail of a murderer. Richardson captures not only the tourist-choked beaches and roads, sensational vegetation such as the towering gunnera (giant rhubarb) and restless ocean of this toe of the Cornish coast, but also the insularity and 'sense of secrecy' here. As sculptor Martha Shaw lies crushed by her own massive granite work of art, it appears that, like Desdemona, she has been 'trapped by evil which eventually destroys her'. It falls to

Robert Richardson brings a touch of drama to the Cornish coast in *The Dying of the Light*.

Maltravers to overcome his scepticism of a local man's psychic powers and to find the link between Martha's death and the mysterious disappearance of the theatre founder and wealthy patron of the 'Porthennis School' in 1951. Although a 'metropolitan sophisticate', Maltravers cannot fail to be impressed by his surroundings:

Minack Theatre, Porthcurno, 220 feet above the sea, could stand in for **Robert Richardson**'s fictional open-air theatre in *The Dying of the Light.*

> Maltravers drove out to where the road immediately dropped, twisting along the cliffs overlooking Porthennis. Miniaturised by distance, its houses fell among trees in a crumpled fan shape from sliding moors and farmland to the focal point of the harbour, stone walls curved like open pincers. From the highest point they could see clear across Mount's Bay, the great scoop of sea grasped in a huge claw where England pushed to its extreme points west and south.

Author Index

(Where writing under a pseudonym, authors real names are given in brackets)
(Page numbers for main text entries are in **bold**)

Places Index

Acknowledgements

Grateful thanks to everyone who provided material and assisted in the research and writing of this guide. Special thanks to our families and friends for their wholehearted support and encouragement, and to Ben, Ruth, Eleanor and Janice at Ben Cracknell Studios, Norwich, for completing this huge and complex project in style and record time. Thanks to Alan Blair, Cromer; Kate Charles; Christopher Dean (D L Sayers Society); Robert Hughes (Chesterton Society); P D James; Michelle Spring; Philip Weller (The International Sherlock Holmes Study Group); the staff at the Suffolk County Library, Ipswich Institute, and British Library – and, last but not least, thanks to the British Tourist Authority and Tourist Boards across the country for their assistance and generosity.

Every effort has been made to ensure the accuracy of the factual and biographical information. The authors would be grateful to learn of any unintentional errors.

Grateful acknowledgements are made for permission to reproduce the illustrations on the following pages. Where there is more than one illustration per page, items are sub-referenced (a,b,c) from top to bottom. All other pictures © Julian Earwaker.

Colour images:

Alan Blair, Cromer: front cover (Ranworth Broad), Middle Fen (nr Ely), Felixstowe Docks, Burford, River Teign, Dartmoor. Clifford Robinson, Leeds (Yorkshire Heather nr Reeth)

Mono images:

Catherine Aird (Anita Clarke): 206a. Margery Allingham Society/Barry Pike: 136a, 184a. Allison & Busby: 38b, 41a, 96b. David Armstrong: 86. Ari Ashley: 246. Anna Baker: 47a. Kathleen Becker: 67, 111, 112a, 112b, 114b, 132a, 147, 160a, 229b. Alan Blair, Cromer: 78, 115b, 197, 205. Janie Bolitho: 247b. British Tourist Authority: 36, 100, 249, 228b, 249. British Waterways

Photo Library: 105. Butetown History & Arts Centre, Cardiff: 80. The Cambridgeshire Collection, Cambridge Central Library: 107, 116. Paul Charles: 167. Chesterton Society: 185b. Constable & Robinson: 37, 120a, 123, 171b. Deborath Crombie: 228a. Judith Cutler: 104. Dartmoor National Park Authority: 241a. Alixe Buckerfield de la Roche: 130a. Derbyshire Record Office: 90. Colin Dexter: 215b. Dumfries & Galloway Tourist Board: 35. Edinburgh & Lothians Tourist Board (Harvey Wood, Douglas Corrance and Marius Alexander): 20a. English Riviera Tourist Board: 241b. Liz Evans: 206b. Anthea Fraser: 227b. Glasgow Herald Newspapers: 31. Glasgow Courts (Jenkins & Marr): 28b. Groombridge Place, Sussex: 201. Guernsey Tourist Board: 234. Guernsey Press Co. Ltd: 234b. Peter Guttridge: 199b, 200. HarperCollins: 37, 44a, 82, 141, 203. Hastings Borough Council (Chris Parker): 202. Headline: 24a, 220. Heinemann: 77a (Don

Williams). The Highlands of Scotland Tourist Board: 15. Ken Hitch (LRPS): 118. Hodder & Stoughton: 24c (Colin Thomas), 110, 211a, 219b (Gloucestershire Echo). Roger Holman, Dorset Picture Library: 230, 231b. Joyce Holms: 23. Helen Hunter: 126. Hutchinson (Jerry Bauer): 196. infocus photography, Corby (Kate Dyer): 102b. Alanna Knight: 20b. Myra Knox: 29b. Lancelyn Green Collection: 164. Christopher Lee: 223b. Frederic Lindsay: 22. Leicester Promotions: 101b. Little, Brown: 125a, 204. Peter Lovesey: 169a. Macmillan: 42, 52a (Clifford Robinson), 101a, 102a, 113a (Red Saunders), 117, 137, 232 (Michael Trevillion). John Kennedy Melling: 177b (Kinsella Studio). The Estate of Gladys Mitchell dec'd (S M Crispin Mitchell): 231a. Gwen Moffat: 12, 76. Cathel Morrison: 11. Museum of London: 173. National Horseracing Museum, Newmarket: 133. National Horseracing Museum, Newmarket/Stilton Advertising Ltd, Ipswich:134. No-Exit Press (Piers Allardyce): 180b. North Norfolk District Council: 121. The Norfolk Museums & Archeology Service (Charles Munday, 1899): 122. Orion: 114a. Oxford Picture Library (Chris Andrews): 208, 210, 214, 218. Anne Perry: 174. Perthshire Tourist Board: 19a. Piatkus: 243b. mrp photography (Martyn Pitt), Nottingham: 44b. Stuart Pawson: 57a, 57b, 58. National Portrait Gallery: 163b. Ann Quinton: 132b. Ken Reah: 59, 60a, 60b. Sheila Radley: 128. Ribble Valley Borough Council: 64. Robert Richardson: 248. Clifford Robinson, Leeds: 54, 56b. Martin Russell: 201b. Serpent's Tail: 53, 179a. Somerville College, Oxford: 211b. Stoke-on-Trent Tourism: 94, 95. Dr Alison Taylor: 14. Andrew Taylor: 89. Thanet District Council: 207. June Thomson: 137b. Time Warner: 171a. Treorchy Library: 79. Virago (Charles Hopkinson): 172. Edgar Wallace Society: 177a. Warner: 189. Barbara Whitehead (R E N Newman) 46. Yorkshire Post Newspapers Ltd, Leeds: 55b

Grateful acknowledgement is made for quotations taken from the following editions (London publishers unless otherwise indicated):

Douglas Adams: *Dirk Gently's Holistic Detective Agency* (Pan, 1988). Margery Allingham: *Tiger in the Smoke* (Penguin, 1957). J R L Anderson: *A Sprig of Sea Lavender* (Gollancz, 1978). Janie Bolitho: *Snapped in Cornwall* (Constable, 1997). Stephen Booth: *Black Dog* (HarperCollins, 2000). Christianna Brand: *Green for Danger* (Michael Joseph, 1973). Christopher Bush: *Murder at Fenwold* (Heinemann, 1930). Kate Charles: *Evil Angels Among Them* (Headline, 1995). Glyn Carr: *Death Under Snowdon* (Bles, 1954). Peter Cheyney: *The Urgent Hangman* (Pan, 1964). Brian Cooper: *The Blacknock Woman* (Constable & Robinson, 1999). Natasha Cooper: *Out of the Dark* (Simon & Schuster, 2002). David Craig: *Bay City* (Constable & Robinson, 2000). Edmund Crispin: *The Moving Toyshop* (Penguin, 1958). Barbara Crossley: *Rollercoaster* (Virago, 1994). P C Doherty: *Satan in St Mary's* (Headline, 1990). Anabel Donald: *The Glass Ceiling* (Chivers, Bath, 1995). Arthur Conan Doyle: 'The Resident Patient', in *The Adventures and The Memoirs of Sherlock Holmes* (Penguin, 2001); *The Hound of the Baskervilles* (Penguin, 2001). Martin Edwards: *All the Lonely People* (Hodder & Stoughton, 2000). Raymond Flynn: *A Fine Body of Men* (Hodder & Stoughton, 1998). Dick Francis: *Twice Shy* (Michael Joseph, 1996). David Frome: *Mr Pinkerton has the Clue* (Longmans, 1936). Frances Fyfield: *Deep Sleep* (Heinemann, 1991). John Gano: *Inspector Proby's Christmas* (Allison & Busby, 1997). Ann Granger: *Shades of Murder* (Headline, 2001). Cynthia Harrod-Eagles: *Bill Slider Omnibus* (Warner, 1998). Reginald Hill: *Pictures of Perfection* (HarperCollins, 1999). John Buxton Hilton: *The Anathema Stone* (St Martin's Press, New York, 1980). Alan Hunter: *Gently Down the Stream* (Constable, 1996). Graham Hurley: *Turnstone* (Orion, 2000). Michael Innes: *Death at the President's Lodging* (Penguin, 1988). P D James: *Unnatural Causes* (Penguin, 1989). Michael Jecks: *A Moorland Hanging* (Headline, 1996). Katherine John: *Without Trace* (St. Martin's Press, New York, USA, 1989). Paul Johnston: *Body Politic* (Hodder & Stoughton, 1998). H R F

Keating: *The Hard Detective* (Pan, 2000). Mary Kelly: *The Spoilt Kill* (Virago, 1999). Alanna Knight: *The Inspector's Daughter* (Constable, 2000). Frank Lean: *The Reluctant Investigator* (Arrow, 1998). Christopher Lee: *The Killing of Cinderella* (Orion, 1999). Roy Lewis: *The Cross Bearer* (HarperCollins, 1994). Gillian Linscott: *Dance on Blood* (Virago, 1998). Nigel McCrery: *Faceless Strangers* (Simon & Schuster, 2001). Jessica Mann: *Hanging Fire* (Constable, 1997). J J Marric: *The Gideon Omnibus* (Hodder & Stoughton, 1964). Ngaio Marsh: *Off With His Head* (HarperCollins, 2000, ©1957). Jennie Melville: *Windsor Red* (CT Publishing, 1998). John Milne: *Alive and Kicking* (No-Exit Press, 1998). Gwen Moffat: *Miss Pink at the Edge of the World* (Ulverscroft, 1975). Stuart Pawson: *The Mushroom Man* (Headline, 1995). David Peace: *Nineteen Eighty* (Serpent's Tail, 2001). Anne Perry: *The Whitechapel Conspiracy* (Headline, 2001). Ian Rankin: *Mortal Causes* (Orion, 2000). Derek Raymond: *Hidden Files* (Little, Brown, 1992). Danuta Reah: *Silent Playgrounds* (HarperCollins, 2001). Dilwyn Rees: *The Cambridge Murders* (Gollancz, 1945). Robert Richardson: *The Dying of the Light* (Magna Print, Long Preston, 1991). Mike Ripley: *Angel City* (HarperCollins, 1994). Robert Robinson: *Landscape with Dead Dons* (Penguin, 1963). Dorothy L Sayers: *Five Red Herrings* (Hodder & Stoughton, 1984). Manda Scott: *No Good Deed* (Headline, 2001). Gillian Slovo: *Close Call* (Virago, 1996). Michelle Spring: *Nights in White Satin* (Orion, 1999). Jean Stubbs: *Dear Laura* (Macmillan, 1973). Andrew Taylor: *The Office of the Dead* (HarperCollins, 2000). Josephine Tey: *The Singing Sands* (Heinemann, 1967). Leslie Thomas: *The Complete Dangerous Davies* (Methuen, 1995). Mark Timlin: *A Street that Rhymed at 3am* (Vista, 1998). Peter Turnbull: *Deep and Crisp and Even* (Ulverscroft Large Print, Leicester, 1982). Martyn Waites: *Mary's Prayer* (Piatkus, 1997). Jill Paton Walsh: *A Piece of Justice* (Hodder & Stoughton, 1995). Colin Watson: *Coffin, Scarcely Used* (Chivers, Bath, 2001).

Selected Bibliography

London publishers unless otherwise stated.

Crime Fiction Reference

Barnes, Melvyn *Murder in Print – A Guide to Two Centuries of Crime Fiction* (Barn Owl Books, 1986)

Cooper, John & Pike B A *Detective Fiction – The Collector's Guide* (Scolar Press, Aldershot 1994)

Craig, Patricia and Cadogan, Mary *The Lady Investigates – Women Detectives & Spies in Fiction* (Gollancz, 1981)

Gerrard, David *Exploring Agatha Christie Country* (Agatha Christie Ltd/English Riviera Tourist Board, Torquay, 1996)

Heising, Willetta L *Detecting Women* (3rd edition; Purple Moon Press, Dearborn, Michigan, USA, 2000)

Hendershott, Barbara Sloan/Dale, Alzina Stone (eds.) *Mystery Reader's Walking Guide – London* (Passport Books, Lincolnwood, Illinois, USA, 1995)

— *Mystery Reader's Walking Guide – England* (Passport Books, Lincolnwood, Illinois, USA, 1996)

Herbert, Rosemary (ed.) *The Oxford Companion to Crime & Mystery Writing* (Oxford University Press, Oxford, 1999)

Keating, H R F *Crime & Mystery – The 100 Best Books* (Xanadu, 1987)

— *Whodunit? – A Guide to Crime, Suspense & Spy Fiction* (Windward, 1982)

McLeish, Kenneth and Valerie (eds.) *Bloomsbury Good Reading Guide to Murder, Crime Fiction & Thrillers* (Bloomsbury, 1990)

Mann, Jessica *Deadlier Than The Male. Investigations into Feminine Crime Writing* (David & Charles, 1981)

— 'Dons and Detection' in: Evans, John D. et al. (eds.): *Antiquity and Man. Essays in Honor of Glyn Daniel.* (Thames & Hudson, n.d.)

Pederson, Jay P (ed.) *St James Guide to Crime & Mystery Writers* (St James Press, Detroit, USA, 1996)

Swanson, Jean & James, Dean *Killer Books – A Reader's Guide to Exploring the Popular World of Mystery and Suspense* (Berkeley Prime Crime Books, New York, USA, 1998)

Symons, Julian *Bloody Murder – From the Detective Story to the Crime Novel: A History* (Viking, 1985)

Watson, Colin *Snobbery with Violence* (Eyre Methuen, 1979)

Woeller, Waltraud and Cassidy, Bruce *The Literature of Crime and Detection – An Illustrated History from Antiquity to the Present* (Ungar, New York, USA, 1988)

Biographies & Studies by subject (author)

Johnson, Roger & Pike, B A *The Albert Memorial – A 100th birthday tribute to Mr Albert Campion* (The Pyewacket Press, Chelmsford for the Margery Allingham Society, 2000)

Wolff, Robert Lee *Sensational Victorian – The Life and Fiction of Mary Elizabeth Braddon* (Garland, 1979)

Chesterton, G K *Autobiography* (Hutchinson, 1969)

Coren, Michael *Gilbert – The Man Who Was G K Chesterton* (Jonathan Cape, 1989)

Christie, Agatha *An Autobiography* (HarperCollins, 1993)

Keating, H R F (ed.) *Agatha Christie – First Lady of Crime* (Weidenfeld and Nicolson, 1977)

Osborne, Charles *The Life and Crimes of Agatha Christie* (HarperCollins, 1999)

Stashower, Daniel *Teller of Tales. The Life of Arthur Conan Doyle* (Allen Lane/The Penguin Press, 2000)

Weller, Philip: *The Hound of the Baskervilles* (Devon Books, Tiverton, 2001)

Ross, Thomas W *Good Old Index. The Sherlock Holmes Handbook* (Camden House, Columbia, SC, USA, 1997)

Francis, Dick *The Sport of Queens – An Autobiography* (Michael Joseph, 1999)

Lord, Graham *Dick Francis – A Racing Life* (Chivers, Bath, 2001)

Stewart, J I M *Myself and Michael Innes* (Gollancz, 1987)

Waugh, Evelyn *Ronald Knox* (Chapman & Hall, 1959)

Lewis, Margaret *Ngaio Marsh: A Life* (Chatto & Windus, 1991)

Marsh, Ngaio *Black Beech and Honeydew* (Collins, 1966)

Moffat, Gwen *Space Below My Feet* (Sigma, Wilmslow, Cheshire, 2001)

Thorogood, Julia *Margery Allingham – A Biography* (William Heinemann, 1991)

Whiteman, Robin and Talbot, Rob *Cadfael Country*, Foreword by Ellis Peters (Macdonald, 1990)

Whiteman, Robin *The Cadfael Companion*, Foreword by Ellis Peters (Macdonald, 1991)

Phillips, Mike *London Crossings – A Biography of Black Britain* (Continuum, 2001)

Rhea, Nicholas *Heartbeat of Yorkshire* (Jarrold, Norwich, 1993)

Brabazon, James *Dorothy L Sayers: The Life of a Courageous Woman* (Gollancz, 1981)

Roy, Sandra *Josephine Tey* (Twayne Publishers, Boston, USA, 1980)

Wainwright, John *Wainwright's Beat* (Ulverscroft Large Print, Leicester, 1988)

Lane, Margaret *Edgar Wallace* (Hamish Hamilton, 1938)

Travel and General Reference

Andrews, Robert *The Rough Guide to Devon & Cornwall* (Rough Guides, 2001)

Drabble, Margaret/Stringer, Jenny (eds.) *The Concise Oxford Companion to English Literature* (Oxford University Press, Oxford, 1990)

Earwaker, Julian and Becker, Kathleen *Literary Norfolk* (Chapter 6 Publishing, Ipswich, 1998)

Hardyment, Christina *Literary Trails: British Writers in Their Landscapes* (National Trust, 2000)

Scotland – Insight Guides (APA Publications, Singapore)

Hudson, Roger *Fleet Street, Holborn & the Inns of Court* (Haggerston, 1995)

Tagholm, Roger *Walking Literary London* (New Holland Publishing, 2001)

Various *AA Touring Guide to Britain* (The Automobile Association, Basingstoke, 1981)

Britain – The Rough Guide (Rough Guides, 2001)

Cambridge – Official Guide (Jarrold, 2000)

Great Britain (Dorling Kindersley Eyewitness Travel Guides, 1999)

Great Britain – The National Geographic Traveler (National Geographic/AA Publishing, Southampton, 1999)

London (Dorling Kindersley Eyewitness Travel Guides, 1995)

The English Landscape (with an introduction by Bill Bryson, Profile)

Varlow, Sally *A Reader's Guide to Writers' Britain* (Prion, 1996)